D0152748

TREATING
MIND & BODY

TREATING
MIND & BODY

Essays in the
History of Science,
Professions, and
Society Under
Extreme Conditions

GEOFFREY COCKS

with a foreword by
Peter J. Loewenberg

Transaction Publishers
New Brunswick (U.S.A.) and London (U.K.)

Copyright © 1998 by Transaction Publishers, New Brunswick, New Jersey 08903.

All rights reserved under International and Pan-American Copyright Conventions. No part of this book may be reproduced or transmitted in any form or by any means, electronic or mechanical, including photocopy, recording, or any information storage and retrieval system, without prior permission in writing from the publisher. All inquiries should be addressed to Transaction Publishers, Rutgers—The State University, New Brunswick, New Jersey 08903.

This book is printed on acid-free paper that meets the American National Standard for Permanence of Paper for Printed Library Materials.

Library of Congress Catalog Number: 97-20184
ISBN: 1-56000-310-3
Printed in the United States of America

Library of Congress Cataloging-in-Publication Data

Cocks, Geoffrey, 1948–
    Treating mind and body : essays in the history of science, professions, and society under extreme conditions / Geoffrey Cocks ; with a foreword by Peter J. Loewenberg.
        p. cm.
    Includes bibliographical references and index.
    ISBN 1-56000-310-3 (alk. paper)
    1. Psychotherapy—Political aspects—Germany.   2. Psychoanalysis—Political aspects—Germany.   3. National socialism and medicine—Germany. 4. Social medicine—Germany—History—20th century.   5. Germany—History—1933–1945.   I. Title.
RC450.G3C64   1997
616.89'00943'09043—dc21   97-20184
                                                                                              CIP

Contents

Foreword

Peter J. Loewenberg

I well remember the Hamburg 34th Congress of the International Psychoanalytic Association in late July 1985, the first meeting of international psychoanalysis in Germany since 1932. Geoffrey Cocks had just that spring published *Psychotherapy in the Third Reich,* his groundbreaking book on the adaptations and compromises of German psychoanalysts with Nazism.[1] Cocks was present in Hamburg and active in the formal and informal discussions. A Congress exhibit for the first time explored the opportunism, complicity, and betrayals of integrity of "Aryan" psychoanalysts who remained in Germany.[2] Klaus von Dohnanyi, Hamburg's lord-mayor, addressed the Congress describing the psychoanalysts' slippery slope of expedient loss of principle to a totalitarian regime: "Every step rational and yet in a false direction. Here a compromise with individuals, there with substance: always in the vain hope of preserving the whole—which had ceased to exist.... In most cases freedom is lost in tiny steps."[3]

Cocks is an American whose specialties are the history of Germany and Austria, psychohistory, the history of science and of the professionalization of medicine, psychiatry, and psychoanalysis. His work has attained multiple translations and wide resonance in Europe. While researching his dissertation Cocks made a major historical discovery— that psychotherapeutic clinicians in the Third Reich adapted psychodynamic theory, clinical technique, and nomenclature to the demands of Nazism under the aegis of a German Institute for Psychological Research and Psychotherapy (the Göring Institute) founded in 1936 by Dr. Matthias Heinrich Göring, a neuropathologist and psychotherapist, and a cousin of Reich Marshal Hermann Göring. Psychotherapy was termed Seelenheilkunde and attributed to Völkisch Germanic sources. Cocks' book was a pathbreaking work of scholarship which won wide acclaim both in Germany and in the U.S. for its bold re-delineation of the story of psychotherapy in Nazi Germany. His research also opened an acrimonious intergenerational discussion about various heritages of compromise with Nazism among German physicians and psychoanalysts.[4]

Following Hitler's seizure of power the major issue in German psychoanalysis was whether to close up shop or to try to insure its institutional survival by coercing the Jewish members of the German Psychoanalytic Society (Deutsche Psychoanalytische Gesellschaft, DPG) and the Berlin Psychoanalytic Institute (BPI), in the 1920s and 1930s the world's premier psychoanalytic training institute, to "voluntarily' resign. The "Aryanization" proceeded in three steps: first, the exclusion of Jews from the DPG Executive in the fall of 1933; second, the exclusion of all Jews from membership in the DPG in 1935; third, the amalgamation of the DPG and the BPI as a division of the Göring Institute in 1936.

The Jewish members had been the founders, and were a large majority of the membership of both organizations. In the early 1930s leading figures in international psychoanalysis, including Franz Alexander, Therese Benedek, Siegfried Bernfeld, Helene Deutsch, Max Eitingon, Otto Fenichel, Erich Fromm, Frieda Fromm-Reichmann, Karen Horney, Edith Jacobson, Sandor Lorand, Sandor Rado, Wilhem Reich, Theodor Reik, Hanns Sachs, Ernst Simmel, René Spitz, and Edith Weigert were distinguished graduates of, or teachers of, psychoanalysis in Germany. By August 1934, twenty-four of the thirty-six full members had already emigrated from Germany. The teaching staff was reduced from twelve to two. Attendance at lectures fell from 164 in 1932 to thirty-four in 1934. A total of seventy-four psychoanalysts fled Germany.[5]

In May 1933 Oskar Pfister wrote Freud: "Last week I was briefly in Germany and was so nauseated that it will be a long time until I recover.... Cowardly towards the outside world, it turns its infantile rage on defenseless Jews and even plunders the libraries. Good luck to him, who still has the strength to be a healer of souls, in the face of such dishonorable idiocy."[6] Freud responded with: "There is little reason to alter my judgment of human nature, especially the Christian-Aryan variety."[7]

Freud's position was to maintain the existence of the institutions of psychoanalysis in the Third Reich, even under its racial laws excluding Jews. He wrote to Max Eitingon in March 1933:

> Let us assume nothing happens to the Institute, but you, as a foreigner, etc. [as a Russian-born Jew of Polish nationality] are removed from the directorship.... In this case, I think you cannot close the Institute. True, you founded it and stayed in

charge the longest, but then you handed it over to the Berlin group to whom it now belongs. You cannot close it legally, but it is also in the general interest [of psychoanalysis] that it remains open, so that it may survive these unfavorable times. In the interval [until the end of Nazism], someone who is indifferent, such as Boehm, can lead it.[8]

Boehm visited Freud in Vienna on April 17, 1933 and reported:

Freud presented his position to me that changing our board would not prevent the government from banning psychoanalysis in Germany, "they will ban it in any case." But if not altering our Board could serve as a handle for the government to proceed against psychoanalysis in Germany, then we should avoid giving the government this handle, i.e., then we should change the Board in the sense of the current government [im Sinne der jetzigen Regierung].[9]

In January 1937 Boehm came to Vienna and described the situation of psychoanalysis in Germany to the Freud group at great length. According to Jones:

Boehm talked for three hours until Freud's patience gave out. He broke into the exposition with the words: "Quite enough! The Jews have suffered for their convictions for centuries. Now the time has come for our Christian colleagues to suffer in their turn for theirs. I attach no importance to my name being mentioned in Germany so long as my work is presented correctly there." So saying he left the room.[10]

Freud was clearly more interested in preserving the organization and presence of psychoanalysis in the Third Reich than he was in the dignity and self-esteem of his Jewish colleagues or in the conditions that are necessary for psychoanalysis to function as a clinical therapy.

The initial response of German psychoanalysts was to refuse to submit to National Socialist racial legislation. An Extraordinary General Meeting of the DPG membership on May 6, 1933 rejected the proposals of Felix Boehm and Carl Müller-Braunschweig to "Aryanize" the Board.[11] Ernest Jones, then president of the International Psychoanalytical Association (IPA), showed a callous insensitivity to the feelings and situation of Jewish colleagues whom he had advised to resign from the German group. In anticipation of the forthcoming 13th International Psychoanalytic Congress in Lucerne, he wrote to Felix Boehm in Berlin:

You are not likely to know the strength of the storm of indignation and opposition which is at present agitating certain circles, especially among the exiles from Germany. This may easily take the form of a personal vote of censure against yourself or even a resolution to exclude the German Society from the International Association.

> You will know that I myself regard these emotions and ultra-Jewish attitude very unsympathetically, and it is plain to me that you and your colleagues are being made a dumping-ground for emotion and resentment which belongs elsewhere and has been displaced in your direction.[12]

While the Nazis were forbidding their psychologists to address any sessions where Jews were present at the annual C.G. Jung "Eranos" conference at Ascona, Jones, on behalf of the IPA, was pressuring Jews to withdraw from their German professional organizations and identitites. He sent a telegram reading: "Urgently advise voluntary resignation" to Therese Benedeck, a spokesperson among those who fought against "voluntary" resignation.[13] Eva Rosenfeld articulated the dynamics of humiliation, saying "they could not resign voluntarily because too high a degree of masochism would be involved, as though they had voluntarily to become their own executioners."[14]

It is painful and mortifying to read the record of how the leaders of an honored institution, in order to save the organization and promote the careers of the new successors to leadership, humiliated and cast out a large majority of its members to accommodate to a totalitarian state. That a "scientific," or for that matter a "humanistic," society would exclude qualified members for ethnic, racial, religious, or other extrinsic grounds for the sake of the existence of the institution, defies the autonomy of science from political ideology and the morality of valuing individuals that is the humane liberal essence of psychoanalysis itself.

Cocks' chapter on the social history of illness in Nazi Germany promises to decisively redefine our understanding of the social dynamics of Nazi Germany.

During the Third Reich and since, the Jews were in German psychoanalysis and medicine, as Cocks elegantly puts it, "the presence of an absence." Meanwhile, Felix Boehm, putatively an authority on homosexualiy, was by 1944 authoring reports "on criminal cases of unnatural and immoral sexual practices" that read: "The starting point should be that from the medical point of view there is no reason to treat homosexuals differently from other offenders..."[15]

Cocks takes us into the living hell of experimentation on humans in Nazi science. He relates the fear of a typhus epidemic carried by prisoners of war, slave laborers, and returning Wehrmacht troops from the East. The infamous typhus barracks at Buchenwald which the S.S. avoided "like the plague," is the setting of an extraordinary resistance which evinced heroic achievements of intellect over a monopoly of brute force. In Blocks 46 and 50 the S.S. gathered an international scientific "collective" of scientists to make a typhus vaccine for the combat troops of the Waffen S.S.. Their scientific leader was Ludwik Fleck, a Polish Jewish immunologist, who describes a international scientific "collective" working on a typhus vaccine for the S.S. in Buchenwald, consisting of a Pole, two Austrians, a German, a Dutchman, and two Czechs.[16] The prisoner group made two kinds of typhus serum, a large batch of approximately 600 liters of inert vaccine with which around 30,000 S.S. men at the front were injected, which did neither harm nor good, and a small batch of six liters of top quality serum for prisoners in exposed positions who were in constant danger of laboratory infections.[17] They were never betrayed—which would have meant certain death. According to Eugen Kogon:

> We produced two kinds: one which had no value and was perfectly harmless, we produced in large quantities; this vaccine was sent to the front; the other, produced in very small quantities, and very effective, was used in special cases—for example for ourselves and our comrades who were working in special parts of the camp.... the adventure continued until March of 1945.[18]

The Germans remained ignorant of the deception until the war's end.

Cocks invites us into the historian's world without showing us the scut work of his painstaking archival research. He grants us the delight in discovery, the thrill of shrewd inference that in his skilled hands is pursued toward evidence. Cocks takes us into the life of Heinz Kohut, whose letters he edited.[19] Kohut was one of the few post-Freudian psychoanalysts to make major theoretical and clinical innovations in the last quarter century. Cocks' biographical essay in this volume provides us with a textured, new view of Kohut as a person, a father, a psychoanalytic politician and theorist, and an intellectual in the modern world. Kohut's Viennese cultural origins are apparent in what he, as a man and father, valued. Kohut's correspondence with American politicians, such as Chicago's Mayor Richard Daley, bears the nostalgic memory and political resonance of Das Rote Wien, the Red Vienna, in which the Social Democratic city government of the 1920s built outdoor swimming facilities in each neighborhood where the populace to this day enjoys a daily swim. There is no American baseball "Dad" here. He wished to introduce his son, now an accomplished historian, to the opera, and specifically to *Die Meistersinger,* just as his father had introduced him to that opera in Vienna. He piled pressure on Tom for his "radical" college political activism, which was not so radical. Tom demonstrated against the Vietnam War, he was not a Weatherman robbing banks or blowing up buildings. Kohut came down hard on Tom, laying caution and guilt on his son like the good bourgeois, or *bürgerlich,* European father that he was.

Cocks was the first to tease out, reconstruct, and publically reveal that Kohut's paradigm case of self psychology, "The Two Analyses of Mr. Z," was autobiographical.[20] To the consternation of many self psychologists, Cocks concluded that Kohut was "Mr. Z" and that the second analysis of "Mr. Z" was a self-analysis. I am persuaded by Cocks' reconstruction and the evidence he marshals, as well as by my own inquiries among Kohut's closest adherents. I am not appalled at the idea of Kohut using his subjective self-reflection for his profoundest insights, including narcissistic rage, mirroring, and self-object transferences. I believe that psychoanalysis is a hermeneutic "science," signifying that we must acknowledge the secondary and tertiary revision and the imputation of meaning to all reported clinical material. Indeed, I would argue the subjective source gives Kohut's discoveries a greater validity and conviction. Is there any kind of psychodynamic knowledge that is more reliable? George Devereux developed a principle of method on the acknowledgement that self-experience is our best psychoanalytical and behavioral science data:

> The scientific study of man.... must use the subjectivity inherent in all observation as the royal road to an authentic, rather than fictitious, objectivity.... When treated as basic and characteristic data of behavioral science they are more valid and more productive of insight than any other type of datum.[21]

This is what Freud did. We have Erik Erikson's account that his personal journey through adolescence is the source of his "discovery" of the moratorium and the identity crisis.[22] In my view the most compelling psychoanalytic data we have are the subjective descriptions of experience and insight by self-reflective clinicians such George Engel who described the prodromal events to his own coronary, and Lawrence Freedman's depiction and reflections on his cerebral concussion.[23] I believe this is true of all the best psychoanalytical insights: they are first intuited subjectively, then elaborated according to positivistic criteria. What is important is that Freud, Erikson, and Kohut formulated their original subjective insight in the discourse of the prevailing psychodynamic paradigm, which they then reconceptualized, enlarged, and generalized, to make the insight useful to the world. The new insight was then validated in the concurrent clinical workshops of many others who found it enlightening theoretically and useful in pursuing research and clinical work.

Kohut was aware that his innovations in clinical technique and theory did not come without a political and personal narcissistic price. He was denied the presidency of the International Psychoanalytical Association in 1969, which caused him "waves of resentment and hurt pride."[24] At the time he was running for the presidency he was preaching wariness and circumspection to his son Tom who was at Oberlin College protesting the Vietnam War. Kohut wrote his son to be cautious and to avoid being provocative, and, he assured Tom that if he used provocative methods, he could be ruthlessly suppressed:

> Please don't throw away your chances for a productive and happy future on the basis of an impulse, or even on the basis of a presently held strong conviction. To be a militant on campus does entail risks which may be greater than you allow yourself to know.... I believe that you should think long and hard before committing yourself to extreme causes and, especially, to extreme means of furthering them.[25]

Kohut was voted off of the Psychoanalytic Education Council, the Chicago Institute's governing board in 1978, though he was reelected in 1980. He felt the need for prudence in formulating and expressing clinical departures to prevent psychoanalytic and institutional marginalization and isolation.

At the very historical moment that Heinz Kohut was pursuing his psychoanalytical researches at the Institute of Psychoanalysis, another Central European intellectual, only slightly older than Kohut, was also in Chicago developing an influential model of the transmission of ideas. Leo Strauss (1899-1973), a political philosopher who held the Hutchins Chair in Political Science at the University of Chicago from 1949 to 1968, developed the case that writing in the Western tradition since Plato has functioned on two levels, a public exoteric level and behind that an esoteric level of meaning open to those who know how to read it.[26] Although the structure may be familiar as manifest and latent content, in the case of Strauss both levels are very conscious. Science and the world are changed by subversive texts that constitute a disguised critique of prevailing assumptions but are only understood by the cognoscenti. Since Socrates was given the hemlock, said Strauss, it has been too dangerous to tell the truth as it is: "Philosophy and philosophers were 'in grave danger'.... The exoteric teaching was needed for protecting philosophy. It was the *armor* in which philosophy had to appear. It was needed for political reasons" (my italics).[27] The psychoanalytic meanings of "armor" takes us back to Wilhelm Reich of Berlin who because of his radical politics and unorthodox method was read out of the DPG in 1933 and refused the right to present a paper at the Lucerne International Psychoanalytical Congress in 1934.[28]

The price of detection is persecution, which Strauss defined in the most nuanced form to include not only exile and destruction, but being ostracized or marginalized within a group:

> Persecution covers a variety of phenomena, ranging from the most cruel type, as exemplified by the Spanish Inquisition, to the mildest, which is social ostracism.[29] Persecution cannot prevent independent thinking. It cannot prevent even the expression of independent thought. For it is as true today as it was more than two thousand years ago that it is a safe venture to tell the truth one knows to benevolent and trustworthy acquaintances, or more precisely, to reasonable friends. Persecution cannot prevent even public expression of the heterodox truth, for a man of independent thought can utter his views in public and remain unharmed, provided he moves with circumspection. He can even utter them in print without incurring any danger, provided he is capable of writing between the lines.[30]

Those trusted benevolent minds who are the initiates to this encoded esoteric knowledge constitute an elite who carry on a disguised discourse whose secret texts are public, but whose revolutionary levels of meaning can only be comprehended by those who know how to read them.

The problem laid open by Cocks' work is Kohut's intellectual and theoretical stratagems used to conceal his originality as he developed self psychology. I cite two examples from a letter to the Ornsteins in 1975, four years after *The Analysis of the Self* (1971), and while he was bringing to completion *The Restoration of the Self* (1977), which would appear in two years:

> I have come to prefer the term "separate" line of development to the term "independent" line of development when I speak of the development of narcissism from its rudimentary archaic beginnings to its mature forms.... There is nothing in the psyche that could be called "independent" in this sense. But at any rate, as *a self-protective measure,* I suggest that we use the word "separate" and not the word "independent".... I am more and more inclined to replace the term "narcissism" with the term "self." I prefer, for example, the term "self-object transferences" to the term "narcissistic transferences".... (My inclination, by the way, to use the term "narcissism" up to now, is related to *my attempt to prevent a sudden break with tradition.*)[31] (My italics)

Kohut is avowedly writing to avoid perceived persecution by the Chicago, American, and international psychoanalytic establishments which he knew would compensate his clinical and theoretical originality and doctrinal independence with ostracism as he pursued his project of building a developmental psychology of the self that, as Robert Stolorow has put it most sharply, attempts "to reframe psychoanalysis as pure psychology."[32]

Now, due to Cocks' scholarship we may see the personal and inside story of Heinz Kohut's tensions and covert strategies of esoteric writing as he worked, suffered, and claimed his originality as a psychoanalytic clinician and theorist. Cocks enables us to read new levels of the explorations of Heinz Kohut. As the Straussian model demonstrates, scholarship is a truly priceless commodity because it cannot be purchased, traded, returned, undone, or made an article of commerce.

Cocks' work demonstrates the particular rewards of scholarship on the intellectual *limes*—the term Romans used to indicate a boundary line, often marked by a pathway or road, or a stone wall. In Roman law the limes was also a distinction or a difference between two cases or concepts *(judicium brevi limite falle tuum)*. Cocks chooses to take his stance on the limes, the crossways between disciplines of history and psychoanalysis, politics and the histories of science, medicine, and the professions. His writing and interpretations in this book have benefited from the unique vantage of those boundary paths, and sometimes walls, between disciplines and cultures. He is neither a physician nor a clinical psychoanalyst, nor a Freudian, a Jungian, nor a Kohutian. Cocks is therefore a detached observer who analyzes relationships and appraises actions with a cool judiciousness. As an American he writes about his research on the highly controversial subject of psychotherapy in Nazi Germany, "I decided that I should take advantage of the fact that I was a foreigner who had no other purpose than to describe accurately and dispassionately the history of this group of aspiring professionals." While detached from special pleading, Cocks is not without feeling or emotional commitment. He writes with ethical and moral sensibility, recognizing and bringing to the page "the pervasive social intimacy of human experience." What makes the questions he poses powerful and his answers compelling is his supple awareness that "human society is as much about desire, fantasy, and irrationality as it is about interest, reality, and reason." The limes are not for everyone, they may be an exposed and insecure position. For Cocks, and therefore happily for his readers, the limits between disciplines and cultures are a premier vantage point for casting new visions of the broad sweep of emotional context in history.

Notes

1. *Psychotherapy in the Third Reich: The Göring Institute* (New York: Oxford, 1985, second ed. revised, New Brunswick, N.J.: Transaction Publishers, 1997).
2. Karen Brecht, Volker Friedrich, Ludger M. Hermanns, Isidor J. Kaminer, Dierk H. Juelich, Hella Ehlers (for the English ea.) eds., Christine Trollope and Joyce

Crick, trans., *"Here life goes on in a most peculiar way..." Psychoanalysis before and after 1933* (Hamburg: Kellner Verlag, 1985). The title is a quotation from a letter by John F. Rittmeister to the Storch family in Munsingen, Switzerland, October 15, 1939: "Hier geht das Leben auf eine sehr merkwurdige Weise weiter, namlich teilweise so, wie wenn garnicht wäre." (p. 187) Rittmeister, a Berlin psychoanalyst, was active in an anti-Nazi resistance group and was executed by the Gestapo at Berlin-Plötzensee on May 13, 1943.

3. Fritz Stern, "Fink Shrinks," *New York Review of Books* (December 19, 1985), p. 48, n.3.

4. Regine Lockot, *Erinnern und Durcharbeiten: Zur Geschichte der Psychoanalyse und Psychotherapie im Nationalsozialismus* (Frankfurt am Main: S. Fischer, 1985); and *De Reinigung der Psvchoanalyse: die Psychoanalytische Gesellschaft im Spiegel von Dokumenten und Zeitungen (1933–1951)* (Tubingen: Diskord, 1994); Volker Friedrich, "Psychoanalyse im Nationalsozialismus: Vom Widerspruch zur Gleichschaltung," *Jahrbuch der Psvchoanalyse,* XX (1987), 207–233; Bernd Nitzschke, "Psychoanalyse als "un"-politische Wissenschaft, " *Zeitschrift für psychosomatische Medizin und Psychoanalyse,* 37:1 (1991), 31–44; *Annemarie Dührssen, Ein Jahrhundert Psychoanalytische Bewegung in Deutschland: Die Psychotherapie Unter dem Einfluss Freuds* (Göttingen: Vandenhoeck und Ruprecht, 1994). For a German New Left view, see Helmut Dahmer, *Libido und Gesellschaft: Studien über Freud und die Freudische Linke* (Frankfurt am Main: Suhrkamp, 1973, 1982).

5. Brecht, et al., p. 72, including a list of psychoanalyst emigres from Germany.

6. Pfister to Freud, May 24, 1933, Sigmund Freud-Oskar Pfister, *Briefe 1909–1939* (Frankfurt am Main: S. Fischer Verlag, 1963), p. 151.

7. Freud to Pfister, May 28, 1933, *Ibid.,* p 152.

8. Freud to Eitingon, March 21, 1933, in Brecht, et al., p. 112.

9. Felix Boehm, *"Ereignisse 1933–1934,"* (Report of August 21, 1934), in Brecht, et al., p. 119. This document is, of course, a selfjustification by the author. In his Freud biography Ernest Jones emphasizes Freud's and his own distrust of Boehm's motives, see *The Life and Work of Sigmund Freud,* Vol. 3, *The Last Phase- 1919–1939* (New York: Basic Books, 1957), pp. 182–183.

10. Jones, *Freud,* Vol. 3, 187.

11. Brecht,et al.,p. 112.

12. Ernest Jones to Felix Boehm, July 28, 1934, in Brecht, et al., p. 78.

13. Ernest Jones to Therese Benedek, early December 1935, in Brecht, et al., p. 136. In 1957 Jones wrote: "On December 1, 1933...the few remaining Jews volunteered to resign so as to save the Society from being dissolved. Opinions have since differed about this step, and some have thought it would have been more dignified for all the members to resign in protest, as the Dutch colleagues did later on a similar occasion. But there was still a little hope that something could be saved. " Jones, *Freud,* Vol. 3, p. 186.

14. Memorandum by Felix Boehm, December 4, 1935, in Brecht, et al., p. 137.

15. To the Consultant Psychiatrist of the Armed Forces Health Inspector, "Expert report on criminal cases of unnatural and immoral sexual practices," Berlin, (December 15, 1944), in Brecht, et al., pp. 170–171.

16. "Problems of the Science of Science" (1946), in Robert S. Cohen and Thomas Schnelle, eds., *Cognition and Fact: Materials on Ludwik Fleck* (Dordrecht: D. Reidel Publishing Co., 1986), p. 118.

17. Ludwik Fleck in a 1958 unpublished manuscript quoted in Thomas Schnelle, "Microbiology and Philosophy of Science, Lwow and the German Holocaust: Stations of a Life—Ludwik Fleck, 1896–1961," in Cohen and Schnelle, *Cognition and Fact,* pp. 3–36. The quotation is on p. 26.

18. Cohen and Schnelle, *Cognition and Fact*, p. 27.
19. Geoffrey Cocks, ed., *The Curve of Life: Correspondence of Heinz Kohut, 1923–1981* (Chicago: University of Chicago Press, 1994).
20. "The Two Analyses of Mr. Z.,"*International Journal of Psycho-Analysis*, 60 (1979), 3–27. Reprinted in Paul H. Ornstein, ed., *The Search for the Self: Selected Writings of Heinz Kohut: 1978–1981*, Vol. 4, (Madison, CT: International Universities Press, 1991), 395–446.
21. George Devereux, *From Anxiety to Method in the Behavioral Sciences* (the Hague: Mouton, 1967), pp. xvi–xvii.
22. Erik H. Erikson, "Autobiographic Notes on the Identity Crisis," *Daedalus*, 99:4 (Fall 1970), 730–759.
23. George L. Engel, "The Death of a Twin: Mourning and Anniversary Reactions. Fragments of 10 Years of Self-Analysis," *International Journal of Psychoanalysis*, 56 (1975), 23–40; Lawrence R. Freedman, "Cerebral Concussion," in Harvey Wendell and Howard Spiro, eds., *When Doctors Get Sick* (New York: Plenum Publishing, 1987), pp. 131–138.
24. Kohut to Ruth Eissler, February 10, 1969, in Chapter Six of Cocks, *Treating Mind and Body*.
25. Heinz Kohut to Thomas Kohut, November 17, 1968, in Cocks, ed., *Curve of Life*, p. 217. See also the letter of February 5, 1969, *Ibid.*, pp. 226–228.
26. Leo Strauss, *Persecution and the Art of Writing* (Glencoe, Illinois: Free Press, 1952).
27. Strauss, pp. 17–18.
28. Nitzschke, pp. 35–36.
29. Strauss, p. 32.
30. Strauss, pp. 23–24.
31. Kohut to Anna and Paul Ornstein, February 11, 1975, *Curve of Life*, pp. 317–18, passim.
32. Robert D Stolorow, "Subjectivity and Self Psychology: A Personal Odyssey," *New Therapeutic Visions*, 8 (1992), 241–250. The quotation is from p. 245.

Introduction

As a historian of Germany, psychoanalysis, and medicine, the subject matter of my work has been comprised largely of doctors, dreamers—and demons.[1] For me, Freud was the first doctor and the first dreamer. His doctoring of his dreams helped lead me to other dreamers, to other doctors, and to demons. Through a variety of forms and subjects my writing reflects an abiding interest in the intersections of psychology and history. This interest rests in two relatively new, closely related, but also distinct fields of historical research, one of method and the other of subject matter. The method is that of what since the 1960s has been known among historians—admiringly, ambivalently, or pejoratively—as psychohistory. The subject matter—of equally recent origin and constituting the subject matter of this volume—is that of the history of psychotherapy, psychoanalysis, and medicine, particularly in Germany. The essays in this book, save for the correction of errors, some updating of citations, and the occasional sharpening or smoothing of language, appear in their original form. An introduction allows me to revisit the essays in order to place them in newer and richer contexts.

This introduction also permits me to provide the reader with a complementary sketch of some of the relevant elements in the evolution of psychohistory. The method—as applied here in the case of English writer A. A. Milne—is a part of the history of psychoanalysis explored throughout this collection of essays. This initial exercise in psychobiography also led me to an appreciation for the history of the discipline—psychoanalysis—upon which this new interdisciplinary method was based. At the same time—with, however, later effect—this first psychohistorical attempt at a life also introduced—or reintroduced—me to the pervasive social intimacy of human experience so vital to historical understanding. This reminder greatly informs my ongoing work in the social history of illness (see chapters 7, 8, and 9).

Freud observed that in human affairs there are no accidents. In this, of course, he was expressing his own intellectual commitment to psychic determinism. (He did, perhaps, maintain some perspective, a sense of humor, and—to be sure—a degree of defensiveness about this: A dedicated cigar smoker, he once—allegedly and maybe aprocryphally—responded to a query about the sexual significance of smoking by saying: "Sometimes a cigar is just a cigar.") At any rate, the matter of accident is germane to my initial work in the field of psychohistory. My memory is that in the autumn of 1972 I quite by accident came across A. A. Milne's autobiography in the UCLA library. But the book caught my eye because—or *also* because—I was familiar with Milne's books for children from my own childhood. There seemed to be a fit between what I was reading in Milne's life and work and the theories of Melanie Klein and others about the early relationship between the infant and its parents, especially the mother. I was therefore not deterred by Frederick Crews' use of Milne's Winnie-the-Pooh for a famous parody of gassy literary criticism, including a memorable send-up of the Freudian variety.[2] A life is a life, even for a writer of children's works who lived behind the stately Victorian facade of bourgeois emotional reserve. Moreover, subsequent research on the Victorian age has demonstrated the vigorous emotional life residing behind that facade.[3]

Peter Loewenberg pointed out at the time that more needed to be done with the later ego defensive dynamics of Milne's work and life, particularly the denial of rage and aggression.[4] Melanie Klein in particular had stressed the early instinctual in her work with and on infants, but at the same time her work and that of others pioneered a new emphasis on the pre-oedipal stages of psychological development. This work eventually led away from a drive psychology preoccupied with intrapsychic sexual conflict and toward the study of the psychodynamics of external object relations. This turn joined with growing psychoanalytic interest in the psychology of the ego to orient psychoanalysis increasingly toward the interaction between individual psyche and social environment from the earliest years of life onward. The object relations emphasis on the pre-oedipal has also worked against the traditional androcentric orientation of orthodox psychoanalysis and contributed to greater understanding of the origins of the similarities and differences in the psychology of men and women.[5]

Two general observations may be made in light of all this. The first is that psychoanalytic thought has not been monolithic. It has grown in ways that have brought it into increasingly fruitful contact with other fields and in ways that are particularly useful to the eclectic and holistic interests of the historian. The second is that lately historians are discovering—or rediscovering—that human society is as much about desire, fantasy, and irrationality as it is about interest, reality, and reason. This is one fruitful result of the turn among historians in the latter half of the twentieth century toward a more inclusive social history "from the bottom up." It is upon such ground that history, psychoanalysis, and other disciplines can most fruitfully meet and combine.

My modest little essay on Milne did not explicitly address, much less explore, such issues, but inherent in the material and approach was an interest in the relationship between neurosis and creativity as well as the elucidating power of psychoanalytic thought.[6] The work of Phyllis Greenacre was especially useful in this regard, however limited it is by its early instinctual point of view. More generally, in the portrayal of Milne as one who artistically exploited his own psychological struggles with life the essay also followed to a distinct degree the neo-Freudian and post-Freudian emphasis upon strength and development in place of Freud's concern with conflict and disability. More specifically along these lines, one might profitably apply Heinz Kohut's psychoanalytic self psychology to Milne's infancy and childhood. Kohut argues that the infant's development of a cohesive self depends on the quality of relationship with the parents. This perspective in particular might more fully elucidate Milne's professed childhood struggles with questions of masculine and feminine identity as part of a more general struggle to distinguish and develop his own self independent from that of his mother.

Milne's writings yield evidence of his unconscious desire to make reparation for fantasied infantile rage against his mother, rage aggravated by his mother's own relative aloofness and the mediation of a string of governesses. (A similar "managerial" style of mothering in Victorian families is embodied, to cite another literary instance, by Bertie Wooster's Aunt Agatha in the stories of P. G. Wodehouse.[7]) This reparation subsequently took the form of wishing to provide the little girl for whom Milne's mother (after two boys) had wished and in general attempting to please women and little girls. (There is of course also a cultural factor in this, since Victorian society indulged the "angelic nature" of little girls; one immediately thinks, for example, of the life of Charles Dodgson who as Lewis Carroll transformed such indulgence into *Alice in Wonderland*.) For example, in 1919 Milne wrote to one of the proprietors of *Punch* that his "chief pleasure" in the production of *Belinda*, one of his first plays, was "in meeting [lead actress] Irene Vanbrugh."[8] And in a book of essays published in 1925 and dedicated to his elder—and dying—brother, Milne typically expresses himself in terms of oral demand and dependence:

> I have often longed to be a grocer. To be surrounded by so many interesting things—sardines, bottled raspberries, biscuits with sugar on the top, preserved ginger, hams, brawn under glass, everything in fact that makes life worth living; at one moment to walk up a ladder in search of nutmeg, at the next to dive under a counter in pursuit of cinnamon, to serve little girls with a ha'porth of pear drops and lordly people like you and me with a pint of cherry gin—is not this to follow the king of trades?[9]

This pattern of reparation to the mother included, I noted in the original essay, the wish to sire a daughter. Why, then (I did not ask at the time), did Milne and his wife not have another a child after the birth of their only son, Christopher Robin? The answer came in a 1990 biography: A terribly difficult birth left Daphne Milne "'determined never to repeat the performance.'"[10] Milne's reparative pattern would not only have contributed to the honoring of his wife's decision, but also, as we know, compelled him to look elsewhere in his life and work for a "daughter." Milne's feelings of loss and conflict concerning the place of his mother in his childhood and his adult life must have been sharpened at this particular time because of his mother's series of illnesses ending with her death in 1921.[11] Another discovery seemed to confirm a breezy, undocumented assertion I made about the illustration of another oral fantasy at the center of Milne's 1930 work, *When I Was Very Young*. It seemed to me even more obvious than probable that Milne and illustrator E. H. Shepard would confer on the drawings to be included in Milne's works—and important in the case of the dead woman depicted at the door of the candy store in *When I Was Very Young*. Correspondence between Milne and Shepard at the Victoria and Albert Museum appears to confirm the assumption of consultation, however breezy at the time.[12] His father's death in 1932, documented in the Public Record Office then at Somerset House in London, surely contributed to the pall of the 1930s I describe. As with his mother's death, Milne in his autobiography makes no mention of the death of his father.

Finally, a second book by Milne's son published after my essay appeared demonstrated that his father's psychologically significant predilection for the letter J and the name John in his writing had—consciously and/or unconsciously—become a family tradition: Christopher Milne notes that the first helper in his book shop in 1952 was named John, "the first of sixteen whose names began with a *J*."[13] As I discuss in the essay, Milne was preoccupied with his brother Kenneth John, who took ill in 1924 and died in 1929. In no small measure, Milne's famous cycle of children's books written for and about his son Christopher Robin were also an attempt to deal with both the psychological joy and the psychological pain of his relationship with Kenneth John Milne. Milne's guilt over supplanting Ken as the writer of the family was likely one of the reasons that Milne, whose work appeared in *Punch* regularly from 1904 to 1919, published poems there from *When We Very Young* from January to June 1924 but did not contribute again until August 1934, and only then under a pseudonym.[14] It was Ken who was a regular contributor to *Punch* from the latter part of 1924 until February 1929. His last contribution was a typically gentle Milnean skewering of the medical profession in "Things My Illness Has Taught Me."[15]

Psychotherapy

Once everyone knew that the Nazis had banned psychoanalysis as another "Jewish science" and that no organized psychotherapy could possibly have existed in a land ruled by racial biology. But once historians began studying the complexities of the domestic history of the Third Reich it turned out that on this score everyone was substantially wrong. This new research was a result of an expansion of interest and study from the traditional areas of politics, government, diplomacy, and the military. Historians now were constructing a more comprehensive and critical social history of the period.[16] The study of professions demonstrated—sadly—that professionals in Germany did not require a democratic environment in order to function effectively in service to the state. Such findings have serious implications for other modern societies. This is especially the case with the field of medicine, which at the time was becoming a particularly fruitful area of historical investigation. Doctors were everywhere in the Third Reich and the old German excuse of the "few rotten apples" who had conducted experiments on human beings in the concentration camps (see chapter 9) was being put aside in favor of a study of the integrity of the whole professional barrel. And then there were the psychotherapists who, as it turned out, had experienced a surprising rise in their professional fortunes after 1933. They were needed, and their discipline had some scientific and organizational momentum from the First World War and the 1920s. They also had enemies: the powerful psychiatric establishment in the universities and in the state bureaucracy. But there was also a psychotherapist named Matthias Heinrich Göring, a relative of Hitler's beefy lieutenant, Hermann Göring. In this case, therefore, the sort of traditional historical research on the Third Reich concerned with the men at the top combined with the new social history of individuals and groups mobilizing from below to protect and advance interests in a system as complex as it was corrupt.

The original question was whether—like the Cheshire cat—the history of psychotherapy in the Third Reich, and not just the smile of its promise, was really there. It was, though of course not in the sense of scientific progress.[17] This was a study rather in terms of the even more morally ambiguous and objectionable dynamics of institutional accommodation, consolidation, and advance. The resulting dissertation (1975) and the subsequent book (1985) helped prompt some young German psychoanalysts to examine the history of their field. These critical (in both senses of the word) efforts were paralleled by increasing organized interest in the history of psychoanalysis and psychiatry among historians and practitioners in other countries. Such collective efforts at further documentation and analysis aided immeasurably my own ongoing research, all of which contributed to a second, revised and expanded edition of my book on the Göring Institute.[18] Chapters 1 and 2 are the direct result of this work, while chapter 3 explores the history of the postwar rewriting—to the point, for many, of discovery—of this history.

A German Studies Association conference in Washington, D.C. in 1985 brought together scholars who had been studying various German professions and formed the basis for the book of essays, *German Professions, 1800–1950* (1990), edited by Konrad Jarausch and myself. In my contribution I was able to think more deeply about the more general social context of the Third Reich. Detlev Peukert's *Volksgenossen und Gemeinschaftsfremde* (1982) was especially valuable in this respect. Peukert had, to my mind, demonstrated the surprising complexity and significance of the social order under Nazism. It is not his purpose to ignore the murderous purposes and actions of the Nazi regime or to relieve Germans in general of moral responsibility for the crimes committed in their name and with their consent. Rather, Peukert explores the social conditions that he believes allowed Auschwitz to happen. Peukert's work constituted for me a valuable parallel my earlier reliance on Martin Broszat's *Der Staat Hitlers* (1969), which had organized my view of the often chaotic inner workings of Nazi governance in their effects on German psychotherapists. I would now add the work of Michael Geyer, who has written probingly on the complicated conditions under which individuals and groups do or do not and can or cannot oppose tyranny.[19] The subject of professionalization itself has provided a way not only to understand an important social dynamic of modern Germany. The history of German professions has also opened up the prevailing Anglo-Saxon model of professionalization to greater consideration of the role of the state. This is one of the continuities in modern German history which, therefore, places the Third Reich more firmly not only into the course of German history but that of the West as well. This is a topic I take up more extensively—and ambitiously—in chapter 9. In that essay I move from the somewhat dualistic metaphor I use in chapter 1 drawn from Jean Renoir's film *Grand Illusion* (1937) to a unitary analysis of the differences and similarities between the history of modern Germany and the West.

The revisiting of the topic of psychotherapy in the Third Reich has also allowed me to correct a few mistakes in the book. Chief among these is my earlier conclusion that the army and the air force had adopted the same harsh policy toward homosexuals in 1944. In fact, the Luftwaffe policy reflected a psychotherapeutic emphasis on the "cure" of homosexuality. What I had earlier interpreted as an argument by a Luftwaffe psychotherapist had in fact become the policy; a document discovered by a German colleague demonstrated this. This, happily, made my original argument about the significant influence of the psychotherapists in the Luftwaffe, and in German society in general, that much stronger. Similarly, recent research on the treatment of war neuroses during the First World War has confirmed in even more penetrating fashion the effects of the psychogenic point of view among and around psychiatrists in Germany.[20]

The short paper on Jung, too, came about as a result of my book on psychotherapy in Nazi Germany. The association of Carl Gustav Jung with the Nazi regime was one of the few things historians and psychoanalysts knew about the subject of psychotherapy in the Third Reich. The gap between Jungians and Freudians had been deepened into a chasm by what the latter saw as final, damning proof of Jung's anti-Semitism and so the final justification for Freud's expulsion of his erstwhile heir-apparent from the psychoanalytic movement on the eve of the First World War. For their part, Jungians have attempted to explain Jung's involvement in the affairs of psychotherapy in Germany under Hitler as an attempt to "save what could be saved." In a Jungian vein, they have argued that Jung was engaging the "shadow" of racism in order to destroy it. Placing Jung in the context of the institutional history of psychotherapy in the Third Reich, however, leads to four conclusions: (1) Jung's psychology indeed displays some affinities with the racism of the Nazis; (2) Jung's rhetoric in the early years of the Third Reich certainly can be construed as having given "aid and comfort" to the Nazis; (3) he played no significant part in the institutionalization of psychotherapy in Nazi Germany; and (4) the German psychotherapists used Jung more than he used them.

Jung's "timeless," archetypal approach to human psychology, in contrast to Freud, offers little to the historian and psychohistorian in search of the specific motives of individual human beings at specific junctures in time. The historian's question is not the philosopher's or theologian's broad "Why?" It is, as Loewenberg has so cogently and correctly put it, "Why now?" Jung's approach is also fraught with the danger of awed fascination with all things, including evil, in place of Freud's sober and critical rationality. As Jeffrey Moussaieff Masson puts it in terms of Jungian analysis,

> the essence of the defect of Jungian psychotherapy is the attempt to avoid touching on those issues that are most concrete, most real, most related to the body and to a specific moment in history.... Jung could not afford to urge his patients to examine their pasts, for he needed to avoid thinking about his own past, tainted as it was by collaboration with the Nazis.[21]

While I argue that Jung's "collaboration with the Nazis" was not as straightforward as Masson believes, there is a dynamic in Jung's case that is philosophically and morally problematical. But I put it the other way around: the same airy approach to human experience manifest in Jungian therapy that Masson sees as caused by collaboration with the Nazis was, rather, a style of thought that led to Jung's rhetorical and organizational flirtation with the Nazis.

As with the history of Nazi Germany in general, the subject of resistance to Hitler has undergone significant revision in recent years. Historians are no longer content to chronicle the isolated acts of military conspirators. There was much more—and much less—going on along these lines than such—politically exploitable—portraits suggested. Besides expanding the boundaries of the subject matter from military officers to workers, to students, and to the "everyday" in general, this field of study has also begun to ask new questions about the nature—within and beyond the Third Reich—of "the social processes of undoing despotic regimes."[22]

Especially for Germans, the subject of resistance against the Third Reich—and here "resistance against" has a historiographical meaning as well as a historical one—has most often been a matter of constructing a "usable past." This was certainly the case with German psychiatrists, psychotherapists, and psychoanalysts after 1945. Members of each of these disciplines repressed, distorted, or ignored their field's history between 1933 and 1945. Mythologies of survival, persecution, and disengagement were nurtured—when the subject came up at all. Critical inquiry began only during the 1960s and then only in a general and political way. More specific scholarly inquiry surfaced inside and outside Germany during the ensuing decades as both young professionals in West Germany and historians from abroad started to conduct primary research on the history of the behavioral and medical sciences under Nazism. The struggles over this history during the past twenty years have been as involved as the history itself.[23]

The repression of, and challenge to, memory was most evident among German psychoanalysts. As we shall see in part II of this volume, the historical reality was much more complicated—and disturbing—than the traditional view of the simple Nazi repression of psychoanalysis allowed.[24] In fact, the traditional view by its very existence undermined itself. This was because this traditional view was held by a large number of practicing psychoanalysts and non-Freudian psychotherapists in postwar Germany. Where had all these psychoanalysts and psychotherapists come from? From exile? No. Even psychoanalyst Alexander Mitscherlich, who was credited by many for bringing Freud back into German culture after the Second World War, had spent the years 1937 to 1945 under Gestapo watch in Heidelberg. In fact, the psychoanalytic and psychotherapeutic talent in both postwar republics after 1949 was homegrown. Had these practitioners therefore simply gone into other fields of work from 1933 to 1945? If so, how then to explain the relatively large postwar number of young practitioners and even students with some recent training in psychoanalysis and psychotherapy? Such questions as these were not asked, much less answered, until many years after the war. So the traditional view undermined itself silently, standing as a mute and hollow shell impervious to query. The truth was repressed in a rush away from history and toward significant ongoing professional development in a reconstructing society and polity.

Where the truth threatened to break through the official repression in these years, it manifested itself as professional conflict between the two main psychoanalytic groups, the German Psychoanalytic Society (DPG) and the German Psychoanalytic Union (DPV). The DPG had originally been founded in 1910 and then refounded in 1945. The DPV was formed in 1950 and was comprised of orthodox psychoanalysts who had seceded from the DPG, which included "unorthodox" psychoanalysts such as the self-proclaimed "neo-analyst" Harald Schultz-Hencke. The DPG analysts tended to favor short-term therapies that could be covered under the state health insurance system. They were also ecumenical in trying to attract Adlerians, Jungians, and other psychotherapists into a common society and institute. The DPV, which in 1951 was recognized as a member of the International Psycho-Analytic Association, maintained the traditional exclusivity of long-term Freudian psychoanalysis. Both societies, however, contained members who had been active as psychoanalysts during the Third Reich. Each society, therefore, had behind the official silence an official version of the history the silence was designed to hide. The DPG, which carried on the enforced ecumenical policy of psychoanalysts and psychotherapists from 1933 to 1945, maintained the belief that psychoanalysis had been "saved" during the Nazi years. The DPV, on the other hand, took the position that genuine psychoanalysis had been suppressed under Hitler.

A younger psychoanalytic generation, however, raised on the historically critical consciousness and confrontations of the 1960s, began to question the traditional view beginning in the 1970s. In this, they were aided by two other developments. The first was that the older and heretofore silent generation of psychoanalysts and psychotherapists was at the same time entering the age of personal retrospection, a phenomenon predictably more pronounced among those whose profession was the analytic and therapeutic excavation of human memory. As a result, memoirs of previously unexamined areas of the history of psychoanalysis and psychotherapy in Germany began to appear.[25] These memoirs, however, were not critical but apologetic and lacked treatment of the necessary historical contexts. These shortcomings were compensated for by the second development, the fact that historians were starting to explore previously unexplored areas of the Third Reich. One of these areas was the history of psychotherapy and psychoanalysis. This was in turn the result of two recent developments in the field of history, the trend toward social history on the one hand and the trend toward interdisciplinary history on the other.

What has emerged in the twenty years since has been a detailed examination of the history of the German Institute for Psychological Research and Psychotherapy, the so-called "Göring Institute. In this institute in Berlin and at its branches around Germany and in Vienna psychoanalysts and psychotherapists established an unprecedented professional capacity in collaboration with agencies of the Nazi party, the Reich government, private business and industry, and the military. The result, along with ethical ambiguities and outrages both small and large, was a continuity of professionalization of the discipline that laid the basis for further professional developments in the immediate postwar era and beyond. This continuity had begun with the emergence of the psychodynamic movement in psychiatry led by Freud at the turn of the century and pursued in Germany after the First World War not only by psychoanalysts in Berlin but by the General Medical Society for Psychotherapy founded in 1926. It was the continuity of unacknowledged professional development under Nazism that was confronted for the first time in a comprehensive and critical fashion thirty years after the end of the war.

Most recently, Annemarie Dührssen has ignited a firestorm of controversy with her book on "a century of the psychoanalytic movement in Germany." Dührssen, who is a past director of the Institute for Psychotherapy in Berlin and a former professor of psychotherapy and psychosomatic medicine at the Free University Berlin, was a student of Schultz-Hencke who received her training during the war at the Göring Institute. As such, she is an impassioned defender of the eclectic psychotherapeutic tradition represented by the DPG. In her book she attempts to justify the professional direction taken by the DPG in moving away from an international psychoanalytic movement she characterizes as sectarian and elitist. She claims that the 1992 designation of a medical specialty in psychotherapy in Germany represents a culmination of a century of psychoanalysis. This is a dubious claim for a number of reasons. Freud himself was an exponent of lay analysis because he feared that, if left to doctors, psychoanalysis would become just another medical specialty instead of a scientific and therapeutic mode of inquiry into human nature and behavior. More generally, the introduction of medical specialization in psychotherapy involves not the culmination of a single line of development but rather is the historical product of conflict and compromise among various interests such as academic psychologists, lay therapists, and various positions on psychotherapy and psychosomatic medicine among general medical practitioners, internists, neurologists, and psychiatrists.

That Dührssen herself was a leader in the campaign for such a medical specialization gives her account the cast of special pleading instead of careful historical analysis. Once again, the multifarious—and, in this case, also nefarious—complications of history are ignored, or at least underplayed, in pursuit of the justification of present developments in accord with the author's professional point of view. She argues that in the early 1930s in Germany psychoanalysis was in great financial difficulty and that therefore National Socialism alone cannot be blamed for the destruction of the autonomous psychoanalytic movement there.[26] She thereby ignores the increasingly fascist political environment in Germany and in Europe that caused many psychoanalysts and others to flee even before 1933. In the same vein, she ignores the moral ambiguities of the DPG's and IPA's "acceptance" of German psychoanalysts joining the Göring Institute as well as the resignation and anger with which Freud gave his "approval" to this decision.[27] In any case, it is not clear that psychoanalysis was on the verge of collapsing in Germany. True, the Depression had hurt the psychoanalysts and their patrons, but the passing of the economic crisis would have reinvigorated the movement. Contrary to Dührssen's assertion that the growth of psychoanalysis in the United States was purely exceptional,[28] subsequent developments everywhere in the West have seen an increase in the demand—and funding—for psychological services of all kinds. This meant competition, not extinction, for psychoanalysis.

Dührssen argues that the results of collaboration within the Göring Institute were beneficial in the long run for psychoanalysis in Germany. On the one hand, according to her, the Göring Institute "saved" lay analysts in Germany from "a severe existential crisis" through its creation of officially recognized "attending psychologists."[29] On the other hand, the Göring Institute also allegedly did psychoanalysis a service by stripping it of a pernicious "psychoanalytic group dynamic" that had rendered it an "elitist, conspiratorial sect" while preserving the "spirit of enlightenment" that allowed its (non-Jewish) representatives in the Third Reich to continue the fight against "that irrational mysticism disseminated in a disturbing way at the time by the Jung group in their closeness with Nazi ideology."[30] Such a polarization of good (ecumenical Freudians, like Dührssen, at the Göring Institute) and evil (Nazi Jungians) distorts the historical record. Collaboration with the Nazis crossed psychotherapeutic school lines. The Freudians at the Göring Institute were at the very least no less involved than the Jungians in providing psychotherapeutic "goods and services" for Hitler's regime in the form of presumably less neurotic and thus more productive soldiers and workers. Significantly in this respect, Dührssen as well has nothing to say about the rhetorical concession to Nazi aims by her mentor Schultz-Hencke's opportunistic paean in 1934 to the human "fitness" (*Tüchtigkeit*) produced by psychoanalytic treatment.[31]

In Dührssen's happy professional scenario, the psychoanalysts at the Göring Institute learned to work with the other psychotherapeutic groups and to abandon their previous exclusive commitment to long-term psychoanalysis in favor of short-term therapeutic methods that could help integrate psychotherapy and psychoanalysis into medicine and the state health insurance system. This, for Dührssen, constitutes another step on the way to the realization of the medical specialization in psychotherapy that in her view justifies the existence of psychoanalysis. Dührssen also upbraids later critics of these actions for not understanding—from the comfort and security of a democratic environment—what it was like to have to deal with a dictatorship.[32] She has a point here, but it is a very small one. It is the responsibility of people to look back on history and make judgments, not simply to "understand" to the point of exculpation. This is of course especially the case when contemplating such a destructive phenomenon as the Third Reich.

Most distressingly, Dührssen takes her analysis in the wrong direction by way of an extended—and tortured—exposition on psychoanalysis as an "(allegedly) Jewish science."[33] While she puts her chapter title in the form of a question, "Was Psychoanalysis a Jewish Science?," Dührssen's treatment of the issue reveals a great deal of objective and subjective confusion and bias. There are two questions to pose about this tack: First, what are Dührssen's motives? Second, what does it contribute to the history of psychoanalysis in Germany? Dührssen's motives have been subjected to extremely critical analysis by many of her German colleagues. One review has argued that psychoanalysts of Duhrssen's generation in Germany have been traumatized by their professional exploitation of the expulsion of Jewish colleagues and the poor training in psychoanalysis they received at the Göring Institute, especially the reduction in self-analysis hours from 250 to 150.[34] This argument is hard to document convincingly and has at least the whiff of the ad hominem about it. Another, private, speculation is that Dührssen—for both unconscious personal and conscious political reasons—is making an appeal to aspiring East German psychoanalysts who are seeking a German professional identity and who also are afflicted with anti-Semitic feelings inherited from both the Third Reich and the East German regime.

It is clear that Dührssen's misbegotten foray into racial stereotype contributes little to the historical record. Understanding this, however, allows us to do two things: one, pick out what is valuable in Dührssen's account, and two, discern again the central historical determinant of her bias. As to the first, Dührssen is correct to place psychoanalysis within a larger context of developments in the realm of medical psychology in the twentieth century. And there is nothing wrong—though also nothing new—in critiquing the psychoanalytic movement for its elitist tendencies and its—hardly unique—organizational incestuousness and infighting. That the early psychoanalytic movement was dominated by Jews who—like their Gentile colleagues—were extraordinarily devoted to Freud is also a well-established fact. Dührssen's other argument—that Freud himself was failing during the 1920s and 1930s as a result of his cancer—is true, but it is also overdrawn, ignoring, among other things, Freud's significant intellectual contributions in those years. The first four chapters of Dührssen's book offer a sketch of Freud and the psychoanalytic movement that breaks no new ground. Indeed, Dührssen's discussion of Freud's identification with Don Cipion, Hannibal, Joseph, Moses, and Sophocles' Oedipus ignores the many rich debates in the literature about the extent and nature of Freud's "Jewishness."[35]

We also see that Dührssen's own professional interests in this approach are clear. Dührssen pursues with single-minded vigor her theme of how the orthodox psychoanalysts increasingly diverged from the great stream of history leading to the inevitable and desirable end of a medical specialization in psychotherapy. Dührssen's attempt to tease out the "Jewish" characteristics of the psychoanalytic movement, besides being offensive—or at the very least misleading—in the context of the history of Germany in the twentieth century, is simply too rough a measure to provide any significant historical insight. It is significant in this regard that Dührssen never directly answers her own question, "Was Psychoanalysis a Jewish Science?". But any genuine sensitivity at all on Dührssen's part would have led her put the words "Jewish Science" in her question in quotation marks. This lack of sensitivity, whatever its personal origins, is also reflected in her use of the word *Rasse*—both with and without quotation marks on one page—to describe the Jews.[36] Such an approach leads Dührssen, to cite the most egregious example, into an unfruitful, irrelevant, inexplicable, and objectionable comparison between the Orthodox Jewish prohibition of intermarriage with Gentiles and the Nazi race laws, a comparison she insensitively labels as "black humor."[37] Dührssen's overriding concern about the hostile and undesirable "Other" in her view of the history of her discipline, finally, compels her too see conspiracy in opposing accounts. She detects, for instance, a "cover-up" (*Vertuschungspolitik*) in the fact that the Nazi party membership of DPV psychoanalyst Gerhard Scheunert was not revealed in earlier studies by myself and Regine Lockot.[38] Lockot has fully discussed Scheunert's party membership in her most recent book,[39] while I did not report it earlier because at the time the evidence I had on it was conflicting.[40]

In any case, the—or a—better question about the early years of psychoanalysis is: Why was it primarily Jews—and not just Jews but German Jews—who in Vienna and elsewhere pioneered in particular the early work in psychoanalysis? Such a question leads us into the realms of society and culture rather than those of racial (mis)characterization. Psychoanalysis is a human activity, practiced and undergone by people of all religions, races, and social classes. There was as much variety—and conflict—among the early Jewish practitioners of psychoanalysis as among many a culturally homogeneous group. Is it, for example, more significant for the history of psychoanalysis that Freud and Adler were both Jews or that they differed in their ideas to the point of personal and scientific rupture? The subsequent history of psychoanalysis in Germany is, in any case, one largely marked by the absence of Jews. For a painfully obvious reason, both the postwar DPV and DPG have always had relatively few Jewish members. This fact too renders Dührssen's obsession with the possible "Jewishness" of prewar psychoanalysis useless for historical purposes.

Psychoanalysis

In 1990 the International Association for the History of Psychoanalysis held a conference in London on the involvement of psychoanalysts in the society and politics of Europe in the twentieth century. This represented a conceptual and temporal broadening of the earlier conferences that was appropriate as well for the recent revolutionary developments in Eastern and Central Europe. The most striking evidence of these developments at the conference was the presence of young psychoanalytic scholars from a Soviet Union then in the process of disappearing. Psychoanalysis had a brief and difficult history in the Soviet Union, its initial enthusiasms buried under tons of Pavlovian indifference and Stalinist hostility. Now there was talk in London of the KGB wanting to return documents seized from the Russian Psychoanalytic Society in the 1920s and of a current renaissance of psychoanalytic thinking and practice in Russia.

My paper argues that psychoanalysis in the first forty years of the twentieth century was not in a position either theoretically or organizationally to do much in the realm of social or political reform. Freud himself was anything but a revolutionary and the psychoanalytic emphasis on the "individual contemplative" was out of step with the "group manipulative" ethos of the political right, left, and center of the era. Psychoanalysts necessarily were more concerned with securing a professional place in the face of significant professional and cultural opposition. Still, psychoanalysis has always retained a rebellious element in its conception of the individual at instinctual war with society. In this respect, Freud is like Hegel: His epigoni could take his thought in opposite directions. Like the Right Hegelians who emphasized the rational justice of the status quo, mainstream psychoanalysts have followed Freud's lead toward mitigation of suffering and the upholding of civilized restraints and achievements against the disruptive forces of the id. Like the Left Hegelians, chief among whom was Marx, a smaller group of radical psychoanalysts have stressed the need to bend or break the social order for equality of individual freedom and happiness.

The second paper on the history of psychoanalysis reprinted here was presented in Paris in 1987 at the first conference of the International Association for the History of Psychoanalysis, a meeting devoted to the subject of psychoanalysis during the Second World War. The focus of the paper is on historical context since (1) the systematic historical study of the history of this field was new we all needed to remind ourselves of proper historical procedure; (2) the psychoanalysts who made up the bulk of the participants in the conference were not professional historians and lacked the necessary background in subject matter and history; and (3) psychoanalysts in particular often tend—out of a combination of embattled defensiveness and a tendency toward intellectual clannishness—not to take other contexts as seriously as they should. The paper also reflects research on the larger contexts of the mobilization of psychology for industry and war and the social place of illness in general in modern German society. This research uncovered a coincidence of striking coincidence between historical subject matter and its treatment. In 1943 Matthias Heinrich Göring, the director of the German Institute for Psychological Research and Psychotherapy in Berlin, lectured in Paris on the "The Foundations of Psychotherapy" at Maison de la Chimie, in the same auditorium in which the IAHP had just held its inaugural conference in 1987.[41]

In 1987 as well I was given the opportunity to edit the correspondence of Chicago psychoanalyst Heinz Kohut, who was a leader of the postwar American psychoanalytic establishment. He pioneered new work on narcissism and eventually developed his own version of psychoanalysis called self psychology which has remained influential in psychoanalysis and in a variety of other disciplines, including history. Kohut was born in Vienna in 1913 and was forced to emigrate in 1939 following the annexation of Austria by Nazi Germany.[42] Kohut's history therefore coincided well with my areas of interest and expertise. His correspondence is rich in scientific and historical significance, but the most surprising discovery receives no mention in the correspondence. According to Kohut's wife and son, Kohut himself was the subject of his most famous case study, "The Two Analyses of Mr. Z." According to this view, the first of the two analyses was Kohut's own training analysis from the 1940s and the second was a self-analysis from the 1960s. The claim is a controversial one. Some friends and colleagues of Kohut think it is likely, while others dispute it. Concerns have been raised about the propriety of such a deception and about the effect of such a claim, whether true or not, on the fortunes of self psychology.

Did Kohut in fact analyze himself? His son says he did and Kohut's correspondence at the time refers on more than one occasion to periods of introspection during and after his American Psychoanalytic Association presidency. The second analysis in the case study begins in the mid-1960s, placing it squarely in the time period when Kohut was undergoing his self-analysis.[43] Some argue that Kohut projected his own experiences into the case, that Mr. Z.'s life resembled his own, or that Kohut consciously used details of his own life to camouflage the identity of the real patient.[44] In my view, there are simply too many parallels in the case to Kohut's life to be just camouflage or countertransference. I also think that instances of what some have seen as "the failure to comment on what appear to be extraordinary similarities between Mr. Z's life and his own"[45] is evidence of Kohut's unwillingness to reveal himself as the analysand. The same reason lies behind the fact that "absolutely nothing is said about the nature of [Mr. Z's] father's sickness,"[46] since this would be the camouflage for Kohut's father's absence during the First World War.

Kohut was clearly aware of the similarity of his own venture to Freud's self-analysis as reported in *The Interpretation of Dreams* and its centrality to the discovery of psychoanalysis. Kohut finished his own study of Freud's self-analysis in early 1973, emphasizing the link between self-examination and scientific discovery. That same year Kohut wrote a letter to German colleague Tilmann Moser which appeared as a preface to the original German edition of Moser's book of reflections on his own analysis, concluding:

> The greatest present danger to analysis, as I see it, is the loss of the spirit of adventure, of exploration, of the courage to undertake new forays into the still unknown regions of the psychological universe.[47]

That self-analysis and science were deeply personal experiences for Kohut at the time is, in my view, further indicated by several of the passages in the essay, "Creativeness, Charisma, Group Psychology: Reflections on the Self-Analysis of Freud," published in 1976. Freud's self-analysis merits an enthusiastic redundancy of prose in the first two paragraphs, an enthusiasm born of identification and recent personal experience: "a unique event in the history of human thought.... without precedent in the history of human thought," Kohut writes.[48] And there is, I think, as much Kohut—child, youth, young adult, and adult—as Freud in this generic assessment from the final paragraph of the essay:

> I am certain that decisive progress in the area of depth psychology is tied to personal acts of courage by the investigator who not only suffers anxiety but tends to be maligned and ostracized.[49]

And is it only a coincidence that Kohut's first book, published in 1971, is entitled *The Analysis of the Self*?

But is a complete and successful self-analysis possible at all? Freud himself entertained some doubts about this, writing to Wilhelm Fliess: "True self-analysis is impossible, else there would be no illness"; but he obviously felt that for him at least a significant degree of self-analysis was feasible, for he went on to Fliess: "the most important patient for me was my own person."[50] He undertook such a self-analysis using his free associations, dreams, memories, and slips of tongue and pen. This self-analysis, undertaken in the mid-1890s, provided much of the data for *The Interpretation of Dreams*. As he wrote again to Fliess on October 15, 1897: "My self-analysis is in fact the most essential thing I have at present and promises to become of the greatest value to me if it reaches its end."[51] He proceeded with it in spite of deep personal reservations:

> I should have to reveal to the public gaze more of the intimacies of my mental life than I liked, or than is normally necessary for any writer who is a man of science and not a poet.[52]

In fact, Freud found the process so distressing that he had to put off the publication of *The Interpretation of Dreams* for more than a year-and-a-half.[53] But in that book he offered an extended defense of the virtues of self-observation:

> I have noticed in my psycho-analytical work that the whole frame of mind of a man who is reflecting is totally different from that of a man who is observing his own psychical processes. In reflection there is one more psychical activity at work than in the most attentive self-observation, and this is shown amongst other things by the tense looks and wrinkled forehead of a person pursuing his reflections as compared with the restful expression of the self-observer. In both cases attention must be concentrated, but the man who is reflecting is also exercising his *critical* faculty; this leads him to reject some of the ideas that occur to him after perceiving them, to cut short others without following the trains of thought which they would open up to him, and to behave in such a way towards still others that they never become conscious at all and are accordingly suppressed before being perceived. The self-observer on the other hand need only take the trouble to suppress his critical faculty. If he succeeds in doing that, innumerable ideas come into his consciousness of which he could otherwise never have got hold. The material which is in this way freshly obtained for his self-perception makes it possible to interpret both his pathological ideas and his dream-structures.[54]

But if Freud's self-analysis was feasible, was Kohut's? Peter Gay has observed that Freud's self-analysis was "by its very nature...unduplicable."[55] But Gay is comparing Freud to the members of the Freud circle in Vienna who had not yet been analyzed. Kohut—thanks to Freud and his self-analysis—had been analyzed three times before, twice incompletely in Vienna and a full analysis in America. He could use this experience, as well as his years of psychoanalytic study, as a point of departure for a self-analysis. Such a self-analysis would, moreover, have been much less problematic in terms of accuracy and professional ethics than the countertransference on Kohut's part that some have charged. Kohut's self-analysis arguably could have been more thoroughgoing than Freud's given the historical advantages. Freud never explored the pre-genital relationship with his mother and his "mother's power over him."[56] Freud was never analyzed and his self-analysis remained uncompleted. As he wrote to Fliess on February 9, 1898: "My self-analysis is at rest in favor of the dream book."[57] As for the objection that Kohut's turn to self psychology was a defense against unresolved Oedipal wishes from the first analysis, it can be argued that both the successes as well as the failures of the first analysis could have inspired Kohut to build a new psychoanalytic paradigm on the basis of the old through his self-analysis.

There is another possible confirmation of the real identity of Mr. Z. Kohut was not down to the last letter of the alphabet: K and S, as far as

I can tell, were never used. Perhaps, therefore, Z as the last, the ultimate case? Perhaps. K would have been appropriate, but too obvious as well as too derivative of Kafka, one of Kohut's favorite authors. But historians know as well as psychoanalysts that human actions are overdetermined and there is a compelling—because historically specific—reason for Z, I think. Another of Kohut's favorite authors was Italo Svevo, a Trieste businessman who lived from 1861 to 1928 and whose real name was Ettore Schmitz. Of German-Austrian-Italian-Jewish ancestry, Schmitz—like his hometown Trieste—was a product of what historian Michael Geyer has called the permeability of national borders, particularly in Central Europe. Partly as a result of this, Svevo's fiction was concerned with questions of identity and the self and his most famous novel—and the one with which Kohut was most familiar—was the autobiographical *Confessions of Zeno*. This book was first published in Italy in 1923. Although Kohut could read Italian, it is likely he either read one of the two German editions published in Basel in 1929 and 1930, or the 1928 German translation of the first chapter, also published in Basel as *Psychoanalysis of the First Cigarette*, or one of the postwar English translations. Kohut told Tom that he particularly enjoyed the cigarette chapter—photographs of Kohut with his analyst August Aichhorn show him with cigarette in hand—and it is this chapter which forms the core of Svevo's book. The protagonist, Zeno Cosino, has pledged to give up cigarettes and he seeks the help of a psychoanalyst to do it. But he gives up on the psychoanalyst on May 3, 1915—by striking coincidence the date of Kohut's second birthday—and embarks upon a self-analysis. There are other large and small features of the book that no doubt struck resonant chords in Kohut's psyche. As with Kohut's own published accounts of his childhood and youth, in the novel there is scant mention of the mother while the entire second chapter is devoted to "The Death of My Father." Among the smaller clues is the name of Zeno's wife, Augusta, suggestive of Kohut's Viennese analyst, August Aichhorn, for whom Kohut gave his son the middle name August. Taken together, these elements argue for *Confessions of Zeno* being the alphabetic inspiration for Mr. Z. as well as a strong clue that the second analysis in the case study is a self-analysis following upon an unsuccessful psychoanalysis.

Why would Kohut disguise himself? First of all, because he was a private person and one who had witnessed how German colleague Tilmann Moser had endured brickbats for reflecting on his own analysis in print. But perhaps he was also concerned about heightening criticism of a nascent self psychology already attracting hostile criticism from orthodox Freudians. Loewenberg has argued perceptively that Kohut employed conscious stratagems "to conceal his orignality as he developed self ¬sychology."[58] Loewenberg's text is political philosopher Leo Strauss, who held the Hutchins Chair in Political Science at the University of Chicago from 1949 to 1968. There is no record of Kohut contact with Strauss; the latter does not appear among Kohut's correspondents. And while they were contemporaneous colleagues at the University of Chicago, Kohut by 1949 was moving away from his medical positions at the university toward more intensive involvement with the Institute for Psychoanalysis uptown. But Strauss's argument in *Persecution and the Art of Writing* (1952) that, in Loewenberg's words, "[s]cience and the world are changed by subversive texts that constitute a disguised critique of prevailing assumptions"[59] can be seen as an accurate assessment of Kohut's attempts to camouflage his growing disagreement in the late 1960s and early 1970s with fundamental psychoanalytic assumptions. This tendency was strengthened both by Kohut's own ambivalence about challenging psychoanalytic orthodoxy (and authority in general) and by the actual and perceived ostracism he suffered as a result. Moreover, while Kohut was a confirmed political liberal, his experience as an assimilated Jew in Austria and the United States—assimilated to the degree that he became nominally a Unitarian!—had lent him a proclivity for leftist politics of tolerance and empathy born of the Jewish experience of exclusion and persecution.

Kohut thus most likely felt ambivalent about casting himself as the new Freud in using a self-analysis as the foundation for his theory, while also fearing that attendant charges of hubris—combined with a history of charges of plagiarism against Kohut—would further prejudice the reception of his ideas. He also would not have wanted to embarrass his friend Ruth Eissler, the analyst in the first—failed—case, who was still alive at the time. Are the disguises used in the case study so extensive as to preclude the possibility that Kohut was Mr. Z? While the parallels to Kohut's life are striking, so are the differences. For example, in the case study the father leaves home when the boy is three-and-half-years old and is away without interruption for a year-and-a-half; Kohut's father left for the war when Heinz was only fifteen months and did not return for good until Heinz was five. As a layperson with regard to psychoanalysis, I cannot judge the relative amount of camouflage in this case study as compared to others or what amount might be too much. For a historian, the altering of detail is unacceptable. But the clinician has the luxury of changing details for purposes of confidentiality after the conclusion of the analysis when the disguise can be tailored so as not to distort the findings. And if the degree of disguise in "The Two Analyses of Mr. Z." is high, it may only confirm Kohut's conscious and unconscious desire to keep his identity secret.[60]

Medicine

In 1993 the German Historical Institute in Washington, D.C. sponsored a conference on the history of medicine in modern Germany. This conference brought together historians and physicians from Germany, England, and also North America. In my introduction to the published papers (chapter 7) I emphasize the strong gravitational pull exerted on historians of Germany by the Third Reich and argue that the newest research on subjects such as doctors and medicine helps to pull Nazi Germany out of historical isolation from the history of Germany and of the West during the modern period. This does not diminish historical acknowledgment of the awful immorality of the Third Reich. This is particularly the case in the history of medicine, since it has already been well established—and reemphasized by a number of the papers read at this conference—that doctors and the field of medicine not only played an inordinately large role in the racial policies of the Nazi regime, including the Final Solution, but had as a whole displayed significant degrees of anti-Semitism and allegiance to the Nazis before 1933. Some historians have nevertheless expressed the concern that study of any "gray areas" of the Nazi era will lead—or has led—to a relativization and normalization of the Holocaust.[61] My view is that historians must be morally responsible and accurately responsive to their material and not place conditions on the complexity of history. No serious person can dispute the central unique importance of the Holocaust and serious historical study can only contribute to an understanding of how such an atrocity could be allowed to happen. Moreover, detailing the history of German society under Nazism and establishing the continuities as well as the discontinuities in German—and Western—history draws the *differentiated* circles of contribution and responsibility more widely and not more narrowly.[62] More, if more or less subtle, connections can be drawn between the darkest deed of the Nazis and other groups, individuals, and trends. Once again, the critical social history of medicine is a particularly significant example of this process.[63]

The growth of interest in the history of the professions in Germany has in part been a function of recent scholarship on the history of the bourgeoisie in nineteenth-century Europe. This research complemented earlier historical attention to peasants and the urban working class. The new social history threw open the doors to a deep and wide preoccupation with all facets of modern history. The professions in Germany were a major feature of the development of the *Bildungsbürgertum* in the nineteenth and twentieth centuries. The "rise" of the bourgeoisie and of secular liberal culture also meant greater opportunities for Jews.[64] While these opportunities had established limits and while the new era also brought about the eventually murderous phenomenon of modern anti-Semitism, Jews, as elsewhere in Europe, made significant contributions to professional and academic life in Germany. Other work on the history of professions had also touched on the matter of client reaction to professional position and advance. Moreover, historians had become increasingly aware of the crucial place of medicine in Nazi plans and projects. For example, from 1934 onward the regime had required regional medical officers to provide narrative reports of health conditions in their areas in addition to the usual statistics on major diseases. This not only revealed utilitarian and racist Nazi concern with popular health and productivity, it represented an important new source of information not only on the entire range of illnesses but also persisting and changing perceptions of and attitudes toward illnesses among the members of the population and various state and party agencies.

Jews of course had been expelled from the German medical profession in 1938, but some Nazi medical officials subsequently considered the possibility of allowing Jewish physicians to treat non-Jewish patients. It is unlikely much, if anything, actually came of this, but an initiative of this sort is surprising nonetheless since Jewish doctors had been deprived of their license to practice in 1938. Such spotty but lingering reconsideration arose from the growing shortage of doctors, which became especially acute with the widening of the war in 1941. This is significant not because it changes our view of the Nazi persecution of Jews or the persistent associations in many German minds between Jews and disease, but because it demonstrates the ongoing importance and the complexity of the social place of medicine in German history between 1933 and 1945.

The subject of Nazi medical experiments on human beings has an extensive literature in English as well as German. These works include: the early documentary account by Alexander Mitscherlich and

Fred Mielke, translated as *Doctors of Infamy* (1949); a recent psycho-historical study by Robert Jay Lifton, *The Nazi Doctors* (1986); two even newer histories of medicine in Nazi Germany by Michael Kater, *Doctors Under Hitler* (1989); and Robert Proctor, *Racial Hygiene* (1988); and a collection of essays edited by George Annas and Michael Grodin, *The Nazi Doctors and the Nuremberg Code* (1992).

The newest historical research addresses questions of continuity in German history through the Nazi years as well as the nagging issue of differences and similarities between the history of Germany and that of the West in general in the modern period. Chiefly as a result of the two world wars, Western scholarship for a long time regarded Germany as a tragic departure from the successful path of liberal bourgeois democratic development in the West. According to this view, the Germans, politically crippled by a "feudal" authoritarian past preserved through the unification of Germany by Prussia, never experienced the successful bourgeois revolution that had created liberal democracy elsewhere in Europe. The result was Hitler. This *Sonderweg* thesis has undergone considerable revision in recent years and in my paper I attempt to recast the debate to take account of the evidence and argument on both sides. My conclusion, based on the history of the Nuremberg doctors, is that modern Germany *was* different from the West but as a *combination* of old ("feudal") and new ("bourgeois") that *anticipated* what I describe as the corporatist features of Western postliberal industrial statism.[65]

Notes

1. Geoffrey Cocks, "The Hitler Controversy," *Political Psychology* 1 (1979): 67–82.
2. Frederick C. Crews, *The Pooh Perplex: A Freshman Casebook* (New York, 1963); but cf. Benedict Nightingale, "Pooh's Perplexers," *The Guardian*, March 18, 1964; and Ann Thwaite, *A. A. Milne: The Man Behind Winnie-the-Pooh* (New York, 1990), pp. xix, 301.
3. Peter Gay, *The Bourgeois Experience: Victoria to Freud*, 4 vols. (New York, 1984–96); Roy Porter and Lesley Hall, *The Facts of Life: The Creation of Sexual Knowledge in Britain, 1650–1950* (New Haven, 1995).
4. For a definitive working explication of psychohistory, see Peter Loewenberg, *Fantasy and Reality in History* (New York, 1995).
5. See, for example, Nancy Chodorow, *The Reproduction of Mothering: Psychoanalysis and the Sociology of Gender* (Berkeley, 1978).
6. Geoffrey Cocks, "A. A. Milne: Sources of His Creativity," *American Imago* 34 (1977): 313–26; see also idem, "War, Man, and Gravity: Thomas Pynchon and Science Fiction," *Extrapolation* 20 (1979): 368–77; and idem, "Bringing the Holocaust Home: The Freudian Dynamics of Kubrick's *The Shining*," *Psychoanalytic Review* 78:1 (1991): 101–23.

7. Jean Strouse, "Alice James: A Family Romance," in William McKinley Runyan, ed., *Psychology and Historical Interpretation* (New York, 1988), p. 89.
8. Milne to Philip Agnew, February 20, 1919. *Punch* archives, London.
9. A. A. Milne, "At the Bookstall," in idem, *Not That It Matters* (New York, 1925), p. 110.
10. Thwaite, *A. A. Milne*, p. 214.
11. Ibid., p. 222.
12. Letters and other material relating to the illustration of 'Winnie-the-Pooh' and 'Now we are six'. London, 1925–26. Box V.86.DD (XIII). Victoria and Albert Museum, London. See also Thwaite, *A. A. Milne*, pp. 294–5.
13. Christopher Milne, *The Path Through the Trees* (New York, 1979), p. 183. As I note in the essay, for A. A. Milne the name John incorporated imagoes of both his father and his brother, but it could also—it occurs to me now—represent a defense by nominal indirection of too great a confrontation with his guilt over surpassing his brother Kenneth John.
14. Thwaite, *A. A. Milne*, p. 382. Milne's other contributions were made in 1939–40 and 1946; Ken's youngest daughter Angela was a contributor to the magazine in 1941.
15. *Punch*, February 13, 1929, p. 187.
16. Thomas Childers and Jane Caplan, eds., *Reevaluating the Third Reich* (New York, 1993); David F. Crew, ed., *Nazism and German Society, 1933–1945* (London, 1994); Richard Bessel, *Life in the Third Reich* (London, 1987).
17. Ludger M. Hermanns, "Bedingungen und Grenzen wissenschaftlicher Produktivität bei Psychoanalytikern in Deutschland 1933 bis 1945—mit einem exemplarischen Versuch über Alexander Mette und sein Novalis-Projekt," *Jahrbuch der Psychoanalyse* 25 (1990): 28–54.
18. Geoffrey Cocks, *Psychotherapy in the Third Reich: The Göring Institute*, 2nd, rev. ed. (New Brunswick, NJ, 1997).
19. Michael Geyer, "Resistance as Ongoing Project: Visions of Order, Obligations to Strangers, and Struggles for Civil Society," in idem and John W. Boyer, eds., *Resistance Against the Third Reich, 1933–1990* (Chicago, 1994), pp. 325–50.
20. Paul Lerner, "Rationalizing the Therapeutic Arsenal: German Neuropsychiatry in the First World War," in Manfred Berg and Geoffrey Cocks, eds., *Medicine and Modernity: Public Health and Medical Care in 19th and 20th Century Germany* (Cambridge, 1997), pp. 121–48.
21. Jeffrey Moussaieff Masson, *Against Therapy: Emotional Tyranny and the Myth of Psychological Healing* (New York, 1988), p. 123.
22. Geyer, "Resistance as Ongoing Project," p. 327.
23. For general treatments see Alf Lüdtke, "'Coming to Terms with the Past': Illusions of Remembering, Ways of Forgetting Nazism in West Germany," *Journal of Modern History* 65 (1993): 542–72; and Ian Buruma, *The Wages of Guilt: Memories of War in Germany and Japan* (New York, 1994).
24. Geoffrey Cocks, "The Politics of Psychoanalytic Memory in Germany," *Psychohistory Review* 24 (1996): 207–15.
25. Ludwig J. Pongratz, ed., *Psychotherapie in Selbstdarstellungen* (Berne, 1973).
26. Annemarie Dührssen, *Ein Jahrhundert Psychoanalytische Bewegung in Deutschland* (Göttingen, 1994), pp. 165–6.
27. Ibid., p. 176.
28. Ibid., p. 166.
29. Ibid., pp. 116, 179.
30. Ibid., pp. 182, 183.
31. Ibid., pp. 207, 215–16.
32. Ibid., p. 173.

33. Ibid., p. 133.
34. Ulrich Schultz-Venrath, "Der Missbrauch von Geschichte als transgenerationelles Traumatisierungsphänomen," *Psyche* 49 (1995): 398–9.
35. See Peter Loewenberg, "The Pagan Freud," in idem, *Fantasy and Reality in History*, pp. 9–32.
36. Dührssen, *Jahrhundert Psychoanalytische Bewegung*, p. 196.
37. Ibid., p. 140.
38. Ibid., pp. 210–11.
39. Regine Lockot, *Die Reinigung der Psychoanalyse: Die Deutsche Psycho-analytische Gesellschaft im Spiegel von Dokumenten und Zeitzeugen (1933–1951)* (Tübingen, 1994), pp. 227–8, n. 59.
40. Berlin Document Center, Ermittlung von Unterlagen, November 5, 1973; and Daniel P. Simon, personal communication, September 4, 1985.
41. "Les conferences de l'Institut allemand," *Oeuvre*, November 19, 1943, PC 5, reel 102. Wiener Library, London; see also Alain de Mijolla, "Documents inedits. Les psychanalystes en France durant l'occupation allemande, Paris, Novembre 1943," *Revue Internationale d'Histoire de la Psychanalyse* 2 (1989): 463–73; and German Captured Documents/Reichsforschungsrat, reel 102, folder 12850. Manuscript Division, Library of Congress, Washington, D.C.
42. See Nathan G. Hale, *The Rise and Crisis of Psychoanalysis in the United States: Freud and the Americans, 1917–1985* (New York, 1995), pp. 360–79; and Edzard Ernst, "A Leading Medical School Seriously Damaged, Vienna 1938," *The Annals of Internal Medicine* 122 (1995): 789–92.
43. Susan Quinn, "Oedipus vs. Narcissus," *New York Times Magazine*, November 9, 1980, p. 126; see also Heinz Kohut, *How Does Analysis Cure?* (Chicago, 1984), p. 87: Here Kohut places the last stages of the first analysis "with my first attempts to escape from the inner conflicts...by making diversionary moves toward organizational and administrative tasks" (pp. 87–88).
44. Doris Brothers, "Dr. Kohut and Mr. Z: Is This a Case of Alter Ego Countertransference?" in Arnold Goldberg, ed., *A Decade of Progress*, Progress in Self Psychology, vol. 10 (Hillsdale, NJ, 1994), pp. 100–101.
45. Ibid., p. 100; this would also be consistent with Kohut's firm rejection of any unnoticed countertransference in the case: see *Cure?*, p. 87.
46. James W. Hamilton, "Some Comments on Kohut's 'The Two Analyses of Mr. Z'," *Psychoanalytic Psychology* 11 (1994): 528.
47. Heinz Kohut, "Letter to the Author: Preface to *Lehrjahre auf dem Couch* by Tilmann Moser," in idem, *Search for the Self*, ed. Paul Ornstein (New York, 1978), 2:735–6.
48. *Search*, 2:793, 794.
49. Heinz Kohut, "Creativeness, Charisma, Group Psychology: Reflections on the Self-Analysis of Freud," (1976) in idem, *Search for the Self*, Paul Ornstein, ed. (New York, 1978), 2:843.
50. Quoted in Peter Gay, *Freud: A Life for Our Time* (New York, 1988), p. 96.
51. *The Complete Letters of Sigmund Freud to Wilhelm Fliess*, Jeffrey Moussaieff Masson, ed. and trans. (Cambridge, Mass., 1985), p. 270.
52. Sigmund Freud, *The Standard Edition of the Complete Psychological Works of Sigmund Freud*, James Strachey, ed. (London, 1952), 4:xxiii–xxiv.
53. Ibid., 5:477.
54. Ibid., 4:101–2.
55. Gay, *Freud*, p. 177.
56. Ibid., p. 505.
57. *Freud to Fliess*, p. 299.

58. Peter Loewenberg, "Discussion of Professor Geoffrey C. Cocks 'From K to Z: European Roots of Heinz Kohut's Psychology'," Southern California Psychoanalytic Institute, March 18, 1985, p. 9.
59. Ibid., p. 8.
60. See also *Psychoanalytic Books* 6:1 (1995): 1–11.
61. Saul Friedländer, "Some Reflections on the Historization of National Socialism," *Tel Aviver Jahrbuch für deutsche Geschichte* 16 (1987): 310–24. The related danger in art as well as history would be the danger of trivializing the Holocaust through inappropriate comparisons and genres of expression: see James Diedrick, "Apocalypse Now: *Einstein's Monsters, London Fields, Time's Arrow*," in idem, *Understanding Martin Amis* (Columbia, South Carolina, 1995), p. 173.
62. Ian Kershaw, *The Nazi Dictatorship: Problems and Perspectives of Interpretation*, 2nd ed. (London, 1989), pp. 158–67.
63. See, for example, Götz Aly et al., *Cleansing the Fatherland: Nazi Medicine and Racial Hygiene*, trans. Belinda Cooper (Baltimore, 1994).
64. Reinhard Rürup, *Emanzipation und Anti-semitismus: Studien zur "Judenfrage" der bürgerlichen Gesellschaft* (Göttingen, 1975).
65. See also Cocks, *Psychotherapy in the Third Reich* (1997), chapter 16; and idem, "The Ministry of Amusements: Film, Commerce, and Politics in Germany, 1917–1945," *Central European History* 30:1 (1997). See also Karl Heinz Roth, "Die Modernisierung der Folter in den beiden Weltkriegen," *The Origins of Nazi Genocide: From Euthanasia to the Final Solution* (Chapel Hill, North Carolina, 1995), pp. 79, 113–14, 155–56; Peter riedesser and Axel Verderber, *"Maschinengewehre hinter der Front": Zur Geschichte der deutschen Militärpsychiatrie* (Frankfurt am Main, 1966); and Stephen Fritz, *Frontsoldaten: The German Soldier in World War II* (Lexington, Kentucky, 1995), pp. 156–86, 194, 206–10.

Part I

Psychotherapy

1

The Professionalization of Psychotherapy in Germany, 1928–1949[1]

On October 23, 1942, a letter from the office for science in Alfred Rosenberg's Nazi party organization for the overseeing of doctrine was sent to the party chancellery in Munich. This letter concerned the deputy director of the German Institute for Psychological Research and Psychotherapy in Berlin, Johannes Heinrich Schultz. Rosenberg's office had no objection to Schultz giving public lectures on psychotherapy since he was a noted psychotherapist and displayed no political, philosophical, or personal blemishes. Moreover, the letter went on, the institute with which Schultz was associated was directed by Matthias Heinrich Göring, "a close relative of the Reich Marshal."[2] In Nazi Germany, to be a relative of a powerful figure like Hermann Göring was a political imprimatur or, for a rival, most often a sign that nothing was to be done. In this case, Schultz, whatever his own merits as far as the Nazis were concerned, was safe and even favored because of his association with the Göring name.

The role played by Matthias Heinrich Göring, who was a neurologist and psychotherapist from Wuppertal-Elberfeld in the Ruhr, in the history of psychotherapy in Germany is a prime example of the importance not only of the individual but also of historical accident. Göring provided the protection and prestige necessary for the institutionalization of a marginal medical discipline between 1936 and 1945. The accident of a Göring connection, however, brought to partial professional fruition a number of dynamic intellectual and institutional trends in the realms of medicine, psychology, and social policy in Germany during the first half of the twentieth century.[3]

The Third Reich accelerated a process of professionalization among German psychotherapists that had begun in 1928 with the founding of the General Medical Society for Psychotherapy. This society, which by 1930 counted almost 500 members, was the chief organizational expression of a strong new trend among physicians, especially neurologists (*Nervenärzte*), that stressed the importance of psychological influences in mental and physical illness. This trend, which was embodied most significantly in the psychoanalytic movement emerging from Vienna at the turn of the century,[4] had been strengthened during the First World War when cases of "shell shock" were successfully treated by psychoanalytic methods. This was a direct challenge to the reigning psychiatric establishment in Germany, which regarded mental illness as physical in origin and rejected "psychodynamic" interpretations as unscientific and indulgent of supposed conflict in the patient's mind. Although the German wartime government displayed some interest in this new approach, after 1918 German psychiatry retained its dominant position in the universities and the state medical bureaucracy. Among other things, the great majority of psychiatrists continued to view "war neuroses" as manifestations of either congenital defect or a lack of will and continued to reject in their role as government consultants such applications for disability pensions.[5] During the war, psychiatrists had practiced "disciplinary therapy" determined by a "moral view of neurosis."[6] Nevertheless, after the war the psychoanalysts established training institutes and clinics, at Berlin in 1920 and at Vienna in 1922.

Although the General Medical Society for Psychotherapy had embraced a diversity of views on the status and role of psychotherapy in medicine, it was led after 1933 by those who since its founding had sought professional autonomy for the discipline. The Nazis in their campaign against "the Jew" were to destroy the autonomous Freudian movement and favor traditional psychiatry in a ruthless "biological" program of sterilization and "euthanasia" against a broad grouping of the "incurably insane,"[7] but conditions in Hitler's Germany also benefited the professional ambitions of the psychotherapists who had reorganized themselves under Göring's leadership. Aside from Göring, opportunistic psychotherapists exploited the organizational disorder of the Third Reich as well as the Nazis' interest in an Aryanized field of psychology to ensure the "care and control" (*Betreuung*) of a loyal and productive *Volk*. The resultant professional gains provided for a continuity of institutional development along the disciplinary boundaries between medicine and psychology after 1945. This has created a tie between past and present, which had been earlier obscured by professionally protective claims for either the complete suppression of psychology in medicine under the Nazis or its clandestine preservation.[8] So even though psychotherapists in the Third Reich had the unique professional advantage of the Göring name, their experience between 1933 and 1945 also shows that basic characteristics of professional life in Germany were compatible with the Nazi dictatorship.

The traditional Anglo-American model of professionalization stresses the reality and desirability of professional autonomy from state sponsorship or control. It is the practitioners themselves who organize, practice, and regulate their profession for the benefit of their clients in terms of expertise and standards and for themselves in terms of market control—the latter either through a classic liberal free market or by restricting the number of practitioners. The German (and Continental) tradition of strong state claims on education, law, commerce, and health offers a different model of professionalization but one that reminds us that even in Britain and the United States the modern bureaucratic state has been a necessary part of professional development. This does not mean that the state, even in Germany, has determined the process of professionalization. Research into the history of the professions in Germany has to some extent supported recent studies in German social history which have revealed the surprising degree of organizational initiative and autonomy "from below" of groups advancing and defending their ideas and interests within a complex industrial society and economy. Although special German statist and authoritarian traditions still played a role, especially within the political elite, more universal features and forces of modern industrial society worked a powerful influence.

Integration into the state system was the ultimate goal of the psychotherapists at this time. In terms of achieving these ends, their record was dismal. Not only did they face significant established opposition, but their very success in establishing themselves in various occupational realms also aggravated the problem of differentiating themselves from other professions, especially medicine, and of finding a disciplinary identity among the numerous fields scattered between medicine and psychology. Coupled to this was the chronic theoretical and practical disunity among psychotherapists concerning the cause, nature, and treatment of psychological disorders as well as an equally chronic division over the question of lay therapy. Without such differentiation and concomitant unity, psychotherapy could never achieve licensure by the state as a profession. Only one of their number won a post (and a minor one at that) teaching psychotherapy at the university level. They failed to have psychotherapeutic treatment included under the state health insurance scheme. Furthermore, the medical offices of the Reich Ministry of the Interior never acknowledged an autonomous psychotherapy, remaining firmly in the hands of traditional university psychiatry. Professional development along such lines would come only in the postwar successor states.

But the extralegal nature of the Nazi regime made such formal victories superfluous for the short term, because the Göring Institute received de facto recognition through the support of various agencies of the regime, the military, and industry. Moreover, such autonomy prevented absorption by official state and university psychiatry, allowing the freedom to set standards for training, including the trademark "training analysis," and practice. It was this very fear of domination by established psychiatry that in 1943 occasioned the Göring Institute's refusal to affiliate with the medical faculty of the Friedrich Wilhelm University in Berlin.[9] The therapists' small numbers also spared them the market difficulties experienced by larger and more developed professions such as lawyers and doctors in general. And it was only during the war that rival psychiatrists attempted to compete with the psychotherapists by introducing electroshock and drug therapy into German asylums.[10] This was done to meet heightened Nazi demands for productivity from members of the "master race," to try to limit the growing competence of the Göring Institute (which by 1945 would have 290 members, 215 training candidates, and branches in several cities), and to escape the professional blind alley of the murder of mental patients suffering from "hereditary" disorders. In 1944 an article in Joseph Goebbels's prestige paper *Das Reich* accurately reported the de facto professional status of psychotherapy in the Third Reich: "Psychotherapy…has made great strides in the last decade and in Germany has been visibly acknowledged by the state through the recent elevation of the German Institute for Psychological Research and Psychotherapy (in Berlin) to a Reich Institute in the Reich Research Council."[11]

The initiative of the psychotherapists under Göring exploited the realities of Nazi governance. *Gleichschaltung*, the process by which individuals and groups were "coordinated" in service to the regime, was not simply imposed from above by a monolithic totalitarian state but was to a great extent self-imposed from below by various groups defending their interests and seeking their places in the new order. Göring, for instance, was not forced on the psychotherapists by Nazi officials either within the party or state medical bureaucracy, but was drafted by anxious and opportunistic colleagues who rightly saw him as a valuable means of protection and promotion. One of them in the fall of 1933 was moved as a result of Göring's assumption of leadership to speak of the "genuinely favorable prospects"[12] for psychotherapy in spite of continuing attacks from Nazi ideologues and from psychiatrists. Even the founding of the institute in 1936 resulted from a combination of Göring's own efforts to mobilize Adlerians, Jungians, and various independents and the desire of the Ministry of the Interior to close down the "Jewish" Berlin Psychoanalytic Institute. The solution was to give to Göring and his entourage the old Freudian institute along with its non-Jewish members. State authority and power were of course not absent from these transactions, but organizational initiative from outside the government, particularly when it stemmed from patriotic and solidly bourgeois experts, often received the regime's sanction at the expense of those within the Nazi party who called for radical and violent overthrow of traditional elites and institutions. In general, below the bloody arenas of Hitler's *grosse Politik*, there was a signal lack of unified direction from the regime with regard to specific reforms or programs; far more typical was the building of satrapies and the clash of interest groups.[13] This process of "incomplete" revolution provided opportunities for certain old and new groups to advance their interests, creating a significant degree of functional unity among experts in service to the regime in place and alongside of Nazi rhetoric about *Volksgemeinschaft*.[14]

The Third Reich offered a chance for some professions to advance their status, such as doctors who resented the corporate system of sickness funds under the national health insurance program and sought to change their status from that of a trade to that of a profession.[15] The Nazis also appeared to offer the possibility for the "reprofessionalization" of such professions as teachers and lawyers, who had been disadvantaged during the Weimar Republic. However, the long-term trend under National Socialism was one of "deprofessionalization" through the deterioration of educational standards, the perversion of professional ethics, and the assertion, however chaotic, of ideological and governmental control.[16] Had the Nazis won their war, it is likely that such a trend would have intensified, although some countervailing pragmatism might have protected technical professions.

The psychotherapists without Göring (who turned sixty in 1939) certainly would have shared this fate. The protection afforded by the Göring name and its bearer's relatively unassertive nature and modest intellectual gifts, along with the sterility of any concept of a "German" psychotherapy and the Nazis' short-term pragmatism, allowed for a significant degree of theoretical and practical autonomy for psychotherapists. Nevertheless, they compromised professional ethics for personal and professional gain, beginning with the exclusion of Jewish colleagues and patients between 1933 and 1938. Some psychotherapists continued to treat Jewish patients and train Jewish students: On December 11, 1939, Göring issued a directive complaining about such violations and reminding institute members that such activity was illegal.[17] Individual psychotherapists could protect patients from the Nazis, and psychotherapy offered in general a relatively humane option to a deadly Nazified psychiatry. But at the other extreme existed the possible betrayal of patients who expressed disloyal or defeatist sentiments. This constituted a violation of that confidentiality that, while not unqualified in a lawful society, is the indispensable basis for trust in a psychotherapeutic relationship. A former member of the institute remembers one such case involving Göring's reporting of a patient to the authorities, although Göring was apparently unable to implement within his institute a 1942 Hitler decree suspending medical confidentiality in cases of "national security." Most of the specific actions and inactions along these lines were based on mixtures of fear, prudence, indifference, patriotism, and some degrees of personal integrity and pride. Though allegedly protecting some mental patients from the Nazis, for example, Göring was on the other hand not willing to endanger his position or his institute by supporting two colleagues' protests against the "euthanasia" program.[18]

Aside from such abuses and the more general problem of the exploitation of professional knowledge and expertise by evil regimes, the ethical dimension inherent in professional work is especially crucial in the very practice of medical psychology. This situation was even more pronounced under a regime that made murderous distinctions between health and illness, usefulness and uselessness, and loyalty and disloyalty.[19] Psychotherapists, to the extent that they were utilized by the Nazi regime, were engaged in a curative task but one that also met the regime's need and desire to exercise control over its people. Such exploitation by the Nazis of both therapist and patient aggravated an inherent ambiguity in the practice of psychotherapy, especially as organized under the model of practitioner control. On the one hand, psychotherapists "are committed to the absolute priority of the interests of the individual patient."[20] On the other hand, however, there is no profession in which the relationship between practitioner and client is more subject to the insinuation or imposition of social norms and values on the part of both the therapist and political, social, and economic third parties. The more successful the individual treatment, the greater the concession and contribution to collective entities and aims. In Nazi Germany, the communitarian ethos of a romantic intellectual tradition among the psychotherapists, along with a general tendency toward political conservatism and anti-Semitism, combined with the more universal trend within the discipline toward socially useful and professional promotional adjustive therapy to produce a means of social control congruent with explicit Nazi aims and the implicit dynamics of an industrial society.

The psychotherapists at the Göring Institute repeatedly claimed that psychotherapy could quickly and inexpensively return people to health, to work, and to military service. In 1943, the institute signed an agreement with an association of private health insurance carriers for white-collar employees, which in its implementation guidelines contained the following stipulation: "The admission of patients is to be handled with the greatest caution. Only socially and biologically valuable patients with positive prospects for a successful cure over the short term may be treated."[21] It is difficult to determine the precise proportion of racist rhetoric to racist conviction in this statement, What is clear, however, is the convergence of professional, financial, and political interests in the speedy dispatch of psychological disorders. Thus, to speak of the "Nazification" of disciplines and professions is not to describe a simple and direct process of dictatorial control and imposition of doctrine but rather an exploitation of systems, characteristics, and trends.

There were two levels on which the means toward the Nazi exploitation of medicine in general rested. First, the Nazis "had recognized and correctly assessed the special political and social importance of physicians in their state-supporting, ideology-promoting role, as well as in their manysided functions of social control, especially distinct with regard to the German system of social security."[22] The Nazis, moreover, drew upon a long history in Germany of the "medicalization" of social problems and potentials[23] and of Social Darwinism in viewing society generally in racist terms of health and illness. At the same time, on the level of the medical profession itself, structural and institutional conditions produced a convergence with National Socialism. Thus, the violation of "professional" and moral standards by physicians, psychologists, psychotherapists, and psychoanalysts[24] under Hitler cannot be understood only in terms of individual moral dereliction but rather also as a function of structures and processes. In addition to the materialistic, technical, and nonphilosophical nature of modern medicine, doctors are "a social group under the greatest possible pressure to emphasize the useful."[25] Such an emphasis on the useful is magnified by the social role that doctors have as servants of not just individual patients but also of functional groupings of the population that are "represented" by agencies of the state, military, and the economy. Moreover, almost no nonmedical therapists were in private practice in Germany; most were employed outside the Göring Institute in the public or private sector, while the war brought most physicians out of their practices into the military. Although the provision of medical care is in itself good and is enhanced in various ways (e.g., education, research, standards) by professional associations and supported financially and served organizationally by state and private agencies, the cumulative effect of such bureaucratization can be to diminish or even lose altogether the importance of the individual patient's interests, to entangle the lines of society's interests with those of professional and governmental oligarchies, and to modify the application and supervision of praxis.

In publicly distinguishing "German" psychotherapy from "Jewish" psychoanalysis after 1933, the leadership of the newly renamed German General Medical Society for Psychotherapy was, among other things, responding to Nazified psychiatrists' attempts to destroy the new organization.[26] On October 7, 1933, Göring wrote to colleague Walter Cimbal that "we must not allow ourselves to be taken in tow by the old ossified psychiatrists."[27] Cimbal replied on October 19, expressing the fear that the new regime's desire for centralization and unification of professional groups for service to the state might result in the dissolution of the psychotherapeutic society and its incorporation into the German Association for Psychiatry under the prominent Nazified psychiatrist Ernst Rüdin.[28] Ernst Kretschmer, former president of the General Medical Society, had proposed such a union to Göring in a letter dated October 6.[29] Kretschmer had resigned as president earlier in the year. Though an anti-Nazi, he believed that psychotherapy had to remain under the control of psychiatrists and not become an autonomous discipline or profession.

In 1935 the psychotherapists rejected a similar proposal that their society join the new German Society of Neurologists and Psychiatrists, an organization that was dominated by old-school psychiatrists.[30] In subsequent discussions they declared their willingness only to become an autonomous part of an informal umbrella organization and to participate in joint congresses for the purpose of sharing knowledge.[31] This organizational struggle continued into the war years when the position of the psychotherapists had been enhanced by the founding of the institute and its funding since 1939 by the German Labor Front and the Luftwaffe. At a meeting on May 10, 1941, chaired by Herbert Linden of the Ministry of the Interior, Göring and Rüdin assumed opposing positions, Göring arguing that psychotherapy was related to all medical disciplines, especially internal medicine and pediatrics, and Rüdin asserting that psychotherapy was a matter for psychiatrists.[32] Such a confrontation illustrates the realities of professional conflict in the field of medicine behind the Nazi facade of national and professional unity.

This conflict had an influence on an ongoing debate among the psychotherapists. Most physicians felt that psychotherapy should be practiced only by doctors since, they argued, medical training was necessary to distinguish somatic from psychological complaints. Though a physician himself, Freud had been a leading advocate among those who feared that medical monopolization of the treatment of medical disorders would lead to a functional and technical narrowing of the field from a means of humane insight to that of a mechanical "cure." In 1933 the statutes of the German General Medical Society were revised to allow special membership for nonmedical psychotherapists, and the Göring Institute trained lay therapists and accorded them status as regular members of the institute. Indeed, by 1941 nonmedical candidates and members outnumbered physicians at the institute. Göring himself was among those who believed psychotherapists should have medical training, but he was compelled to cultivate nonmedical practitioners on political grounds. In a letter dated May 28, 1938, to Franz Wirz, who was the Nazi party's chief administrator for university affairs, Göring argued that there were not enough doctors to fulfill psychotherapy's contribution to the Nazi campaign for *Volksgesundheit*.[33] The training of nonmedical therapists by the Göring Institute, including supplementary training for (mostly female) nonacademics in the traditionally female "nurturing" spheres of pedagogy and social welfare, allowed the psychotherapists to increase their numbers and expand their competence and control over all organizational and practical aspects of the field of medical psychology. This was in order to demonstrate their usefulness to the regime, to industry, and to the military as well as to assert themselves professionally against the rival psychiatrists.

Designated by the Göring Institute as "attending psychologists," nonmedical psychotherapists were recognized in 1939 by the Ministry of the Interior as medical assistants who would work under the supervision of a doctor.[34] Even though this compromise left these practitioners, like psychotherapists in general, short of formal state recognition as a profession (the requisite regulations were to have been worked out after the war), the nonmedical therapists thus avoided inclusion under the 1939 Health Practitioners Law with is professionally damaging association with the medically suspect proponents of "natural health." The Göring Institute was also involved with the successful effort by university psychologists to win state certification for their discipline. In 1941 the Ministry of Education approved guidelines for a state examination and awarding of a diploma in psychology. Though opposed vigorously by psychiatrists in the government, the psychologists had the support of industry and the military, which were demanding experts in various fields of applied psychology.[35] For its part, the Göring Institute did not require a degree in psychology for those entering training as attending psychologists, but it did state a preference for such a degree. Thirty years later in both German republics academic psychologists would emerge as strong competitors to the type of "depth psychologists" trained at the Göring Institute; this was a consequence of overlapping expertise in a highly professionalized society and of the demand for economical "behavioral therapy."

These institutional developments served and were served by the trend in psychotherapy toward adjustive therapy—a trend that also reflected and reinforced certain conditions of the social and economic environment of a modern industrial system. Especially as doctors became increasingly interested in psychotherapeutic methods, there was a tendency among its advocates to encourage more short-term, less sophisticated, and less expensive means of treating psychological disorders. Such methods would, it was argued, allow for a wider and more flexible use of psychotherapy by medical specialists, general practitioners, and lay therapists in fields of social work, education, religion, business, and industry. They would also ease the way for the inclusion of psychotherapeutic treatment in public and private health insurance schemes and in general provide for the integration of psychotherapy into state, society, and economy. Altruism also played a part in the process as, for example, among the "social Freudians" who wished to extend the benefits of sophisticated, rigorous, and expensive psychoanalytic therapy to the broader social task of alleviating everyday neurotic complaints and promoting healthy, happy, and productive adjustment to family, work, and leisure. This trend also reflected the multiplication of theories and practices and their influence and origins in various allied disciplines in an increasingly crowded field of professional expertise along the boundaries between health and illness. These intellectual and medical resources would be significantly exploited by the major Western industrial nations during and after the Second World War.

It might seem at first glance that the brutality inherent in the Nazi belief system would rule out any indulgence of the "sick" or the "neurotic." It was indeed the case that any lack of enthusiasm or effectiveness could lead to a deadly branding as a traitor, a parasite, a malingerer, an asocial, an antisocial, or a psychopath. However, given their belief in "Aryan" superiority, their totalitarian tendency toward "care and control," and the presence of professional experts from the Göring Institute, the Nazis also sought the option of psychological repair for racial comrades engaged in the common struggle for national survival. Intellectual dissidence had to be eliminated by murder or expulsion to protect the community from contamination with undesirable ideas.[36] Psychological disorder, however, could be labeled as involuntary, preventable, and curable. The Göring Institute's lucrative relationship with the German Labor Front was founded upon this conviction, and even late in the war the Nazis accompanied threats against shirkers with calls for the psychological cultivation of the will to work.[37]

This insistence on productivity and the application of various means to cultivate it produced a surprising reliance on the virtues of individual achievement and competition.[38] Psychotherapists could be expected to play a role in managing the stress arising from such an environment. Even though the Nazis made much of the virtues of prevention through healthful *völkisch* living, the pace of life, service, and sacrifice—especially during the war—made exploitation of individual performance the order of the day under Hitler. For example, despite much debate among medical experts including psychotherapists over their effectiveness and effects, the use of stimulants such as caffeine and amphetamines was extensive, especially in the Luftwaffe.[39]

This same exploitation of human resources for the state lay behind the extensive use of applied psychology in the selection and training of military officers and specialists. The racism of the Nazis added some complementary appreciation of the virtues of the soldierly character of a warrior people. But the war's turn from blitzkrieg to attrition and the belated Nazi mobilization of the German economy for total war brought an end to almost all institutional psychology in the armed forces. In 1942 the Psychological Section of the Reich Ministry of War was dissolved along with the psychological testing stations in the army and the air force. Apart from the view that such things were now a luxury in a time of necessity, in the army in particular there had always been tension between the psychologists and officers as a result of the traditional emphasis on battlefield operations and the leadership of men and cultivation of character by unit commanders.[40] In the Luftwaffe disagreements between psychologists and the High Command over particular cases as well as the desperate need for pilots helped lead to the jettisoning of psychologists in that branch of the service.[41] Nazi racism in its biological certainties was fundamentally impatient with the niceties and ambiguities of academic psychology. This racism thus also contributed to the decline of psychology in the armed forces. The "racial quality" of Germans was quantified on the basis of the belief in their inherently superior character.[42] Propaganda and terror would bolster martial spirit in an environment of demand rather than professionally supervised incentive.

Unlike the psychologists, psychotherapists did not suffer such a reversal of fortunes during the war. The nature of the turning of the war's tide against Germany increased the need for medical capacities both on the home front and in the field. Whereas the Ministry of the Interior requested on June 21, 1943, that the Göring Institute stop accepting women for training as attending psychologists so that they could be spared for more important work as youth leaders and operating room nurses,[43] attending psychologists in general, as "members of a health profession," were exempt from war work.[44] The psychotherapists nonetheless endured some setbacks. In late 1942 psychotherapists in the Luftwaffe with medical training were transferred to service as regular physicians to meet the immediate crisis of the spiraling numbers of casualties. As the situation grew ever more desperate for Nazi Germany, the military laid greater stress on material projects with the potential for meeting pressing needs. For example, medical research projects recommended for funding by the Reich Research Council in 1944 included one from Matthias Heinrich Göring on personality development and psychotherapeutic training. However, this proposal and others like it were designated as less urgent than research into the physiology of high-altitude flying and the causes of crashes through pilot error, though more important than more *völkisch* studies on mother's milk, medicinal soils, and the psychology of Eastern European peoples.[45]

However, as the war lengthened and intensified and German forces had to endure mounting defeats and losses with the accompanying pressure and strain on the troops, the incidence of mental disorder began to increase. The psychiatric services of the Wehrmacht medical corps were forced to meet this crisis. Ironically, just as in the civilian sector, the psychotherapists' lack of an official institutional status within the military helped them preserve greater influence than the psychologists after 1942. The Göring Institute was an autonomous entity under special protection and maintained a significant if subordinate influence in the medical service of Hermann Göring's Luftwaffe. Its transformation into a generously funded "Reich Institute" in 1944 was also a function of the Göring family tie. The original institute had received financial support from the Reich Research Council ever since the latter had come under the direction of Hermann Göring in 1942.[46]

Although, as in the First World War, the effectiveness of psychotherapeutic methods boosted the professional fortunes of the psychotherapists,[47] the history of their operations in the German military during the Second World War is primarily one of continued professional conflict with their archrivals, the psychiatrists. This conflict did not revolve so much around the psychiatrists' complete rejection of psychotherapeutic methods, since there was a wide range of views on technique among psychiatrists, as around the issues of how they should be applied and by whom. The psychiatrists were compelled by their new competitors and the possible recurrence of the psychological casualties experienced in the First World War to declare their exclusive knowledge of the uses and limits of psychotherapy.[48] The psychiatrists had a strong position in the Wehrmacht medical services, particularly in the army, and jealously guarded it, especially when the problem of "war neuroses" brought with it a strengthened challenge from the psychotherapists under Göring.

The first line of defense for the psychiatrists was to minimize the problem. There was significant evidence of an ebb and flow in the statistics of mental casualties, depending on the intensity of the fighting,[49] but at what level rested on how various complaints were diagnosed and what level of "psychogenic disorders," as they came to be called, was regarded as critical.[50] However, army internists suspected the growing number of chronic stomach disorders included a large percentage of psychosomatic cases. In July 1943 the first of a number of "stomach battalions" was established to deal with the problem not only means of medication and diet but also by "education" to duty and efficiency (*Leistungsfähigkeit*) as well as referral to psychiatrists.[51] As for therapy, the psychiatrists claimed great success for the new electroshock treatment; Friedrich Panse of the reserve hospital at Ensen near Cologne was the leading exponent of this practice.[52]

The clash between psychiatrists and psychotherapists of course was not confined to scientific debate, but had significant institutional dimensions as well. In a letter dated October 25, 1944, to the Army Medical Service Command psychiatrist Max de Crinis, who was a rabid Nazi and relentless critic of the psychotherapists, stressed the importance of maintaining "scientific control in the army" of mental cases requiring therapy.[53] Although his concern about the danger of such men being released from civilian hospitals if discharged from the Wehrmacht was frequently expressed among psychiatrists, de Crinis's emphasis on the army as a bastion of scientific reason also embodied his oft-expressed concern over the competition offered psychiatry by the dilettantish psychotherapists under Göring. De Crinis's colleague at the Academy for Military Medicine, Otto Wuth, had noted two years earlier that unlike in the First World War the Nazi party leadership offered an avenue for appeal to "nondoctors" for cases of "war neurotics."[54] Wuth, who like de Crinis constantly voiced his displeasure at the work of the Göring Institute, was clearly anxious about the leverage the psychotherapists enjoyed within the Nazi leadership and in civilian society as a whole. For Wuth, the party was a place where psychotherapists could impress nonmedical people unable to understand the scientific complexities of psychiatry and who often resented the traditional university elites. In addition, Wuth could distrust the party's general desire to control matters and probably suspected that on the issue of war neurotics it would often prefer to hear the therapeutic optimism of the psychotherapists.

The very debate over the word "neurosis" also displayed the professional struggle going on between psychiatrists and psychotherapists in the military. On June 30, 1944, the head of the Wehrmacht Health Services issued a directive outlining the various terms to be used in place of "neurosis." Terms like "war neurotic," "war trembler," and "war hysteric" were to be avoided at all costs.[55] With some justification, it was claimed that the term "neurosis" was vague and overused, but for psychiatrists it was equally true that its use was associated with, and gave credence to, a psychodynamic view of the mind to which a physicalist psychiatry was opposed. For many psychiatrists and Nazis, moreover, the work recalled the vexing problems of the last war and smacked of medical indulgence of cowardly malingerers. Many psychiatrists of the old school, encouraged by Nazi racial theory, divided those cases not diagnosable or treatable by psychiatric methods into true "psychopaths," or those hereditarily defective, and malingerers, those consciously feigning illness to shirk duty. For psychiatrists in general, neurosis could fall into either category.

Because of the strong psychiatric establishment in the army, the psychotherapists were unable to achieve any position or influence there. The situation was different in the Luftwaffe, where the Göring name "sufficed to open doors."[56] Both Göring and Schultz were medical officers in the air force reserve and led a successful effort to establish a psychotherapeutic capacity within the youngest branch of the armed forces. Luftwaffe medical officers regularly received training at the Göring Institute for service with psychotherapeutic aid stations throughout occupied Europe.[57] The Luftwaffe regarded itself as a select Nazi force and attracted men from the elite of German society among whom, under the peculiar mental strains of combat flying, were often manifested the neurotic conditions linked with the "sensibilities" of the highly educated and the socially favored.

In 1944 the Luftwaffe established a special reserve anti-aircraft battery in Dortmund for those members of the air force suffering from psychogenic disorders.[58] The reaction of the army psychiatrists was predictably harsh. De Crinis commented on December 4, 1944, to the army's medical inspector that psychotherapeutic methods, whatever their past successes, consumed too much time and expense given the pressing demands of the war.[59] In spite of their promotion of short-term methods dedicated to swift readjustment and enhanced productivity, the psychotherapists were vulnerable on this score, especially amid the hysteria generated among the Nazis by the worsening war situation. Within the Luftwaffe itself, psychoanalysis had been discarded as being too time-consuming and demanding on the patient, while air force psychiatrists and neurologists reportedly tended to avoid "the therapeutically and administratively troublesome category of psychoneurosis."[60]

However, the institutionalized influence of psychotherapy persisted in the Luftwaffe, as is evident in the Wehrmacht's confrontation with the important social and medical issue of homosexuality. The Nazi regime had expanded the laws against homosexual activity, sending thousands of homosexuals to their deaths in concentration camps. But many more homosexuals avoided such persecution since, unlike most Jews and communists, they were not usually easily identifiable.[61] Furthermore, even though by 1942 the SS had declared the death penalty for homosexual activity among its members and the party and Nazi youth groups had from the beginning expelled overt homosexuals from their ranks,[62] the Nazis were constrained by the pervasiveness of homosexual behavior in the populace, especially among adolescents, to seek medical assistance in dealing with this problem. Their aims were pragmatic in the sense that they wished to exploit as many socially and sexually productive individuals as possible; they were ideological insofar as the Nazis strove to use the power of biology to overwhelm perversions supposedly cultivated by a decadent and materialistic civilization. Crude and sadistic experiments in the camps were one result. These aims also drew upon the Nazis' desire to exert technical control over all aspects of life, as well as the deep psychological need of many Nazis to assert, out of "their own personal agony of armor-plated self-discipline,"[63] a masculine identity against everything internally and externally that was soft or feminine.

Not surprisingly, psychiatrists and psychotherapists differed on the causes and treatment of what both groups agreed was a serious disorder. The psychotherapists also saw in homosexuality another chance to prove the worth of their discipline and strengthen their claim to professional status. They argued that the great majority of homosexual cases had psychological origins and could therefore be treated and cured. By 1939, in fact, the Göring Institute claimed 500 such cures.[64] The psychiatrists, by contrast, argued that homosexuals suffered from a hereditary disorder and advocated punishments for repeat offenders ranging from imprisonment to castration to death.

Beginning in 1942 the Wehrmacht grappled with the problem of homosexuality and in so doing engaged contending institutional and professional forces in the fields of criminology, medical psychology, and forensic medicine. In 1942, in the case of an officer convicted of homosexual activity, Hitler decreed that since he had been judged to have a hereditarily defective disposition, he must be punished and not be permitted—as he had requested in his appeal for leniency to the Führer—to rehabilitate himself in combat. This decision was passed down from Hitler's headquarters as a precedent, but one that left unanswered a number of important questions. As a result, the Armed Forces High Command sought the views of the Ministry of Justice, the Gestapo, the Criminal Police, and the army psychiatrists. There were a variety of opinions, making it clear that a unified policy would have to be negotiated. The Ministry of Justice, the Gestapo, and the psychiatrists essentially agreed that adult homosexuals were suffering from an incurable hereditary defect, but that homosexual incidents among adolescents might often be the result of pubertal difficulties and/or seduction by a "true" adult homosexual. The psychiatrists warned against discharging homosexuals from the armed forces because this might encourage simulation among "normal" soldiers wishing to escape the front. Only the Criminal Police distinguished between hereditary and environmental homosexual disorders. They pointed out that many homosexuals released into the Wehrmacht from preventive detention had not subsequently engaged in homosexual conduct. In any case, there was not enough room in the concentration camps, the Criminal Police argued, so the armed forces would have to construct their own detention facilities. Since, in the view of the Criminal Police, not all homosexuals were incurable, there was hope that treatment could help to solve the problem. This approach arose from the working relationship between the Criminal Police and the Göring Institute through the psychotherapists' attempts out of the offices of the Reich Air Ministry "to reintegrate such people into the racial community."[65]

The psychotherapists and psychiatrists subsequently confronted each other directly over this issue. The result was that the army and the air force ended up with different policies on homosexuality. On May 19, 1943, Field Marshal Keitel, chief of the Armed Forces High Command, issued guidelines on punishment (including death) for homosexual activity. There were three categories of perpetrators: those congenitally afflicted or suffering from an untreatable drive, onetime offenders (particularly victims of seduction), and those in whom a hereditary disposition was uncertain.[66] On June 7, 1944, the Luftwaffe health service published its own directive. This fourteen-page document emphasized that not every man who committed a homosexual act was a homosexual, that most homosexuals did not manifest a hereditary disposition (*Hang*) but rather a desire (*Trieb*) acquired in life, and that a majority of the latter—and some of the former—could be cured with psychotherapy.[67] The battle lines had been drawn. On December 9, 1944, de Crinis expressed his unconditional opposition to the Luftwaffe guidelines in a letter to the Army Medical Service Command.[68] That the army stood by the 1943 policy is evidenced by the conclusions of a commission studying the use of expert medical opinions in the implementation of those guidelines on December 15, 1944. Furthermore, the culpable fact of the membership in this group of psychoanalyst Felix Boehm, who was a member of the Göring Institute, also underlined the limits of the psychotherapists' influence.[69]

By 1944, as we have seen, the Göring Institute had technically become an official state institution. This status was of course short-lived. The Reich Institute building in Berlin was destroyed by the Russians in April 1945 after a clash with SS men hiding there.[70] Göring was taken prisoner and died that summer in captivity. Survivors from the institute, however, set about reestablishing psychotherapeutic services in the rubble of Berlin with the encouragement of the occupation authorities, who were concerned about the ongoing disruption of people's lives. The years of applying short-term therapy in the Göring Institute's outpatient clinic and the training of lay and medical psychotherapists provided the practical basis for the resumption of work in the immediate postwar period.[71] As early as 1946, two former Freudian members of the Göring Institute had established an outpatient clinic under the supervision and with the support of the state health authority in Berlin.[72] By 1949, with the founding of the West and East German states, individuals and groups formerly associated with the Göring Institute had joined (and competed) with those few colleagues who had returned from exile to lay the organizational basis for the further development of psychotherapy's position.

Problems persisted, however, because the number of psychotherapists remained small and they still faced opposition from within the university medical faculties and the state bureaucracy. Even though training at the Göring Institute was recognized, no comparable institution developed to take its place. Neither postwar regime for various and obvious political reasons was to regard the Reich Institute as a precedent for state institutionalization of psychotherapy. In the case of the Federal Republic, the official reason was that the supervisory Reich Research Council had, as an offshoot of the German Research Society, been created by administrative decree and not by law. Psychotherapists would only gradually win university positions and only much later would psychotherapy be covered by state health insurance systems. The field continued to be rent by divisions. For two years after the war groups in Berlin and Munich fought over the right to be the legal successor to the Reich Institute and thus to the considerable funds taken by the institute's comptroller to Bavaria for safekeeping in February 1945.[73] In the Federal Republic psychoanalysts regained the autonomy lost in 1936, but split into two groups at the end of 1950. These divisions were symptomatic of the lack of theoretical consensus and, especially in the democratic environment of the Federal Republic, would persist as a major impediment to the full professionalization of psychotherapy. As early as June 1945 the Göring Institute was even being declared by some to be a liability because of its opportunistic training of attending psychologists; as always, the issue of lay versus medical training was acute.[74] Because of these unresolved difficulties remaining from the Nazi years, the Göring Institute, while providing for a continuity of professional development for psychotherapy in Germany, was to mark not only the extremity of the discipline's politicization but also the apex of its professional autonomy.

What, then, is the general significance of the history of psychotherapy in Germany between 1928 and 1949? First, this history contributes to a growing body of knowledge about professional life in modern Germany, and about the social, political, and economic dynamics of the educated middle class (*Bildungsbürgertum*). It does this by revealing the institutional structures and processes that were responding to—as well as creating—the demand for technical expertise by the complex industrial society that Germany had become by the twentieth century, often (as was most evident under the Nazis) at the expense of the interests of clients and of higher morality. More specifically, the ultimately incomplete professionalizing project of psychotherapists in Germany typified the importance of the state in German professional life. But in this case, as in others, the state had—and has—been an entity the recognition from which was an indispensable part of the goal for a professional group organizing from below and, in this case, in conflict with a part of the medical establishment within the university system, the state bureaucracy, and the military. The result in the postwar era has been a mix of practitioner dominance that is typical of free market Western systems and, particularly in the German Democratic Republic, a German tradition of socialized medicine. Second, this history reveals much about the structure of government and society under the Nazis, a system that was much more riven with discontinuities than earlier studies of the aims and actions of its leaders had led us to believe. These discontinuities in the structure of National Socialism in power, however, allowed for social and economic continuities with developments before 1933 and after 1945, thus lodging the Nazi years more firmly into the course of modern German history.

There was in general after 1933 a distinct carryover of social and economic conditions and trends along a scale of oppression, opportunity, collaboration, and contribution. These continuities were not merely a function of structure or process, but reflected dynamic and dialectical conditions that resulted in displacements in one way or another in the constellation of forces involved. An excellent relevant example was the success of doctors in achieving recognition from the state as a profession in 1935, which was an occurrence that marked not only the assertion of Nazi control over the medical profession but also the physicians' triumph as a result of the Nazi destruction of socialist and working-class control over the state health insurance system. The professional hegemony won thereby by the doctors over their patients continued, though not without challenge particularly in the Federal Republic, after the war.[75] In the realm of psychotherapy, whereas some prominent older practitioners with Nazi ties were kept from the professional mainstream after 1945, the developments in psychotherapy in both the Federal and Democratic Republics coursed primarily from domestic continuities rather than from foreign influences.

Such lines of continuity are unlike those "peculiar" to a Germany dominated by preindustrial elites. A more recent functional view of modern German history as well as some critical explorations in "the history of the everyday" have uncovered the degrees of influence of modern professional elites in an increasingly industrial and technological social environment. Old elites, as Michael Geyer has shown in the case of the officer corps, were reforming their practices along modern professional lines in response to the institutional and technical demands of the modern era.[76] By the twentieth century the German landscape had been largely transformed into a modern industrial society, although one still bearing some marked traces of specifically German preindustrial ideals, institutions, and influences. In recent times the German's head has often been crowned by a spiked helmet, but, like the German officer von Rauffenstein in Jean Renoir's film *La Grande Illusion* (1937), his body was held erect not only by Prussian rigor but also by braces of steel.

The history of the Göring Institute also offers insight into the dynamics of German society as a whole under National Socialism, which is a phenomenon that has often and necessarily been ignored in the historical literature out of concern for the broad, characteristic extremes comprised of Nazi victimizers and their victims. This was a social environment in which "the overwhelming majority of...citizens...were ready to complain but willing to comply..., maintaining a clear sense of their own interests and a profound indifference to the suffering of others."[77] Nazi policy toward this great mass of *Volksgenossen* was driven by anxiety as well as by arrogance, however. The Nazis recognized that "carrots were needed as well as sticks" to ensure at least the "passive loyalty" required for the privations occasioned by rearmament and war.[78] As a result, Nazi social policy displayed not only the ideological fanaticism applied most gruesomely against "racial enemies" and in service to a fantasized "racial community" they wished to create. It also exercised a pragmatism, however muddled by organizational chaos and individual incompetence, arising from their mastery of a modern industrial society that they desperately as well as callously wished to exploit. The Nazi emphasis on productivity so professionally beneficial to the ambitious and opportunistic psychotherapists also created an environment of competitive individualism that was at odds with reactionary Nazi rhetoric about the comradely *Volksgemeinschaft*. This not only advantaged educated elites but had the effect of subverting opposition throughout society, leaving workers, for example, with vague feelings of cultivated nationalism, self-interest, and a certain resentment over sacrifices, shortages, and, finally, the sufferings brought on by the war.[79]

Since class and occupational identity and interest alone do not suffice to explain the motives of individuals, the complex political motives of human beings within specific cultural and historical contexts[80] describe the limits of the type of structural and institutional history we have pursued here. As much as psychotherapists were motivated by professional aims, each was also a member of a social environment that was filled with the less tangible but no less significant percolations of culture, tradition, and personal experience. Such individual combinations of traits are more historically significant the higher one goes in the social and political hierarchy, especially in the Third Reich, the black core of which can only be grasped through an understanding of the brutal fantasies of individuals with the power to act on them.[81] But to explain how such people came to power, to comprehend the historical ramifications of their rule under the various and complex conditions set by their time and place, and to locate the aspects of their regime in the contexts of German, Western, and human history is the task of an approach that takes into serious account what Max Weber in 1903 saw being constructed, namely, an "iron cage" of institutions.

Notes

1. From *German Professions, 1800–1950*, edited by Geoffrey Cocks and Konrad H. Jarausch, pp. 308–28. Copyright 1990 by Oxford University Press, Inc. Reprinted by permission.
2. MA 116/15. Institut für Zeitgeschichte, Munich.

3. Geoffrey Cocks, *Psychotherapy in Third Reich: The Göring Institute* (New York, 1985).

4. Hannah S. Decker, *Freud in Germany: Revolution and Reaction in Science, 1893–1907* (New York, 1977).

5. Robert Weldon Whalen, *Bitter Wounds: German Victims of the Great War, 1914–1939* (Ithaca, 1984), p. 63.

6. Eric J. Leed, *No Man's Land: Combat and Identity in World War I* (London, 1979), pp. 63–92.

7. Ernst Klee, *"Euthanasie" im NS-Staat: Die "Vernichtung lebensunwerten Lebens"* (Frankfurt, 1985).

8. Regine Lockot, *Erinnern und Durcharbeiten: Zur Geschichte der Psychoanalyse und Psychotherapie im Nationalsozialismus* (Frankfurt, 1985); Karen Brecht et al., *"Hier geht das Leben auf eine sehr merkwürdige Weise weiter...": Zur Geschichte der Psychoanalyse in Deutschland* (Hamburg, 1985).

9. Göring to Sergius Breuer, October 2, 1943, German Captured Documents/Reichsforschungsrat, reel 107, folder 12850. Library of Congress, Manuscript Division, Washington, D.C.

10. Karl-Heinz Roth, "Leistungsmedizin: Das Beispiel Pervitin," in Fridolf Kudlien, ed., *Ärzte im Nationalsozialismus* (Cologne, 1985), p. 173.

11. Heinrich Goitsch, "Heilwege für die erkrankte Seele," *Das Reich*, August 20, 1944, p. 8.

12. Fritz Künkel to M. H. Göring, August 9, 1933, Kl. Erw. 762/2. Bundesarchiv, Coblenz.

13. Peter Hüttenberger, "Nationalsozialistische Polykratie," *Geschichte und Gesellschaft* 2 (1976): 419–42.

14. Konrad H, Jarausch, "The Crisis of German Professions, 1918–1933," *Journal of Contemporary History* 20 (1985): 394.

15. Michael H. Kater, "Professionalization and Socialization of Physicians in Wilhelmine and Weimar Germany," *Journal of Contemporary History* 20 (1985): 677–702.

16. Konrad H. Jarausch, "The Perils of Professionalism: Lawyers, Teachers, and Engineers in Nazi Germany," *German Studies Review* 9 (1986): 107–37.

17. Kl. Erw. 762/4.

18. Frederic Wertham, *A Sign for Cain: An Exploration of Human Violence* (New York, 1966), pp. 178–9; Klaus Dörner, "Nationalsozialismus und Lebens-vernichtung," *Vierteljahreshefte für Zeitgeschichte* 15 (1967): 143; Robert Jay Lifton, *The Nazi Doctors: Medical Killing and the Psychology of Genocide* (New York, 1986), pp. 83, 85–7, 91.

19. Michael H. Kater, "Medizin und Mediziner im Dritten Reich: Eine Bestand-saufnahme." *Historische Zeitschrift* 244 (1987): 350–1.

20. Louise S. Horowitz, "Whose Interests Should the Psychotherapist Represent?" in Raphael Stern et al., eds., *Science and Psychotherapy* (New York, 1977), p. 161.

21. Matthias Heinrich Göring, Ausführungsbestimmungen, January 1, 1943, Kl. Erw. 762/4.

22. Stefan Kirchberger, "Public Health Policy in Germany, 1945–1949: Continuity and a New Beginning," in Donald W. Light and Alexander Sculler, eds., *Political Values and Health Care: The German Experience* (Cambridge, Mass., 1986), pp. 186–7.

23. Ute Frevert, "Professional Medicine and the Working Classes in Imperial Germany," *Journal of Contemporary History* 20 (1985): 637–58.

24. Volker Friedrich, "Psychoanalyse im Nationalsozialismus: Vom Widerspruch zur Gleichschaltung," *Jahrbuch der Psychoanalyse* 20 (1987): 207–33.

25. Sherry Turkle, *Psychoanalytic Politics: Freud's French Revolution* (New York, 1978), p. 49.
26. Karl Hannemann, "Seelenheilkunde und politische Führung," *Völkischer Beobachter* (South German edition), October 2, 1938, p. 12; M. H. Göring, "Deutsche Seelenheilkunde," ibid. (Berlin edition), December 3, 1938, p. 5; Herbert Gold, "Auch die ersten Kindheitseinflüsse bestimmen die Lebensgestaltung," ibid. (Berlin edition), May 14, 1939, p. 5; and Göring to Otto Curtius, October 11, 1938, Kl. Erw. 762/2.
27. Kl. Erw. 762/2.
28. Ibid.
29. Ibid.
30. Microcopy T1021, roll 11, frame 459. National Archives, Washington, D.C.
31. "Tätigkeitsbericht 1935/36," *Zentralblatt für Psychotherapie* 10 (1937): 5.
32. Protokoll der Sitzung mit der Psychiatrischen Gesellschaft unter Vorsitz von Ministerialrat Linden am 10.5.41, pp. 1, 2, 4, Kl. Erw. 762/2. See also Friedrich Mauz to Bernhard Rust, September 27, 1937, Reichserziehungsministerium 2954. Zentrales Staatsarchiv, Potsdam.
33. Kl. Erw. 762/3.
34. Werner Achelis, Rundschreiben, August 7, 1939, Kl. Erw. 762/4.
35. Ulfried Geuter, *The Professionalization of Psychology in Nazi Germany*, trans. Richard J. Holmes (Cambridge, 1992).
36. Alan Beyerchen, "Anti-Intellectualism and the Cultural Decapitation of Germany Under the Nazis," in Jarrell C. Jackson and Carla M. Borden, eds., *The Muses Flee Hitler: Cultural Transfer and Adaptation, 1930–1945* (Washington, D.C., 1983), pp. 39–40.
37. Adolf Friedrich, "Der Rhythmus der betrieblichen Entwicklung," *Völkischer Beobachter*, April 7, 1944, p. 6.
38. Detlev J. K. Peukert, *Inside Nazi Germany: Conformity, Opposition, and Racism in Everyday Life*, trans. Richard Deveson (New Haven, 1987), p. 95.
39. Oberkommando der Luftwaffe, "Leistungssteigernde Mittel bei der Luftwaffe," August 31, 1944, H 20/345. Bundesarchiv-Militärarchiv, Freiburg (hereafter abbreviated as BA-MA).
40. Martin van Creveld, *Fighting Power: German and U. S. Army Performance, 1939–1945* (Westport, Connecticut, 1982), pp. 132–6.
41. D. Russell Davis, *German Applied Psychology*, B.I.O.S. Trip No. 2084 (London, n. d.), pp. 5–6.
42. Georg Lilienthal, *Der "Lebensborn e. V." Ein Instrument nationalsozialistischer Rassenpolitik* (Stuttgart, 1985), pp. 93, 95.
43. Kl. Erw. 762/6. On the failure of the regime to effect the wartime mobilization of women, see Claudia Koonz, *Mothers in the Fatherland: Women, the Family and Nazi Politics* (New York, 1987), pp. 196–7, 394–8.
44. M. H. Göring, Rundschreiben, March 27, 1943, Kl. Erw. 762/4.
45. Werner Osenberg, "Recherche Nr. 31," June 4, 1945, FD545/46, box S243, Speer Collection. Imperial War Museum, London.
46. Cocks, *Psychotherapy in the Third Reich*, pp. 168–71. See also the letter from the dean of the medical faculty in Berlin complaining about the funding of the Göring Institute, September 16, 1943, German Captured Documents/Reichsforschungsrat.
47. Leo Alexander, *Neuropathology and Neuropsychiatry, Including Electro-Encephalography, in Wartime Germany* (Washington, D.C., n. d.), p. 13.
48. Max de Crinis, Miltärärztliche Akademie, October 26, 1944, H20/464. BA-MA.
49. Beratende Psychiater beim Heeres-Sanitätsinspekteur, Auszugsweise, no date, H 20/464. BA-MA.

50. Oberkommando der Wehrmacht, Chef des Santitätswesens, August 24, 1944, H 20/835. BA-MA. See also microcopy T78, roll 183, frame 3999. National Archives.
51. *Bericht über die 4. Arbeitstagung der Beratenden Ärzte vom 16. bis 18. Mai 1944 im SS-Lazarett Hohenlychen* (n. p., n. d.), pp. 206–10.
52. Friedrich Panse, Auszugsweise Abschrift, March 15, 1944, H 20/464. BA-MA.
53. H 20/464. BA-MA.
54. Otto Wuth to Hans Bürger-Prinz, April 24, 1942, H 20/464. BA-MA.
55. *4. Arbeitstagung*, p. 276.
56. Walther Bräutigam, "Rückblick auf das Jahr 1942: Betrachtungen eines psycho-analytischen Ausbildungskandidaten des Berliner Institutes der Kriegsjahre," *Psyche* 38 (1984): 907.
57. See the questionnaire of Hans Suchner, November 6, 1942, Kl. Erw. 762/6. Göring went to Paris in 1943 on Luftwaffe business: see "Les conferences de l'Institut allemand," *Oeuvre*, November 19, 1943, PC 5, reel 102. Wiener Library, London; and Cocks, *Psychotherapy in the Third Reich*, p. 221.
58. Anweisung für Truppenärzte Einzelordnungen Nr. 11, December 6, 1944, p. 4, RL 4 II/304. BA-MA.
59. H 20/464. BA-MA.
60. Alexander, *Neuropathology and Neuropsychiatry*, p. 30.
61. Richard Plant, *The Pink Triangle: The Nazi War Against Homosexuals* (New York, 1986), p. 52.
62. Reichskartei-Warnkartei. Berlin Document Center.
63. Peukert, *Inside Nazi Germany*, p. 169.
64. Johannes Heinrich Schultz, Anweisung für Truppenärzte über Erkennung und Behandlung von abnormen seelischen Reaktionen (Neurosen), n. d., p. 18, RW 2/251. BA-MA.
65. Vortragsvermerk für Herrn Feldmarschall, August 12, 1942, p. 2, H 20/479. BA-MA.
66. H 20/474. BA-MA.
67. Ibid.
68. H 20/479. BA-MA. The copy of the Luftwaffe directive in H 20/474 had been received by the consulting army psychiatrists on November 11, 1944, and is heavily marked with marginalia, mostly agitated exclamation points and question marks.
69. H 20/474. BA-MA. Cf. Franz Seidler, *Prostitution, Homosexualität, Selbstverstümmelung: Probleme der deutschen Sanitätsführung, 1939–1945* (Neckargemünd, 1977), pp. 213–21, which by ignoring the institutionalized disagreements between Wehrmacht psychotherapists and psychiatrists leaves the apologetic impression that by 1944 there was agreement on the less brutal Luftwaffe guidelines regarding homosexuality. Seidler also fails to mention the 1944 commission report on the army policy.
70. Harald Schultz-Hencke, Zweiter protokollarischer Bericht, June 1, 1945, p. 2, Kl. Erw. 762/7.
71. Bemerkungen zum Brief Wiegmann an Kemper vom 12.8.1945, August 17, 1945, Kl. Erw. 762/7.
72. Ludwig J. Pongratz, ed., *Psychotherapie in Selbstdarstellungen* (Bern, 1973), pp. 296–302.
73. Johannes Grunert, "Zur Geschichte der Psychoanalyse in München," *Psyche* 38 (1984): 873–5.
74. Harald Schultz-Hencke, Vierter protokollarischer Bericht, June 12, 1945, pp. 3–5, Kl. Erw. 762/7.

75. Stephan Liebfried and Florian Tennstedt, "Health-Insurance Policy and Berufsverbote in the Nazi Takeover," in *Political Values*, pp. 127–84. This hegemony confronted institutional and popular challenge in all professions: Geoffrey Cocks, "Psychiatry, Society, and the State in Nazi Germany," paper presented at Miami (Ohio) University, February 24, 1989.

76. Michael Geyer, "The Past as Future: The German Officer Corps as Profession," in *German Professions, 1800–1950*, pp. 183–212.

77. James J. Sheehan, "National Socialism and German Society: Reflections on Recent Research," *Theory and Society* 13 (1984): 865, 867.

78. Peukert, *Inside Nazi Germany*, pp. 31, 188.

79. Ibid., pp. 108, 113, 117.

80. Sheehan, "National Socialism and German Society," pp. 858, 860.

81. Peter Loewenberg, "The Kristallnacht as a Public Degradation Ritual," *Leo Baeck Institute Yearbook* 32 (1987): 319.

2

The Nazis and C.G. Jung

In this chapter[1] I shall explore some of the historical context for Carl Jung's words and actions regarding Jews between 1933 and 1940. More specifically, my primary aim is to concentrate on events in Nazi Germany in order to complement the usual and present emphasis on Jung himself. This is why I have titled this chapter "The Nazis and C.G. Jung." The word order of the proper nouns is meant to carry the action from the Nazis to Jung. This is not, as will shortly become evident, an attempt to whitewash a passive or victimized Jung. It is to show both the compromising and extenuating complexities of this fateful era.

There is a tendency among psychoanalysts, and nonhistorians generally, to focus on individuals, especially on the "great" in history and especially in a time, the first half of the twentieth century, when the world was seemingly dominated by larger-than-life figures, both benevolent and malevolent. Clearly, the significance of individuals, such as Freud or Jung—or Hitler—should not be underestimated, but too often forays into recent history by psychoanalysts in particular have slighted proper historical method and exhibited both an ahistorical concern with the anecdotal and, even more troubling, the prejudgments that come with partisanship.

The latter problem is especially acute when it comes to debates between Jungians and Freudians, camps divided by deep philosophical differences, differences that became manifest during the period in Europe between the two world wars. Anti-Semitism of course bulked large in European life in those years and thus unavoidably played a role in the intramural clashes within the psychoanalytic movement. These general philosophical differences and the specific tradition of anti-Semitism also naturally played a part in the reception and use of Jung and Jungian psychology in Germany between 1933 and 1940.

First, I would like to offer a brief survey of Jung's involvement in German affairs during these years and the contemporary and subsequent reactions to it. I do this in order to highlight what I think are the major shortcomings on both sides of the debate about Jung's words and actions during the fascist era. This will also give me the opportunity to present some of my own views on this question.

On June 21, 1933 Jung took over the presidency of the General Medical Society for Psychotherapy from German psychiatrist Ernst Kretschmer. Kretschmer, no friend of the Nazis and an opponent of a psychotherapy or psychoanalysis independent of medical control, had resigned the office he had held since 1930 on April 6. On September 15 a German society was founded under the leadership of psychotherapist Matthias Heinrich Göring as part of what was to become an international society headed by Jung that was formally constituted in May of 1934. Jung had been vice president of the old society, founded in 1926, since 1930. Thus it is not accurate to say, as Nathaniel Lehrman did last spring in a letter to the *New York Times*, that Jung and Göring presided jointly over the same organization. In the attempt to understand Jung's motives historical accuracy is vital. This will be a major theme of the present chapter. That the intentions and attitudes of all concerned were overdetermined is exemplified by Kretschmer himself who, contrary to the common implication of an uncomplicated rejection of the regime, went on to work quietly in Hitler's Germany, publishing as late as 1944 an article in the popular press on the relevance of his theory of constitutional types to increasing war production.[2]

Jung also became an editor of the society's journal, the *Zentralblatt für Psychotherapie*, which was published in Germany by Hirzel Verlag of Leipzig. The journal, like the international society as a whole, was dominated by the large and newly aggressive German group that had formed the bulk and center of the old society. It was in this journal that Jung published his observations on the distinctions between German and Jewish psychology alongside calls by Göring to the Nazi colors. While Jung's words here betrayed habits of mind we shall explore critically in a moment, Jung's opponents have often reduced these pronouncements to proof of unalloyed anti-Semitism and wholehearted collaboration with the Nazis. Such a view, however, ignores Jung's increasing disaffection toward the Nazis and his desire to protect psychotherapists in Germany from dangerous Nazi equations with so-called "Jewish" psychoanalysis. Any dissection of Jung's motives and actions, therefore, cannot be based simply on a recitation and critique of his words in the *Zentralblatt*, as has most recently been attempted by Jeffrey Masson.[3] By 1940, in any case, Jung had resigned as president of an international society rendered moribund by war and had likewise left the editorship of the journal to a now-estranged Göring and his collaborators.

While Jung's critics must be more attentive to historical detail and to multiple and evolving motives on Jung's part, his defenders must be more candid about the disturbing ambiguities in his thought, especially with regard to Jews. As Paul Roazen has rightly observed, "just as Jung shared sexist prejudices toward women, it would not be surprising for him to have uncritically adopted many traditional stereotypes about Jews."[4] There have been two interrelated ways in which insufficiently critical admirers of Jung have attempted to render harmless his expressions of such views in connection with the Third Reich. The first is to quote Jung's postwar reflections on Nazism and to trace the growth of his doubts, beginning with his "Wotan" essay of 1936. The second, and less noted, means of rendering Jung's statements less ambiguous and questionable is through their alteration in translation.

For example, in his 1934 *Zentralblatt* essay Jung twice uses the adjective *arisch* in discussing "Aryan" psychology. In the translation by R.F.C. Hull in the Bollingen Series of Jung's collected works, the German adjective *arisch* is capitalized and placed in quotation marks. In the original, however, the word appears in the lower case and without quotation marks. The translator might argue that current usage demands the quotation marks or that they indicate what Jung really meant or would have said later on, but proper historical inquiry demands fidelity to the primary source. At the time, to be sure, the word Aryan was used often and without quotation marks.[5] The word occurs regularly, for example, in Freud's correspondence, as Peter Gay has shown in his recent biography.[6] Of course, the important matter is what the word meant to its user and in the case of Jung's *Collected Works* one tends to think that the editorial decision was designed to cosmetize and thus alter the historical picture. The same is true of the translation of a footnote to a speech given by Jung in Vienna in November 1932 that was published in 1934 as part of a book entitled *Wirklichkeit der Seele*. The note is to the following text:

> ... the great liberating ideas of world history have sprung from leading personalities and never from the inert mass.... The huzzahs of the Italian nation go forth to the personality of the Duce, and the dirges of other nations lament the absence of strong leaders.[7]

The note itself in the original German reads: "Seitdem dieser Satz geschrieben wurde, hat auch Deutschland seinen Führer gefunden."[8] The translation reads, incorrectly: "After this was written, Germany also turned to a Führer." The latter verb construction implies a neutral-ity or even a disparagement on Jung's part and a resignation or des-peration on the part of the Germans not expressed by the original language. The translation should read: "Since this sentence was writ-ten, Germany too has found its leader." The Jungian cultural specific-ity of the pronoun is missing in the Hull translation, as is the positive connotation of discovery in "has found" that corresponds to the en-dorsement of strong leaders found in the text, a theme to which Jung returned in a 1933 interview on Radio Berlin with German disciple Adolf von Weizsäcker.[9]

Jung, however, did not involve himself unilaterally in the domestic affairs of Nazi Germany. He was in fact sought out by psychothera-pists there who felt his association and endorsement would add luster to their bid for professional autonomy from then dominant nosological psychiatry and dissociate them from Freud in the eyes of the regime. The German Jungians in particular were of course eager to promote Jung for generally defensive as well as specifically partisan purposes. This was precisely the theme, for example, of an article written by a Jungian member of the so-called Göring Institute, Gustav Schmaltz, that appeared in the major Cologne newspaper in 1937.[10] So though Jung could hardly have been averse to the advancement of his school of thought at the expense of that of Freud, he was involved in a project that he could rightly claim served the survival of psychotherapy in general. Should he have anticipated the extent to which psychotherapy could contribute to the repressive aims of National Socialism? Since Jung in the event had little influence on the operations of the Göring Institute, that is a question I shall not pursue here. Rather, I will con-centrate on the specific reception and use of Jungian psychology in Nazi Germany.

Jung's abiding emphasis on the unique collective experiences and memories of the world's cultures, nations, and races provided inspira-tion for various individuals and groups in Nazi Germany. While Freud and his theories were officially disapproved and thus, when used, were cloaked in Aesopian language, Jung's ideas were often evaluated posi-tively in Nazi literature. One article in the journal *Rasse* in 1939 equated Jung's notion of the collective unconscious with the Nazi concept of heredity and race.[11] And this article was listed in the official Nazi party bibliography. This is not to say that in fact Jung's ideas and those of the Nazis were identical, only that such identifications could be and were effected. And while, as Robert Proctor has noted in his recent book on medicine in Nazi Germany, Jung never went on from differentiation to denigration in his cultural relativism, Nazi "racial anthropologists" and physicians sought to elucidate the pernicious peculiarities of "Jewish" science and culture.[12]

Göring and others had originally hoped to use Jung and his followers at the institute in Berlin, individuals such as G.R. Heyer, Wolfgang Kranefeldt, and Olga von König-Fachsenfeld, as a major resource for the construction of a non-Freudian "German psychotherapy." Although this fascistic spirit pervaded the institute, neither a "German psychotherapy" nor Jung's theories by themselves in fact played a predominant role in the psychotherapists' activities. The various practical demands assumed by the psychotherapists in applying and advertising their therapeutic expertise in the realms of German society, industry, and the military took precedence over the more abstract and less pragmatic characteristics of Jungian psychology. Still, such Jungian themes continued to be applied to the events and rigors of the time. In 1943, for example, the *Zentralblatt* published an article dealing with the asserted healing power of the symbols of mother earth and father heaven from the ancient German religion of nature, powers supposedly helpful in strengthening the "feminine" sphere of the home as a refuge for the returning soldier.[13]

The regime itself displayed little scientific interest in Jung or his followers. It did, however, monitor their activities even outside of Germany. This is clear from the files of the former Reich Education Ministry held by the Zentrales Staatsarchiv in Potsdam, East Germany. From 1935 to 1939, various government agencies gathered information on the annual Eranos conferences at Ascona in Switzerland. In 1936 the Ministry refused to grant Germans permission to attend. The next year Göring arranged to have Eranos secretary Olga Fröbe-Kaptayn visit the Ministry to smooth the way for German participation. This intervention proved successful but by 1938 the Nazi Auslands-Organisation was objecting that there were lots of Jews at the meetings, that some of the topics were "politically conflictual," and that in general the whole organization seemed "mysterious." To resolve such doubts, a Ministry official asked Göring to have a report prepared on that year's meeting. On August 23, 1938 Olga von König-Fachsenfeld duly reported that she had heard nothing political at the conference, that the Swiss in particular seemed to have gone out of their way not to criticize Germany, and that while there were a number of Jews in attendance none was on the program. Permissions were given for Germans to participate in 1939 and in December of that year the German consulate in Locarno commented that while the participants at the meeting were certainly "different," the conferences did not seem to serve the interests of foreign powers, Jews, or Masons and that therefore Germans should be allowed to attend. The only restriction was to be that they could not address sessions where Jews were present.[14]

By 1939 Jung, his ideas, and his followers were not an important issue for the Nazis. By that time as well Jung and Göring were at odds over German domination of the international society and Jung was now casting a critical eye over the Nazi phenomenon. The significance of Jung's experiences during these years I think lies less in the question of any overt prejudices on his part than in the various suprapersonal dynamics his words and deeds engaged. Anti-Semitism was endemic in European society but particularly in the German lands where strong nationalism was aggravated by the proximity of the Slavic world and by the migration of *Ostjuden* into Germany and Austria. The traditional elites in Germany, for example, remained closed to Jews. As historian Fritz Stern has put it in describing the homogeneity of the officer corps: "In Germany there was no Dreyfus Affair because there was no Dreyfus."[15] The medical profession was particularly anti-Semitic due to the pervasiveness of Social Darwinist, eugenic, and racist theorizing and, after 1918, as a result of economic pressures which increased jealousy and resentment of the many prominent and successful Jewish physicians in Berlin and other large cities. Thus the Nazis could appeal to doctors and other professionals on the basis of an interlocking grid of nationalism, self-interest, and anti-Semitism.

European anti-Semitism was not usually racist in the Nazi sense, rather the interwar fascist movement capitalized on a more general cultural movement against materialism that often caricatured Jews as lacking "spirituality." Historian George Mosse has shown how pervasive this caricature was, citing as one example the late nineteenth-century Swiss historian Jacob Burckhardt who, while not close to the nascent *völkisch* movement, fulminated against the decline of aesthetics and civilization as evidenced by the machinations, among others, of venal Jews.[16] Jung never expressed himself in this way, but did share the widespread concern about the deterioration of spiritual values that, among other things, led him to see in the mass movements of the 1920s and 1930s elements of what he called liberation. This philosophical stance cultivated degrees of anti-Semitism inherited from the culture, the intensity of which varied with time and event. It must be said that

Jung broke from these notions in a way that suggests a dialectic of prejudice and tolerance within him that was ultimately resolved in favor of the latter. This is not to agree, however, with the argument of Wolfgang Giegerich that all along Jung was purposefully engaging the shadow of racial prejudice in order to extirpate it.[17] Such a judgment naively ignores the plurality of motives and conditions present in any human action, a number of which we have explored in the case at hand. Such a rationalization also turns a blind eye to the negative effects of Jung's lack of vigorous early criticism of Hitler and the possible legitimacy for the regime created in the minds of many or some through Jung's association with it, whatever protective professional capacity he effected or intended.

Jung's outlook also proved to be problematic in a more general way. Although the Nazis exploited modern technical and material resources, including medicine and psychotherapy, they also built their power on yearnings for the mysterious and the transcendent. In so doing, they revealed the perils of fascination among those who must maintain a critical, rational, and ethical distance from destructive enthusiasms, recognizing the crucial difference between saying "this is amazing" and saying "this is wrong."

Notes

1. Aryeh Maidenbaum and Stephen A. Martin, eds., *Lingering Shadows: Jungians, Freudians, and Anti-Semitism* (Boston, 1991), pp. 157–66, with permission of Shambala Publications.
2. Ernst Kretschmer, "Konstitution und Leistung," *Westfälische Landeszeitung*, August 20, 1944, microcopy T78, roll 190, frames 1866–7. National Archives, Washington, D.C.
3. Jeffrey Moussaieff Masson, *Against Therapy: Emotional Tyranny and the Myth of Psychological Healing* (New York, 1988), pp. 94–123.
4. Paul Roazen, *Freud and His Followers* (New York, 1985), p. 292.
5. C. G. Jung, "The State of Psychology Today," *The Collected Works of C. G. Jung* (Princeton, 1953–79), 10:165–6.
6. Peter Gay, *Freud: A Life for Our Times* (New York, 1988), pp. 205–39.
7. C. G. Jung, "The Development of Personality," *Collected Works*, 17:167–8.
8. C. G. Jung, "Vom Werden der Persönlichkeit," in idem, *Wirklichkeit der Seele* (Zurich, 1934), p. 180n.
9. "An Interview on Radio Berlin," in *C. G. Jung Speaking*, William McGuire and R. F. C. Hull, eds. (Princeton, 1977), p. 65.
10. "Die Sprache des Unbewussten," *Kölnische Zeitung*, October 9, 1937; and Paul Feldkeller, "Geist der Psychotherapie," *Deutsche Allgemeine Zeitung*, October 5, 1937, REM 2954. Zentrales Staatsarchiv, Potsdam.
11. Alfred A. Krauskopf, "Tiefenpsychologische Beiträge zur Rassenseelenforschung," *Rasse* 5 (1939): 362–8.

12. Robert Proctor, *Racial Hygiene: Medicine Under the Nazis* (Cambridge, Mass., 1988), pp. 162–3.
13. Frederik Adama van Scheltema, "Mutter Erde und Vater Himmel in der germanischen Naturreligion," *Zentralblatt für Psychotherapie* 14 (1943): 257–77.
14. REM 2797, Zentrales Staatsarchiv.
15. Fritz Stern, "The Burden of Success: Reflections on German Jewry," in idem, *Dreams and Delusions: The Drama of German History* (New York, 1987), p. 108.
16. George L. Mosse, *Germans and Jews: The Right, the Left, and the Search for a "Third Force" in Pre-Nazi Germany* (New York, 1970), pp. 57–60.
17. Wolfgang Giegerich, "Postscript to Cocks," *Spring* 10 (1979): 228–31.

3

Repressing, Remembering, Working Through: The Science and History of Memory in Postwar Germany[1]

In 1949 Alexander Mitscherlich, a lecturer in psychiatry, and Fred Mielke, a medical student, published a book for a research commission formed by the West German Physicians Chambers that documented the recent "doctors' trial" at Nuremberg. The foreword by the members of the working group that sent the commission to Nuremberg observed that of the 90,000 doctors active in wartime Germany, only about 350 had committed medical crimes. This observation was echoed by Mitscherlich and Mielke in the preface, but at the same time they pointed to a larger moral crisis among German doctors as a whole.[2] That this book was largely ignored by the medical profession in Germany indicates the tensions and disagreements existing among physicians regarding their profession's conduct under Hitler.[3]

Wissenschaft ohne Menschlichkeit includes a chapter on the sterilization and murder of mental patients, but in following the trials concentrates on bureaucrats and medical experiments rather than on the role of psychiatrists in the so-called "T 4" program. Mitscherlich, who with his wife Margarete would become a leading psychoanalytic critic of the postwar German denial of the Nazi past,[4] was himself entangled in the skeins of history and memory regarding his own profession's immediate past. This is evident in the small flyer included with *Wissenschaft ohne Menschlichkeit* advertising *Psyche*, a new journal for depth psychology founded by Mitscherlich, who had wintered the Nazi regime in Heidelberg. The flyer claims that *Psyche* is the only German publication carrying on the tradition of earlier journals that had been forced to cease publication by the Nazis. Yet this version of the Year Zero argument for a new beginning after 1945 ignores the fact of significant developments in the field of depth psychology in Germany between 1933 and 1945, developments that carried over into the postwar period. Although *Psyche*, in the words of its subtitle, was transformed in 1966 from *A Journal for Depth Psychology and Anthropology in Research and Praxis* to one for *Psychoanalysis and Its Applications*, its original aim as described in 1949 was to provide a forum for all schools of "*grosse Psychotherapie*." This represented a continuation of the work of the so-called Göring Institute, which, alongside and in line with its stated Nazi goal of establishing a "new German psychotherapy," from 1936 to 1945 attempted to unite the various schools of psychotherapeutic thought, chiefly the Jungian, Adlerian, and Freudian factions. Of the twenty-nine contributors listed in the flyer, eight had been members of the Göring Institute, including one who was director of the outpatient clinic and another who was a member of the Nazi party, as well as at least two others who had trained at or otherwise been associated with the institute.

It is within this context of institutional and personal continuities between the postwar Germanies and the Nazi era that an analysis of the phenomenon of "missed resistance" among psychiatrists, psychotherapists, and psychoanalysts must be conducted. This is especially the case with the professions in general, because between 1933 and 1945 a number of professions displayed "a significant degree of functional unity"[5] in defending, advancing, and sacrificing their interests in service to the Nazi regime. The Nazi era also witnessed a process of "deprofessionalization" insofar as the regime imposed political control over the professions, damaged the educational system, and trampled professional ethics.[6] Physicians, for example, achieved recognition as a profession in 1935, but they paid dearly for this status through the imposition of government control and the erosion of professional ethics. Individual professionals took advantage of the situation by joining the Nazi party (45 percent of all physicians did) or by benefiting from the exclusion of Jewish competitors. And disciplines like psychology and psychotherapy exploited specific conditions created by the Nazi seizure of power to achieve for the first time a significant degree of professionalization.[7] Psychiatrists, psychotherapists, and psychoanalysts all to one degree or another sought professional advantage in competition with one another during the Third Reich, an instance of what in connection with the Holocaust has been called "the nature of modern sin, the withdrawal of moral concerns from public roles in our lives."[8] There are specific reasons why German elites did not resist Hitler, as much of it having to do with greed, ambition, and power as with obedience, fear, and cowardice. Thus reflections on the "missed resistance" on the part of psychiatrists, psychotherapists, and psychoanalysts themselves have taken place (or not) in the context of a continuum of morally ambiguous professional development as well as that of general German culpability.[9]

There are three senses in which the term "missed resistance" can be used to illuminate the ways in which German psychiatrists, psychotherapists, and psychoanalysts have avoided as well as confronted the history and memory of the Third Reich. The first sense is that of the missed opportunity for resistance embodied in the accusations of collaboration made by young Germans in the 1960s. They confronted elders who during the "economic miracle" of the 1950s had lied or remained silent about their actions and inactions under Nazism. The second sense of missed resistance is that of regret/empathy and longing: regret over and empathy with the conditions that rendered resistance problematic as well as regret over the moral derelictions of their own professional ancestors; and longing for a legacy of resistance as redemption of the past and for moral commitment in the present. The third sense constitutes overlooking the nonheroic tradition of quotidian resistance mixed with compromise and even collaboration. Heroism almost by definition describes actions that are too late, while concentrating on heroism devalues "low-level" civil disobedience that if not preempting evil can mitigate it. This is not to celebrate those many who went along at the expense of those few who did not. There is, as Klemens von Klemperer argues, great importance in the example of an individual resister (*Einzelkämpfer*) like psychoanalyst John Rittmeister.[10] But even Rittmeister's life contains instructive ambiguities in terms of his profession: alongside resistance was, as Rittmeister noted in his prison diary, enthusiasm for much of his work at the Göring Institute, where he was director of the outpatient clinic.[11] And a post hoc fixation on resistance heroes can substitute a wish-fulfilling "ego-ideal" for historical inquiry, obscuring lines of continuity between past and present. As we shall see, the figure of Rittmeister has been used in just such a way for conscious political purposes by groups of psychotherapists and psychoanalysts in both postwar German states.

Psychiatrists, psychotherapists, and psychoanalysts have shared in the gradual recapturing of memory after 1945 which has gone through three distinct stages in West Germany. First, there was the repression characteristic of the 1950s, second, the angry generational confrontations of the 1960s, and, third, the more complicated and thoroughgoing recollections of the 1970s and 1980s. To be sure, all three styles have overlapped to some degree and both the criticism and the excesses that arose from the social crises and youth rebellions of the late 1960s and early 1970s largely laid the basis for subsequent professional critiques and self-examinations. But even more important is the fact that avoidance of and confrontation with the past have taken different forms for each discipline. This is so for two reasons. First, the three disciplines have grown increasingly distinct during the twentieth century, especially since 1933; and, second, the experience of each in the Third Reich differed in crucial respects.

Psychiatrists have displayed an almost seamless repression of the field's activities under Hitler, so much so that instances of genuine resistance as well as collaboration[12] were ignored in the silent assertion of general innocence. But recent research has shown the wide extent to which psychiatrists were involved in Nazi campaigns to sterilize and murder mental patients.[13] This collaboration began with the Law for the Prevention of Genetically Diseased Offspring of July 14, 1933. This law mandated the sterilization of those individuals suffering from a wide range of illnesses which, in keeping with Nazi racial theory and the physicalist views of most psychiatrists, were defined as hereditary. These included schizophrenia, manic-depressive insanity, and alcoholism, among others. One of the three chief authors of the expert commentary on the law was the prominent psychiatrist Ernst Rüdin.[14] So-called genetic health courts (*Erbgesundheitsgerichte*) were set up to evaluate such cases. Approximately 400,000 men and women were sterilized under this law,[15] about 95 percent of these before the outbreak of the Second World War in 1939. The radical decline in the number of compulsory sterilizations after 1939 was due to a number of factors, but the most significant was the establishment in that year of the even more radical "euthanasia" program. Under this program, by August 1941 more than 70,000 mental patients had been gassed. Ripplings of public outrage brought an end to this centrally administered campaign, but the killings went on in asylums and hospitals by means of injections, poisonings, and starvation right up to the end of the war. Psychiatrists and doctors assumed the task of murdering mentally ill men, women, and children. In all, over 300,000 people died in this manner. It is important to note that the original act did not order doctors to murder these patients, it only empowered them to do so. There was significant support for this program among psychiatrists while prewar propaganda emphasizing the financial burden placed on society by hordes of mental patients created a significant degree of popular support for the medically supervised termination of "lives not worth living."

In the years immediately following the war, however, only a very few psychiatrists were prosecuted for their roles in this program of involuntary sterilization and murder. Some were even absolved of guilt because German courts ruled that they had acted in the belief that the program was legally constituted.[16] Moreover, there existed a significant demand for medical expertise in rebuilding a devastated society and therefore a distinct carryover of medical personnel from the Third Reich into the postwar republics.[17] So even though the reputation of traditional university psychiatry suffered in Germany both during and after the war because of its involvement with the destructive racial policy of the Nazis, many of its representatives, as well as their students, continued on in positions of authority after 1945. The continuities were not only personal but conceptual. The psychiatric preoccupation with the hereditary determinants of mental illness had been easily exploited by the Nazis. And apart from the authoritarian social and political views commonly held in the German professoriate often linked with this hereditarianism, psychiatrists, like physicians in general, were also heavily influenced by the eugenic thought, Social Darwinism, and racism endemic to Germany during the late nineteenth and early twentieth centuries.[18] The persistence of this way of thinking into the postwar era is evident in the West German disposition of compensation cases for psychic damage caused by Nazi persecution. A number of these claims were rejected on the basis of psychiatric evaluations that declared that these individuals' difficulties were due to hereditary predisposition (*Anlage*), decisions that produced vigorous dissent from psychoanalysts and psychotherapists.[19]

A systematic confrontation with psychiatry's past did not occur until the 1980s. At first, this critique was part of a larger critical "history of the everyday" (*Alltagsgeschichte*) directed "from below" by students and citizens against the silent bastions of academic and political authority. These campaigns took the form of conferences and the collection, exhibition, and publication of documents, recollections, and studies concerning the activities of individuals, communities, and groups under National Socialism. Some of these concentrated on the medical profession, including psychiatry, and constituted criticism primarily from outside the profession from sociologists, pedagogues, historians, theologians, and the like.[20] Much of this critical work has been neo-Marxist or structuralist in orientation and sees Nazi medicine as a culmination of the Western bourgeois trend toward "social control" and eugenic engineering. Especially since the fall of communism in the Soviet Union and Eastern Europe, however, there has also been a greater willingness to confront the abuse of psychiatry by totalitarian socialist regimes.

Only recently have members of the psychiatric community begun to question their collective past. And instead of seeking distance between themselves and their compromised predecessors, as was characteristic of the radical confrontation of the late 1960s with "fascism" at home and abroad, these inquiries have focused with some humility on those processes and structures for dealing with the mentally ill that contribute *now as then* to inhumanity. This does not constitute a facile equation of contemporary society with Nazi Germany but, rather, an attempt to deal with those tendencies toward categorization and evaluation within psychiatry that can stigmatize mental patients as especially disruptive of society and the economy.

Klaus Dörner, one of the very few psychiatrists to address the subject relatively early on,[21] has more lately expressed concern that he had only intellectualized the subject rather than confronting it emotionally and that such an emotional confrontation involved for him an effort to work with relatives of mental patients killed by the Nazis who were denied compensation under the Federal Compensation Law. This effort, Dörner says, has brought him face to face with a continuity of attitude and issue between the Nazi period and the present.[22] Such emotional confrontation, however, has allowed Dörner to buttress his original continuity thesis. Moreover, according to Dörner, such continuity extends back into the late eighteenth century. He has characterized modern European psychiatry as an exercise in "therapeutic idealism" by which "industrial-capitalist bourgeois society" could "deal with those who, by its gauge of rationality, it deems irrational."[23] The coercive social effects of this tyranny of reason ushered in by the Enlightenment and the Industrial Revolution were aggravated in Germany by Prussian authoritarianism. The Nazi period represented the extremity of both of these traditions.[24] In line with this thinking, most recently Dörner's was a strong voice raised in protest against Peter Singer's argument for euthanasia of severely handicapped newborns.[25] Of course, one can support Singer's arguments and "bourgeois society" without espousing Nazism.

A similar ethic pervades the documentation by a group of young mental health care workers of the operations of the asylum at Wittenau in Berlin between 1933 and 1945. The authors ask why they failed during the 1960s to take their teachers to task for their collaboration with the Nazis. The answer, they feel, lies in their own desire to divorce themselves from the horrors of the Nazi era by broadening and thus diluting their criticism into a radical condemnation of society in general and fascism in particular. What they found in scouring the archives at Wittenau was that the procedures and judgments involved in the sterilization and murder of mental patients under Nazi direction blended in rather smoothly with the workings of what up until 1933 had been an institution renowned for its progressive treatment of the mentally ill. This continuity of operation is the reason why documents detailing these measures were found in the archives while documents dealing with Jewish patients had long since disappeared.[26] Investigations and attitudes such as these are in keeping with the second sense of "missed resistance," a regret for failure in the past and the congruent need for commitment in the present.

This is not to say, however, that there are no professional, political, or ideological agendas involved in these efforts at confronting psychiatry's past. Most of the criticism still comes from various left-of-center segments of the German polity who, with considerable justification, see distinct continuities in professional attitudes among psychiatrists before and after 1945. These critiques have most often been part of a general rejection of the conservative West German establishment embodied principally by the Christian Democratic Union which has dominated political life since 1945. Moreover, while this confrontation has to a great extent been one across generations, with the postwar young challenging the wartime old, the more recent concern with the moral ambiguities inherent in the social place of the mentally ill carries with it an implicit critique of professionalization that can be applied to all practitioners, particularly those of the postwar generations who are advancing professionally in a prosperous Germany. At the same time, the unification of Germany has injected a great deal of Marxist-inspired research into the relationships between fascism and capitalism in the Third Reich.[27] Two basic moral positions have evolved out of this combination of Western and Eastern scholarship that pose questions relevant to the debate over the role of psychiatry in Nazi Germany. The first maintains that moral choice is obviated by membership in historically determined collectivities; the second emphasizes individual choices between good and evil that can and must be made: Which is it more important to change, structures or people? Which are more susceptible to change?

While psychotherapists and psychoanalysts have not had to confront direct participation in Nazi atrocities, their history displays some disturbing lines of professional continuity extending through the Nazi years. Under the Nazis this meant some specific as well as general violations of professional ethics, but it also fed into a longer-term and morally ambiguous trend toward adjustment of individuals to the demands of society. Agencies of the Nazi regime, such as the Labor Front, the SS, and the Luftwaffe, funded the Göring Institute generously in their mobilization of expertise to assist in rearmament and war. Between 1936 and 1945 a significant number of the men and women who would constitute the postwar psychotherapeutic movement in both German states were members or trainees of Matthias Heinrich Göring's German Institute for Psychological Research and Psychotherapy in Berlin or at its branches in several other cities. It was in this way that those physicians and lay practitioners in Germany who conceived of mental illness principally in psychological rather than physical terms established themselves as competitors to the dominant university psychiatrists. Some of the impetus for the critical examination of the history of German psychotherapy and psychoanalysis stems from concern over the resultant social identity, role, and responsibility of the field, a concern that also often obstructs understanding of the past.

Psychotherapists have largely ignored their recent professional past, in part because they were busy first surviving the difficult years after the war and then exploiting their newly professionalized position to meet a growing demand for psychological services in both the Federal and the Democratic Republic. It is also true that time is necessary for historical perspective and that psychotherapists, like psychiatrists and psychoanalysts, are not professional historians, but a distinct unwillingness to deal with the legacy of the Nazi years also marks their treatments of the past. The accepted professional view in West Germany was that the "political events following 1933 pushed German psychotherapy...into the background for a long time."[28] In 1977, on the occasion of the fiftieth anniversary of the founding of the General Medical Society for Psychotherapy, its president observed that the only significance of the psychotherapeutic institute in Nazi Germany was the degree of protection and enforced cooperation it provided for those psychotherapists who had not emigrated.[29]

In East Germany an even greater distance was put between postwar psychotherapy and its precedents under German fascism, even though in the socialist republic there was a similar emphasis placed on expert service to the state and a reliance on the short-term methods pioneered in Germany by, among others, Johannes Heinrich Schultz, deputy director of the Göring Institute.[30] Former East German psychotherapists and psychiatrists now face the task of confronting a likewise compromised association with the late communist regime. The difficulty of this task is compounded by the fact that former East Germans in general never had to confront questions of collaboration with the Nazis since by official German Democratic Republic definition all former Nazis lived in the Federal Republic. On the other hand, the infamy and incompetence that prompted the collapse of the communist regimes may combine with the relatively advanced state in the West of confrontation with the Nazi past to produce an easier and quicker coming to terms with this even more recent compromised past. And whatever the psychiatric and psychotherapeutic injustices perpetrated by the East German government in aping its big Soviet brother, they of course pale in comparison to collaboration with the much more evil Nazi regime.

Challenges to the assertion of professional innocence among psychotherapists first came across disciplinary boundaries in West Germany as a result of the professional competition sharpened and even created under National Socialism. In 1960 the director of the German Society for Psychology responded to charges of Nazi collaboration among psychologists by arguing that psychotherapists had compromised themselves to a much greater degree.[31] This type of counterattack, however, raised defenses and not curiosity or consciousness. As a result, the first study of the history of psychotherapy in Nazi Germany came from abroad in the 1970s.[32] By the 1980s some additional work was being done by historians of medicine at the University of Leipzig, but its thematic comprehensiveness is limited by a Marxist-Leninist approach emphasizing a top-down nazification of psychotherapy.[33] By this time as well research in the West had integrated the history of psychotherapy in the Third Reich into the study of professions and professionalization in Germany.[34] This work has had little discernible effect on psychotherapists in Germany, at least partly because the course of their profession's development has scattered them throughout several disciplines and the nature of their practice has oriented them toward issues of application rather than of introspection.

It was the good fortune of this author to have been the first historian to have stumbled onto the subject of psychotherapy in the Third Reich. My major field as a a graduate student at the University of California in Los Angeles was German history and one of my minor fields was in psychohistory, which is the application of psychoanalytic methods to history. As a result, I became interested in the history of psychoanalysis in Germany. In searching for a topic for my dissertation I quite by accident came across some bound volumes of the *Zentralblatt für Psychotherapie*. Upon noticing that the volumes covered the years from 1928 to 1939, I immediately assumed that the journal was Austrian or Swiss, because I already knew that psychoanalysis had been banned in Germany in 1933 and that therefore anything like psychotherapy certainly could not have survived there. I was wrong. The journal was that of the General Medical Society for Psychotherapy, it was published in Leipzig, and the editors included the Swiss, Carl Jung, and a man I had never heard of, Matthias Heinrich Göring. It turned out that Göring's cousin was Reich Marshal Hermann Göring and I immediately understood that the fortunes of psychotherapy in the Third Reich were bound up with the family relations of the second most powerful Nazi in Germany. And I noticed that while there were shrill denunciations of "Jewish" psychoanalysis in the pages of the journal after 1933, there were also articles that incorporated psychoanalytic points of view. So I talked with some psychoanalysts in nearby Beverly Hills who had fled Nazi Germany and they confirmed that some of their non-Jewish colleagues had stayed in Germany and had continued working in the field during the Nazi period.

A year in West Germany conducting interviews with former members of the institute and scouring archives and libraries produced the first history of the Göring Institute. Early in my research abroad I found myself disliking the people whom I was interviewing and about whom I was reading. At the time I had not found evidence that any of the members of the Göring Institute had been involved in atrocities, but I was bothered by an understandable desire on the part of the people I was interviewing to justify and defend their activities in Nazi Germany, including their acquiescence, or worse, in the purging of Jewish colleagues. But I decided that I should take advantage of the fact that I was a foreigner who had no other purpose than to describe accurately and dispassionately the history of this group of aspiring professionals. The wrestling with the moral consequences could be and has been more successfully carried out by professional descendants in Germany. This did not mean that I would not evaluate the social and moral consequences of the professionalization of psychotherapy in Germany between 1933 and 1945. Rather it meant that I would strive to relate all the relevant information I could about psychotherapy in the Third Reich so that as many historical connections as possible could be made by me and by subsequent researchers. It was just about that time that historians of the period were beginning to shift the focus away from the agencies and personalities of Nazi aggression and oppression and toward the broader topic of German society under Nazism in order to understand more fully the ways in which everyday "normal" life was part of the environment that allowed Auschwitz to happen. It would not do simply to label the psychotherapists at the Göring Institute as nothing but just another bunch of Nazis.

I was struck by the amazing success the psychotherapists had in the face of opposition from the powerful psychiatric establishment in the universities, in the government, and in the military. Clearly association with the name Göring helped more than association with the name Freud hurt. And, given the protection and visibility afforded the psychotherapists by Göring, it was also the case that psychotherapists were able to make a significant case for the practical applications of their craft. I was also willing to accept the fact that were wide degrees of collaboration with the Nazis and many levels of culpability. Within this group of individuals there naturally were ranges of collaboration and culpability. But, unlike the psychiatrists, whose collaboration meant the maiming and murder of "racial enemies," psychotherapists had the luxury of working for the enhancement of "racial comrades." This meant that what they were doing as professionals was closer to what professionals in easier and better times usually do. The ethical violations of the psychotherapists as a group were indirect, that is, they helped an immoral regime exploit the capacities of its people for a war of conquest and extermination. As a result, their experience suggests *in extremis* some of the problematic ethical dimensions of professionalization in modern industrial and post-industrial societies. For example, the efforts of psychotherapists and psychoanalysts to "cure" homosexuals represented (1) an attempt to enhance professional status; (2) a desire to "help" the "sick"; (3) support for the regime's insistence on a productive populace; (4) an alternative to the policies of punishment, imprisonment, castration, and extermination carried by psychiatrists, the SS, and the military and (5) a resultant absence of resistance to overall Nazi persecution of homosexuals and thus degrees of participation in an inhumane system.

Unlike the psychotherapists, psychoanalysts in West Germany (psychoanalysis was officially discouraged in the East) have of late confronted their past. This has to do with the distinct history as well as the distinct nature of psychoanalysis. Two versions of the history of psychoanalysis in Nazi Germany were literally institutionalized in the immediate postwar period. The German Psychoanalytic Society (DPG), which had been founded in 1910 and dissolved in 1938, was reestablished in 1946, but was divided between orthodox Freudians and "neoanalysts" influenced by other schools of psychotherapeutic thought within the Göring Institute. By 1951 the orthodox Freudians had seceded to form the German Psychoanalytic Union (DPV) which in that year was recognized by the International Psycho-Analytical Association (IPA). The "official" position of the DPG with regard to psychoanalysis in the Third Reich has been that it had been "saved" by the Freudian members of the Göring Institute.[35] The DPV argued that psychoanalysis had simply been suppressed by the Nazis.[36]

These positions remained unaltered and largely unnoticed until the 1970s when psychoanalytic candidates began questioning these orthodoxies. Chief among them was Regine Lockot who in 1985 published a comprehensive critical study of the Göring Institute. By relying on extensive documentary evidence Lockot demonstrated that psychoanalysis was neither merely suppressed nor simply saved during the Third Reich; rather it was used, compromised, abused, and perverted. On the one hand, Lockot sought to follow what she labelled the *realpolitisch* perspective of the earlier historical work I had done and, on the other, to utilize a psychoanalytic point of view to begin the process of what Freud in 1914 called "working through" (*Durcharbeiten*). Freud had argued that what "distinguishes analytic treatment from any kind of treatment by suggestion"[37] is the process by which the patient *works through* resistances to an understanding of the repressed content behind neurotic symptoms. This didactic aim is furthered by transference, whereby the patient reexperiences feelings toward parents in the relationship with the analyst, and countertransference, whereby the analyst through the emotions created by the relationship with the patient comes to understand the patient's unconscious. Lockot argues that psychoanalysts in particular must work through the repression of their own past and by means of countertransference come to understand not only their history but themselves as well.[38] The alternative is neurotic repetition of actions in place of self-understanding. Lockot argues that this neurotic pattern of behavior was displayed immediately after the war by leading members of the DPG as they struggled with the emotional consequences of a psychoanalytic identity damaged by compromise and collaboration under National Socialism.[39]

It is this psychoanalytic emphasis on repression that in particular characterizes the challenge that young psychoanalysts have raised against their professional elders. All three senses of the "missed resistance" have been present in this challenge: confrontation, regret/empathy, and a tendency to overlook resistance for Resistance. This challenge manifested itself first at a conference in Bamberg in 1980 and was developed by analysts and non-analysts in the pages of *Psyche* between 1982 and 1986. Perhaps predictably for a discipline concerned so much with individual cases and characterized organizationally and emotionally by issues of authority between teacher and student, much of the heat (if less of the light) was generated in a controversy over Göring Institute psychoanalyst Carl Müller-Braunschweig.[40] More recently, the Berlin Forum for the History of Psychoanalysis has begun efforts to deposit documents at the Federal Archives in Coblenz pertaining to the history of psychoanalysis in Germany.

The debate within the DPV has overshadowed the discussions within the DPG, such as those held at DPG conferences in West Berlin in 1985[41] and in Bad Soden in 1989. Young DPV critics see their organization's prior treatment of its past as especially objectionable for two reasons: first, because the notion of the complete suppression of psychoanalysis by the Nazis constitutes silence on the subject; and, second, because collaboration meant forsaking not only the many Jewish colleagues victimized by the Nazi campaign against "Jewish science" but also the ideals embodied in psychoanalytic thought.[42] The DPG, originally displaying the eclecticism in theory and practice which was promoted by the Göring Institute, had been willing to discuss the saving of psychoanalysis but until recently was less willing to examine critically the negative aspects of such salvation. But of late the DPG has been moving away from the "neo-Freudian" position established chiefly by the Göring Institute's Harald Schultz-Hencke toward the orthodox Freudian tradition represented by the DPV and IPA. This movement has been encouraged by increasing contacts among newer members of both groups not divided by traditional rivalries as well as by the growing influence of the DPV both at home and abroad.[43]

Both the DPG and the DPV have attempted to capitalize on the figure of John Rittmeister, the Freudian member of the Göring Institute who was executed by the Nazis in 1943 on charges of having spied for the Soviet Union. There is in this memorialization a distinct sense of "our Rittmeister." For former colleagues at the Göring Institute it is a matter of innocence by association.[44] For younger members of the DPV he has been the counterexample they hold up to their professional elders and from whom they draw inspiration.[45] And Rittmeister's involvement with the communist resistance to Hitler prompted the East German Society for Medical Psychotherapy to create an award in his name in 1979. While Rittmeister is certainly worthy of admiration, concentration on him to the exclusion of the other particulars of the history of psychoanalysis and psychotherapy in the Third Reich has been part of the process of denial and repression characteristic of these groups' perceptions of their collective past until recently. Surely it is a relevant irony that some who lived ethically compromised lives as members of the Göring Institute could at the time and later rationalize their behavior because of small acts of courage and compassion while contemporary critics cannot *do* anything either against the Nazis or for their victims except remember for the sake of memory, their contemporaries, and the future. Under such circumstances the figure of a hero provides a certain degree of vicarious satisfaction and emotional nourishment.

German psychoanalysts have thus been somewhat successful in confronting their history. Psychoanalysis, unlike psychiatry or psychotherapy in general, is based on detailed excavation of the past. Their patients have included those whose lives were directly or indirectly affected by the horrors of the Third Reich, even if for a long time the topic was largely taboo in analytic sessions.[46] Moreover, the DPV in particular is the inheritor of an intellectual tradition that is largely Jewish in origin and many of whose practitioners were persecuted by the Nazis. German psychoanalysts were reminded of this in 1977 when at the Jerusalem meeting of the IPA a proposal to meet in Berlin was turned down. Yet in 1985 the IPA did meet in Hamburg and devoted a day to discussion of "identification and its vicissitudes in relation to the Nazi phenomenon."[47] In conjunction with the congress a group of young German analysts set up an exhibition on the history of psychoanalysis in Germany highlighting the activities of psychoanalysts at the Göring Institute, a history that they see as still being repressed and not worked through by the West German psychoanalytic leadership.[48] But although the DPV has been quite willing to benefit from the international success of the Hamburg exhibition, the IPA has not encouraged confrontation with the discipline's German past, preferring at Hamburg as before to concentrate on technical issues of psychoanalytic theory and practice. This neutral "scientific" posture constituted the original response of the IPA to the depredations of nazism in the 1930s.[49]

The Germans make up the second largest national contingent of psychoanalysts in the IPA, behind only the Americans, a position that certainly will be further consolidated through the unification of Germany. But the popularity of psychoanalysis in West Germany is also due to its being "a Jewish heritage in the German language" uncontaminated by the Nazi past that has served, in the eyes of some, to blind the DPV in particular to its compromised past.[50] Moreover, it can be argued that the introspection inherent in psychoanalysis carries a particular appeal for the German romantic cultural tradition and that such self-absorption can be a means of avoiding rational confrontation with unpleasant truths. Left-wing psychoanalysts such as the Siegfried Bernfeld Group, who wish to realize what they see as the radical social and political implications of psychoanalysis, see contemporary German conservatism in social, political, environmental, and military affairs reflected in the authoritarian practices of psychoanalytic institutes and in the ongoing failure to work through the Nazi past.[51] From this standpoint, the integration of psychoanalysis into the state health care system only aggravated inherent tendencies toward political and social quiescence.[52] Finally, it is anything but clear that Germans in general have laid to rest the legacy of anti-Semitism, particularly with regard to feelings about health and illness.[53]

As with psychiatrists and psychotherapists, psychoanalysts too have tended to concentrate on the actions of individuals independent of the broader context of institutional and professional history, a limitation manifested as well in the anecdotal tendencies of *Alltagsgeschichte*. But in the second sense of "missed resistance," that of regret/empathy, for whose exercise the analytic emphasis on intra- and interpersonal psychodynamics is peculiarly suited, German psychoanalysts have also had to deal with the structural continuities in the history of their discipline to, through, and beyond the Third Reich. Such continuities raise the disturbing question of the ethical problems inherent in a professionalizing society. For all three disciplines, therefore, there exists the task of working through the present as well as the past.

Notes

1. "Psychiatry, Psychotherapy, and Psychoanalysis in Nazi Germany: Historiographical Reflections," in Mark S. Micale and Roy Porter, eds., *Discovering the History of Psychiatry* (New York, 1994), pp. 282–96. Copyright 1994 by Oxford University Press, Inc. Reprinted by permission; "Repressing, Remembering, Working Through: German Psychiatry, Psychotherapy, Psychoanalysis, and the 'Missed Resistance' in the Third Reich," *Journal of Modern History* 64 (1992): S204–16; and in Michael Geyer and John W. Boyer, eds., *Resistance Against the*

Third Reich, 1933–1990 (Chicago, 1994), pp. 312–24. c 1992, 1994 by the University of Chicago. All rights reserved.

2. Alexander Mitscherlich and Fred Mielke, *Wissenschaft ohne Menschlichkeit. Medizinische und Eugenische Irrwege unter Burokratie und Krieg* (Heidelberg, 1949), pp. v, 6. Michael Kater, *Doctors Under Hitler* (Chapel Hill, 1989), pp. 12, 267, fixes the number of wartime doctors in Germany at around 79,000.

3. Robert N. Proctor, *Racial Hygiene: Medicine under the Nazis* (Cambridge, Massachusetts, 1988), p. 309.

4. Alexander and Margarete Mitscherlich, *The Inability to Mourn: Principles of Collective Behavior* [1967], trans. Beverley R. Placzek (New York, 1975).

5. Geoffrey Cocks, "The Professionalization of Psychotherapy in Germany, 1928–1949" in Geoffrey Cocks and Konrad Jarausch, eds., *German Professions, 1800–1950* (New York, 1990), p. 311.

6. Konrad H. Jarausch, *The Unfree Professions: German Lawyers, Teachers, and Engineers, 1900–1950* (New York, 1990).

7. Ulfried Geuter, *Die Professionalisierung der deutschen Psychologie im Nationalsozialismus* [1984], 2nd ed. (Frankfurt am Main, 1988); Cocks, "Professionalization of Psychotherapy in Germany."

8. Rainer C. Baum, *The Holocaust and the German Elite* (Lanham, Maryland, 1981), p. 266.

9. Rolf Vogt, "Warum sprechen die Deutschen nicht?" *Psyche* 40 (1986): 896–97.

10. Klemens von Klemperer, "'What is the Law that Lies Behind these Words?' Antigone's Question and the German Resistance," *Journal of Modern History* 64 (December 1992): S102–11.

11. "Tagebuchblätter aus dem Gefängnis von Dr. med. John Rittmeister," pp. 3, 4, 15, 19, 23. Nds 721 Acc 69/76 Lüneburg, vol. 10, pp. 126–57; Niedersächsisches Hauptstaatsarchiv, Hanover.

12. Dirk Blasius, "Psychiatrischer Alltag im Nationalsozialismus," in Detlev Peukert and Jürgen Reulecke, eds., *Die Reihen fast geschlossen. Beiträge zur Geschichte des Alltags unterm Nationalsozialismus* (Wuppertal, 1981), pp. 367–80.

13. Hans-Walter Schmuhl, *Rassenhygiene, Nationalsozialismus, Euthanasie. Von der Verhütung zur Vernichtung "lebensunwerten Lebens," 1890–1945* (Göttingen, 1987).

14. Arthur Gütt, Ernst Rüdin, and Falk Ruttke, *Gesetz zur Verhütung erbkranken Nachwuchses* (Munich, 1934).

15. Gisela Bock, *Zwangssterilisation im Nationasozialismus* (Opladen, 1986), pp. 230–46.

16. Ernst Klee, *"Euthanasie" im NS-Staat. Die "Vernichtung lebensunwerten Lebens"* (Frankfurt am Main, 1985), pp. 384–86.

17. Kater, *Doctors Under Hitler*, pp. 223–24.

18. Sheila Faith Weiss, *Race Hygiene and National Efficiency: The Eugenics of Wilhelm Schallmayer* (Berkeley and Los Angeles, 1987).

19. Klaus D. Hoppe, "The Emotional Reactions of Psychiatrists when Confronting Survivors of Persecution" *Psychoanalytic Forum* 1 (1966): 187–96.

20. Gerhard Baader and Ulrich Schultz, eds., *Medizin und Nationalsozialismus. Tabuisierte Vergangenheit—Ungebrochene Tradition?* (Berlin, 1980); Projektgruppe "Volk und Gesundheit" eds., *Volk und Gesundheit. Heilen und Vernichten im Nationalsozialismus* (Tübingen, 1982); Kölnische Gesellschaft für Christlich-Jüdische Zusammenarbeit, *Heilen und Vernichten im Nationalsozialismus* (Cologne, 1985). See also Benno Müller-Hill, *Murderous Science: Elimination by scientific selection of Jews, Gypsies, and others, Germany, 1933–1945* [1984], trans. George R. Fraser (Oxford, 1988).

21. Klaus Dörner, "Nationalsozialismus und Lebensvernichtung," *Vierteljahreshefte für Zeitgeschichte* 15 (1967): 121–52.

22. Gerhard Baader et al., "Podiumsdiskussion" in Baader and Schultz, eds., *Medizin und Nationalsozialismus*, pp.23–24.

23. Klaus Dörner, *Madmen and the Bourgeoisie: A Social History of Insanity and Psychiatry* [1969], trans. Joachim Neugroschel and Jean Steinberg (Oxford, 1981), pp. 218, 291. Cf. Robert Brown, "The Institutions of Insanity," *Times Literary Supplement*, January 8, 1982, p. 24. Brown criticizes Dörner's thesis as lacking in evidence.

24. Dörner, *Madmen and the Bourgeosie*, pp. 216–217, 329, n. 157.

25. Johann S. Ach and Andreas Gaidt, "Kein Diskurs über Abtreibung und `Euthanasie'?" Zur Rechtfertigung der Singer-Debatte," *Das Argument* 33 (1990): 769–76. Dörner argues that Singer's view represents a mentality concerning expendable life which replaces or disguises earlier eugenic arguments based on social cost with arguments based on sympathy for severely handicapped newborns. Any discussion of such ideas, Dörner says, provides them with a valuation they do not deserve.

26. Arbeitsgruppe zur Erforschung der Geschichte der Karl-Bonhoeffer-Nervenklinik, eds., *Totgeschwiegen 1933–1945. Die Geschichte der Karl-Bonhoeffer-Nervenklinik* (Berlin, 1988).

27. V.R. Berghahn, "Big Business in the Third Reich," *European History Quarterly* 21 (1991): 97–108.

28. Walter Theodor Winkler, "The Present Status of Psychotherapy in Germany" in Frieda Fromm-Reichmann and J.L. Moreno, eds., *Progress in Psychotherapy 1956* (New York, 1956), p. 288.

29. Walter Theodor Winkler, "50 Jahre AAeGP—ein Rückblick," *Zeitschrift für Psychotherapie und medizinische Psychologie* 27 (1977): 79.

30. Kurt Höck, *Psychotherapie in der DDR* (n.p., 1979), pp. 7, 14; Dietfried Müller-Hegemann, "Psychotherapy in the German Democratic Republic" in Ari Kiev, ed., *Psychiatry in the Communist World* (New York, 1968), pp. 51–70.

31. Albert Wellek, "Deutsche Psychologie und Nationalsozialismus," *Psychologie und Praxis* 4 (1960): 177–82.

32. Geoffrey Campbell Cocks, "Psyche and Swastika: *Neue deutsche Seelenheilkunde*, 1933–1945" (Ph.D. diss., University of California, Los Angeles, 1975).

33. Christina Schröder, "Programm und Wirksamkeit der 'Neuen deutschen Seelenheilkunde'," in Achim Thom and Genadji Ivanovic Caregorodcev, eds., *Medizin Unterm Hakenkreuz* (Leipzig, 1989), pp. 283–305.

34. Geoffrey C. Cocks, "Psychoanalyse, Psychotherapie und Nationalsozialismus," *Psyche* 37 (1983): 1057–1106; idem, *Psychotherapy in the Third Reich: The Göring Institute* (New York, 1985); and idem, "Professionalization of Psychotherapy in Germany."

35. Franz Baumeyer, "Zur Geschichte der Psychoanalyse in Deutschland. 60 Jahre Deutsche Psychoanalytische Gesellschaft," *Zeitschrift für psychosomatische Medizin und Psychoanalyse* 17 (1971): 203–40; Rose Spiegel, Gerard Chrzanowski, Arthur Feiner, "On Psychoanalysis in the Third Reich," *Contemporary Psychoanalysis* 11 (1975): 477–510.

36. Gerhard Maetze, "Psychoanalyse in Deutschland," in Dieter Eicke, ed., *Die Psychologie des 20. Jahrhunderts. Freud und die Folgen*, (Zurich, 1976), pp. 1145–79; Gudrun Zapp, "Psychoanalyse und Nationalsozialismus: Untersuchungen zum Verhältnis Medizin/Psychoanalyse während des Nationalsozialismus" (Inaug. diss., University of Kiel, 1980).

37. Sigmund Freud, "Remembering, Repeating and Working Through (Further Recommendations on the Technique of Psycho-Analysis II)" in James Strachey, ed.

and trans., *The Standard Edition of the Complete Psychological Works of Sigmund Freud* (London, 1958), 12:155–56.

38. Regine Lockot, *Erinnern und Durcharbeiten. Zur Geschichte der Psychoanalyse und Psychotherapie im Nationalsozialismus* (Frankfurt am Main, 1985), pp. 17–38. See also Wolfgang Huber, *Psychoanalyse in Oesterreich seit 1933* (Vienna, 1977).

39. Regine Lockot, "Wiederholen oder Neubeginn: Skizzen zur Geschichte der 'Deutschen Psychoanalytischen Gesellschaft' von 1945–1950," *Jahrbuch der Psychoanalyse* 22 (1988): 218–35.

40. Hans-Martin Lohmann, ed., *Psychoanalyse und Nationalsozialismus. Beiträge zur Bearbeitung eines unbewältigten Traumas* (Frankfurt am Main, 1984), pp. 109–36; "Dokumentation des DPV-Vorstands zum Briefwechsel Ehebald/Dahmer" (DPV, September, 1984, typescript); Hans Müller-Braunschweig, "Fünfzig Jahre danach. Stellungnahme zu den in PSYCHE 11/1982 zitierten Aeusserungen von Carl-Müller-Braunschweig," *Psyche* 37 (1983): 1140–45; and Ernst Federn, "Weitere Bemerkungen zum Problemkreis 'Psychoanalyse und Politik'," *Psyche* 39 (1985): 367–74.

41. Friedrich Beese, "Psychoanalyse in Deutschland. Rückblick und Perspektiven" in Gerd Rudolf et al., eds., *Psychoanalyse der Gegenwart. Eine kritische Bestandsaufnahme 75 Jahre nach der Gründung der Deutschen Psychoanalytischen Gesellschaft* (Göttingen, 1987), pp. 15–29; Geoffrey Cocks, "Psychoanalyse und Psychotherapie im Dritten Reich" in Rudolf et al., eds., pp. 30–43.

42. Volker Friedrich, "Psychoanalyse im Nationalsozialismus. Vom Widerspruch zur Gleichschaltung," *Jahrbuch der Psychoanalyse* 20 (1987): 207–33.

43. Bernd Nitschke, "Psychoanalyse als 'un'-politische Wissenschaft"; and Volker Friedrich, "Die wissenschaftliche und politische Antwort der Psychoanalytiker auf die Herausforderung des Nationalsozialismus und des zweiten Weltkrieges" (papers presented to the International Association for the History of Psychoanalysis, London, July 22, 1990.)

44. Werner Kemper, "John F. Rittmeister zum Gedächtnis," *Zeitschrift für psychosomatische Medizin und Psychoanalyse* 14 (1968): 147–49.

45. Ludger M. Hermanns, "John F. Rittmeister und C.G. Jung," *Psyche* 36 (1982): 1022–31.

46. Lutz Rosenkötter, "Schatten der Zeitgeschichte auf psychoanalytischen Behandlungen," *Psyche* 33 (1979): 1024–38.

47. Edith Kurzweil, "The Freudians Meet in Germany," *Partisan Review* 52 (1985): 337–47. See also Kurzweil, "The (Freudian) Congress of Vienna," *Commentary* 52 (1971): 80–83; and Kurzweil, *The Freudians: A Comparative Perspective* (New Haven, 1989), pp. 231–36, 294–98, 313–15.

48. Karen Brecht et al., *"Hier geht das Leben auf eine sehr merkwürdige Weise weiter..." Zur Geschichte der Psychoanalyse in Deutschland* (Hamburg, 1985).

49. Edward Glover, "Report of the Thirteenth International Psycho-Analytical Congress," *International Journal of Psycho-Analysis* 15 (1934): 485–88; Richard F. Sterba, *Reminiscences of a Viennese Psychoanalyst* (Detroit, 1982), p. 163.

50. Hermann Beland et al., "Podiumsdiskussion: Psychoanalyse unter Hitler—Psychoanalyse heute," *Psyche* 40 (1986): 425; Hans Keilson, "Psychoanalyse und Nationalsozialismus," *Jahrbuch der Psychoanalyse* 25 (1989): 23; and Robert S. Wallerstein, "Psychoanalysis in Nazi Germany: Historical and Psychoanalytic Lessons," *Psychoanalysis and Contemporary Thought* 11 (1988): 360.

51. Janice Haaken, "The Siegfried Bernfeld Conference: Uncovering the Psychoanalytic Political Unconscious," *American Journal of Psychoanalysis* 50 (1990): 289–304.

52. Paul Parin, "Warum die Psychoanalytiker so ungern zu brennenden Zeitproblemen Stellung nehmen," *Psyche* 32 (1978): 385–99.

53. Geoffrey Cocks, "Partners and Pariahs: Jews and Medicine in Modern German Society," *Leo Baeck Institute Yearbook* 36 (1991): 192–205.

Part II

Psychoanalysis

4

On Throwing Dishes from a Window in a Dream: Psychoanalysis in European Society and Politics, 1900–1939[1]

In 1925 Virginia Woolf wrote that the primary focus of interest for humanity in the modern era "lies very likely in the dark places of psychology."[2] Woolf's observation was as much a reflection of her times as a typical expression of the interest in psychoanalysis displayed by members of the Bloomsbury Group. As a culmination to the social and political upheavals of the first decades of the twentieth century, Europe would commit suicide for the second time by putting the gun to its head in September 1939. That same month in London Sigmund Freud died. The war and the death of Freud brought to a close the "classical" period of psychoanalysis. The war also brought suspension of much of the international scientific activity in the field, a deterioration begun in the early 1930s with the emigration of many of its practitioners from Central Europe. While ironically this exodus helped spur the growth of psychoanalysis in Great Britain and the United States, the rise to power of fascism meant the end of autonomous psychoanalytic institutes and societies in both Germany and Austria by 1938. Freud's death itself marked an end not only to an era of pioneering discovery but to psychoanalysis as an intellectual *movement*. After 1939, assisted by the wartime mobilization of science by both the Allies and the Axis, psychoanalysts would enter an age of institutionalization marked by "narrow professionalism...authoritarian control over training"[3] and "intellectual, moral, and political ambiguities."[4]

With the publication in late 1899 of *The Interpretation of Dreams* Freud had "disturbed the sleep of the world" by seeking to understand the dynamics of the unconscious. Dreams, the free association of sleep, became a staple of the psychoanalytic literature. In 1927 the *Interna-

tional Journal of Psycho-Analysis published an account of a dream related by a university student from Canada:

> Last year I taught school in the country. My room was upstairs with a window at the back from which was a fire-escape. One night I dreamt that some men attacked the school and the teacher from downstairs rushed up, followed by all her pupils to climb out of my fire-escape. She carried a dish-pan full of dishes. When she came to the window she threw out the dishes one by one. Then I remember helping the children to climb out. Of course all this was done very quickly, for the attackers were smashing in the doors downstairs. The dream did not end very satisfactorily, as the men did not get in, or we did not get out.[5]

While the accompanying analysis sees this woman's dream as a wish for intercourse and children, the purpose in including it here is to characterize the nature of the psychoanalytic response to European society and politics in the first thirty-nine years of the twentieth century. For the purposes of this chapter the title of this little communication has been rendered as "On Throwing Dishes from a Window in a Dream," while the original reads "On Throwing Dishes from a Window in Dreams." In fact, I originally misread the title this way since I wished (and wish) to argue that while the psychoanalytic emphasis on the irrational was in tune with the times the actual effect of their work on the shattering events of the period was minimal, like both the image and the act of "throwing dishes from a window in a dream."

The psychoanalytic preoccupation with the "individual contemplative" was overwhelmed by the "group manipulative" of the era, much as in the woman's dream the safety of her home above the schoolroom was being threatened by "attackers...smashing in the doors downstairs." It might be said of the first half of the twentieth century, to paraphrase Dickens' *A Tale of Two Cities*: "It was the worst of times, it was the worst of times." More specifically, it was an age of systems designed to change people and society under the leadership of cadres and demagogues. Not only did the *practice* of psychoanalysis not mobilize against these movements, it was alternatively ignored, banished, sacrificed to its competition, or even perverted. Some have even argued that psychoanalysis was among those disciplines coopted by the contemporaneous and relatively benign "liberal-socialist" ethic of medical and psychological intervention in individuals' lives in the name of a rational "therapeutic society."

This is not to argue, however, that psychoanalysis has been irrelevant as a positive factor in the political and social history of our time. Even for all of Freud's gloominess about humanity's nature and prospects, the psychoanalytic emphasis on the individual and its healthy skepticism toward absolute solutions to human problems seems to me especially justified in light of the subsequent breakdown of the systems of fascism (through war) and communism (through popular attrition). This is the argument of Heinz Kohut that a properly empathic psychoanalysis can help lead science and society to a world vastly different from Kafka's nightmare of "regimentations and regularities."[6] The inadequacy and danger of systems of change lacking an appreciation of the individual as means and as end was, to nod again in the direction of the British cultural milieu, given voice by the Beatles in the 1968 Lennon/McCartney song, "Revolution":

> You say you'll change a constitution
> > well, you know
> we all want to change your head.
> You tell me it's the institution,
> > well, you know
> you better free your mind instead.

There are three dimensions to the relationship between psychoanalysis and politics. The first, the features of which we will only briefly summarize here, is the realm of intra- and extramural professional conflict. Personal and factional disputes among psychoanalysts were aggravated by the deep emotional ties produced in training. And, aside from confronting a great deal of opposition from the medical and psychiatric establishments, psychoanalysts in particular were affected by the controversies over the place of psychology inside or outside of medicine. The International Psycho-Analytical Association was itself deeply divided over lay analysis, a division that became organizationally manifest at the 1928 Congress.[7]

The second dimension of the question of psychoanalysis and politics is that of attitudes and reactions *to* psychoanalysis. Particularly after the First World War psychoanalysis became fashionable as well as controversial, so much so that some analysts worried that popularity would dilute and discredit their new science. By 1939 Gregory Zilboorg could write in horror: "There are purple and red neon signs glowing in some streets of Hollywood which proclaim the virtues of psycho-analysis along with those of hair tonics and sure-fire laxatives."[8] But the operations of the outside world upon psychoanalysis were of course not confined to individual supporters, critics, or merchants. The interwar years in particular constituted an age of extremely volatile politics: for example, in Germany, the Soviet Union, and France. One incident involving the intersection of the extended universe of psychoanalysis and the Third Reich illustrates the general conditions of political surveillance under which individuals and groups suffered in a Europe dominated by dictatorships. This incident, moreover, shows not only the lack of concern movements exulting in their power would at times display toward mere intellectuals but also those arenas in which opportunists, exploiters, and even some genuine defenders of depth psychology blunted the edge of fascist oppression and destructiveness. It also shows the degree to which psychoanalytic thought had become an influential fact of European intellectual life by the 1930s.

From 1935 to 1939 various Nazi agencies gathered information on the Jungians' annual August conference at Ascona in Switzerland. In 1936 the Nazi Education Ministry refused to grant Germans permission to attend. The next year, however, the director of the German Institute for Psychological Research and Psychotherapy in Berlin, Matthias Heinrich Göring, arranged to have Eranos secretary Olga Fröbe-Kaptayn visit the Ministry to smooth the way for German participation. This intervention proved successful but by 1938 the Nazi party's Auslands-Organisation was objecting that there were lots of Jews at the meetings, that some of the topics were "politically conflictive," and that in general the whole organization seemed "mysterious." To resolve these doubts, an Education Ministry official asked Göring to have a report prepared on that year's meeting. On August 23, 1938, a Jungian member of Göring's institute, Olga von König-Fachsenfeld, dutifully reported that she had heard nothing political at the conference, that the Swiss in particular seemed to have gone out of their way not to criticize Germany, and that while there were a number of Jews in attendance none was on the program. Permission was given for German participation in 1939 and in December of that year the German consulate in Locarno commented that while the participants in the meeting were certainly "different," the conference did not seem to serve the interests of foreign powers, Jews, or Masons and that therefore Germans should be allowed to attend. The only restriction was to be that they could not address sessions where Jews were present.[9]

As in Germany, psychoanalysis in Russia during this era was at the mercy of a revolutionary regime. The difference was that whereas the Nazis forcefully rejected psychoanalysis as an element of the Jewish world conspiracy, some Bolsheviks originally embraced Freud as part of a modern Western intellectual heritage to which their new state, in dragging Russia out of the dark ages, was making a contribution. This eclectic approach to scientific and medical resources predominated in Russia during the early 1920s but within a very few years was superseded by the Stalinist insistence on party conformity, industrial mobilization, Great Russian chauvinism, and anti-Semitism, all of which combined to reject any indulgence in Western bourgeois psychological fashion and to favor Pavlov's behaviorism. There were those who up into the 1940s argued successfully for psychoanalysis as a therapeutic method for the molding of the new Soviet man. But Russian psychiatrists had long been influenced by the German physicalist school of Kraepelin which rejected psychoanalysis and so this powerful constituency also weighed in against Freudianism.[10]

There had been interest in Freud in Russia before the revolution and a psychoanalytic society had been founded in 1911, but the war interrupted activity in this realm; by 1917, for example, financial problems ended the life of the journal *Psychotherapia*.[11] Nonetheless, the society was reestablished in 1921.[12] And in spite of the growing opposition to psychoanalysis under Stalin, in 1929 Wilhelm Reich addressed the Communist Academy and argued that with the inevitable success of the recently announced Five Year Plan for the forced industrialization of Russia, "Soviet psychiatrists would have plenty of neurotic patients and therefore much need for psychoanalysis."[13] Reich noted that even though Freud's social theory was reactionary, his psychological system was sound. But so-called "Freudo-Marxists" were increasingly swimming against the current in the Soviet Union. In 1934 Reich himself was expelled from the Communist party (as well as from the International Psycho-Analytical Association) and the same year saw the dissolution of the Russian Society.

In the end psychoanalysis came to be regarded as too committed to "the sickly self-absorption of quitters and losers"[14] and thus opposed to the Stalinist stress on social commitment and productivity. Psychiatry's proper role was to provide the necessary fine tuning of the human engines driving the construction of "socialism in one country." This technical and utilitarian orientation toward the problems and responsibilities of the individual was attractive to totalitarian regimes of both left and right committed to crash programs in the spirit of a "culture of impatience."[15] So it was the same type of political pressure that compelled German psychoanalyst Carl Müller-Braunschweig to advertise psychoanalysis to the Nazis as a discipline dedicated to cultivating the strong and not indulging the weak.[16]

In contrast to Germany and Russia, France experienced political continuity during this period. Without the political irruption and hegemony of fascism or communism, France from 1936 to 1940 was even to serve as somewhat of a sanctuary for psychoanalysis on the Continent. The French Society had been founded in Paris in 1926, followed by an institute in 1934 and a clinic in 1936, and in 1936 and 1938 the International Association held its biennial meeting in France. But psychoanalysis in France faced significant opposition, not the least because of anti-German attitudes stemming from the invasions of 1870 and 1914. In 1923 the International Association itself observed that "in France the usual resistances are greatly accentuated by national feeling."[17] This Germanophobia built upon cultural differences and tensions from the even more distant past. Anti-Semitism, highlighted by the Dreyfus Affair at the turn of the century, as well as the pervasive influence of Catholicism,[18] also hindered the acceptance of Freud's theories. And the French psychiatric establishment was closely and powerfully allied in its positivism and anti-clericalism with the government of the Third Republic from the late 1870s onward.[19] The major conduit for psychoanalytic ideas ran through French Switzerland with the work of Jung and his students.[20] Thus it is no less surprising than ironic that it took a Bonaparte, this time in the person of a Greek princess, to conquer France for a German idea. And no less ironic and tragic that cooperation with Germany came in the form of collaboration after 1940, most significantly in the person of René Laforgue who was born in German-occupied Alsace and fought for Germany in World War I.[21]

We must now turn to the third dimension of psychoanalysis and politics before 1939, that is, the ways in which psychoanalysts apprehended and affected the highly volatile political world in which they lived. In general, psychoanalysts, following the lead of Freud, often adopted a long archeological and anthropological view of human society. Like Schliemann at Troy, they worked at excavating the deep layers of human culture just as they explored the remote recesses of the unconscious mind. This is not to say that psychoanalysts were oblivious to the contemporary world; Helene Deutsch, to cite one example, was clearly aware of the relevance of her description of the "as if" personality to political life. And psychoanalytic thought had a profound effect on the work of many disciplines, among them the political science of the day. Harold Lasswell's *Psychopathology and Politics* (1931) reflected as well as illuminated the times with its almost cynical emphasis on the inherently psychopathological nature of styles of political leadership. American political commentator Walter Lippmann, anticipating Deutsch's formulations, stressed the large role played by fiction in political behavior. As early as 1916, Harold Laski complained to Oliver Wendell Holmes: "I wish Walter Lippmann would forget Freud for a little—just a little."[22]

Practically speaking, psychoanalytic theory and its application had little impact on politics. While psychoanalytic insights did inform general intellectual discourse and influenced public opinion as well, this worked no direct or significant effect in the political realm. And psychoanalysts themselves had no access to political leaders in an age dominated by *terribles simplificateurs* and "great men." The closest a psychoanalyst got to Hitler, for example, was Walter Langer's 1943 report for the American Office of Special Services on how Hitler's disordered psyche might be exploited for military ends. This problem was not specific to the time. Politicians may be even more skittish about psychiatry in general than the populace as a whole. Richard Nixon, even though (or because) he apparently consulted a psychiatrist at one time in his career, was reported to hate and fear them.[23] And there are legal, procedural, and ethical impediments to the application of psychiatric diagnoses to public figures. For example, during the 1964 American presidential campaign a magazine published a psychological profile of the Republican candidate Barry Goldwater in which it was asserted that Goldwater was mentally unstable and as president would plunge the world into nuclear war. Goldwater sued the publication and won.[24]

Another reason for the failure of psychoanalysts to affect politics was that they were principally concerned with constructing and perfecting a science in the face of significant professional opposition. We can recall the title of our introductory case study, "On Throwing Dishes from a Window in Dreams," which typically speaks in plural nomothetic terms (dream*s*) rather than the historical and idiographic singular adopted in the title of this essay. The immediate interests and long-term contributions of science superseded the conduct of political or social crusades per se. As Ernest Jones, president of the International Association, put it in 1934 when discussing the repression of psychoanalysts in Germany:

It would be easy to register a protest at the fashion in which these political activities have hampered the work of many of our colleagues, but such a course would be assuredly futile. Moreover, it would be to descend from our own position and participate in the emotional turmoil of others. It will be more dignified, and also more profitable, to contrast this sort of politics with the attitude of Science. When Science is attacked its best answer is simply to restate its tenets.[25]

This is not to say that psychoanalysis is only concerned with people in the abstract; indeed, compared with the hard sciences and with psychology and psychiatry in general psychoanalysis has always displayed a unique emphasis on the understanding and treatment of the individual. But its professional development tended to carry it away from direct political and social action. In the 1920s psychoanalysts found themselves carrying out a threefold policy with regard to treatment: first, to advance psychoanalytic knowledge through practical application; second, to enhance the public and professional standing of the discipline; and, third, to meet a social obligation to treat large numbers of people. The first two components of this policy represented science and propaganda, respectively, while the third involved individual treatment rather than social reform or political confrontation. At the Budapest Congress in 1918, Freud had enthused (and at the same time, one suspects, conceded) that "'when it comes to the application of our therapy to large numbers of people we shall have to mix some alloy with the pure gold of analysis.'"[26] While rejecting the "copper of direct suggestion," psychoanalysts were already on a path toward the neo-Freudian adaptation of didactic analysis to short-term therapeutic applications. This increasingly common practice was informed by altruism and, in many cases, commitment to benign socialist principles, but for some this trend has represented a process whereby the interests of individual patients are compromised for the sake of conformity to social norms and subordination to economic and political elites.[27] For others, this is simply an extension of the benefits of psychoanalysis to those in psychological and financial need.[28]

Zurich analyst Paul Parin has recently enumerated other reasons for an ongoing lack of psychoanalytic involvement with contemporary issues. These include: psychoanalysis as a relic of a cloistered bourgeois Vienna insulated from the outside world, psychoanalysis as a tool of capitalism to pacify the proletariat, and the psychoanalysts' own claim that their insights are won too slowly to affect the immediate present.[29] While these arguments have some merit, they also display serious weaknesses. Carl Schorske, for one, has argued that Vienna was anything but isolated from the burning issues of the new century: rather Austria was, in the words of one of its poets, Friedrich Hebbel, "the little world in which the big one holds its tryouts."[30] And, especially before 1939, many members of the psychoanalytic movement, such as Adler and Reich, in word and deed were anything but servants of monopoly capitalism. And whatever tendency displayed by neo-Freudian therapy toward political quiescence and adjustment of patients to the status quo, its practitioners were most often progressive in their social views and their work involved psychoanalysis more broadly in the life of society.

Three brief "case studies" in psychoanalytic political thought will serve to illustrate at least some of the ways in which analysts responded to larger social and political issues. These are: Freud himself, an essay by Ernest Jones, and similar aspects of the careers of Otto Fenichel, Siegfried Bernfeld, and John Rittmeister.

While Freud was a nineteenth-century liberal who saw change in moral and not social terms and who over time became ever more cynical and authoritarian in his views, he could, in the words of Paul Roazen, "thunder like a modern prophet, challenging the values and practices of Western Christendom" and was in his early years "the heretic who wrote and thought shocking things."[31] There was therefore in Freud a rich ambiguity when it came to the human political order. This ambiguity surfaced in a joke he made to Ernest Jones in 1919. According to an account from unpublished biographical material assembled by Jones and recently recounted by French psychoanalyst Rene Major, Freud claimed to Jones that he had become "half a Bolshevik." He explained that he had been told by a communist that the world was facing a period of bad times but that very good times would follow. Freud told Jones: "I believed the first half."[32] While Freud's true political colors blaze forth here, the ironic phrase "half a Bolshevik" expresses as well the iconoclastic aspect of his life's work.

It was this quality that could attract radicals to Freud's figure even if not to his movement. The American anarchist Emma Goldman was one of these. She admired Freud, even though she saw psychoanalysis as "'nothing but the old confessional.'"[33] As a student she attended lectures by Freud in Vienna before the turn of the century and was in the audience at one of Freud's Clark Lectures in 1909.[34] We do not know if Freud knew Goldman was present, but Gordon Patterson has argued that Freud's famous extended analogy illustrating the dynamics of repression through the "ill-mannered interrupter" who has to be ejected from the hall by "four strong men" is based on Freud's knowledge of the controversy then surrounding Goldman's intention to hold a rally in Worcester, the home of Clark University. The city had tried to prevent Goldman from speaking, but she eventually held the rally in the yard of a private home. Patterson speculates that Freud was using this association as a rhetorical device to cause his audience to identify with the analogy.[35] Although it is not at all clear that this analogy was extemporaneously formulated or adapted or that Goldman attended this particular lecture, it might seem to express Freud's identification with the interrupter, the lonely prophet of psychoanalysis at the mercy of the "strong men" of psychiatry, whether in Vienna or Worcester. Freud and Goldman could identify with each other as Jews who had dared to "move the infernal regions" against "the higher powers" and while Freud was anything but a feminist many of his patients were women who, he recognized, were suffering under the moral and sexual hypocrisy of their day. And the first analyst's lifelong identification with historical figures such as Moses, Hannibal, and Napoleon also demonstrate his conception of himself as a *conquistador* challenging the established order.[36]

Ernest Jones was similar to Freud in that he too was an "outsider," indeed doubly so as a Welshman in England and as a gentile in Freud's circle. He displayed a burning ambition, deployed a ferocious intellect that in argument took no prisoners, and ruled the British Society with an iron hand.[37] Freud described his first impression of him in a letter to Jung in 1908:

> Jones is undoubtedly a very interesting and worthy man, but he gives me a feeling of, I was almost going to say racial strangeness. He is a fanatic and doesn't eat enough.... He almost reminds me of the lean and hungry Cassius.[38]

Jones's ambition stemmed in part from ambivalence concerning his origins. Anna Freud observed that Jones always bore traces of his working-class background.[39] More importantly, although Jones claimed to have experienced a good solution to his oedipal complex involving a mother who "was in every way Welsh" and a father who "took a decidedly English view of life," he did at the end of his life confess "to have never entirely succeeded in achieving a detached attitude toward the callous English acquiescence in assaults on the Celtic language and culture."[40] Jones desperately desired entry into the highest regions of British medicine, but, frustrated in his attempt to win a prestigious position in neurology, he went to Canada. He returned with some measure of defiance to pioneer the analytic movement in Britain. At the same time, Jones reportedly regarded his second-in-command, Edward Glover, as "a mere Scot."[41]

Yet this concern with dominance and authority as well as with national and cultural conflict informed Jones's empathic and perceptive application of psychoanalysis to one of the most vexing and enduring political confrontations in modern European history, that of "the Troubles" in Ireland. Jones presented this paper, "The Island of Ireland: A Psycho-Analytical Contribution to Political Psychology," to the British Society on June 21, 1922. His rather phlegmatic opening sentence communicates some of the personal emotional valence of the subject that he is struggling to control by means of intellectualization:

> It must often have struck *dispassionate* observers as a curious problem that Ireland should differ so profoundly from both Scotland and Wales in her reaction to the *stimuli* provided by England. (Emphasis added)[42]

Jones's ensuing assurance that he is seeking to isolate only one factor in the complex "historical, dynastic, [and] economic" relationship between England and Ireland is not only intellectually sound and prudent but also arguably a defense mechanism. Jones characterizes England and Wales as "two brothers of unequal size" with "good humored tolerance on the one side" and "a combination of petulance and admiration on the other," while portraying English-Irish relations as "dragooning, despoiling and bullying" met by "dogged and contumacious resistance."[43]

Jones argues that the violent difference stems in part from "the tendency of...geographical insularity to become unconsciously associated with particular complexes," specifically "our deepest feelings about birth, death, and mother."[44] That is, islands in particular call up images of the paradise of womb and breast, any threat to which produces bitterness and rage. Jones offers numerous examples of Irish cultural and literary preoccupation with "the idea of an island Paradise."[45] While this psychodynamic analysis is of course not a sufficient explanation for the conflict between Ireland and England, it may well be a necessary one, especially given the ongoing and apparently intractable struggles in Ulster. Whatever the deficiencies of Jones's brief study, its approach not only underscores the importance of the role of the intimate joys and terrors of human life in the history of individuals and peoples but also the utility of emotion for the intellectual enterprise, a sensitivity born of experience both reflected upon as well as defended against.

In 1935 Otto Fenichel and Edward Glover engaged in a brief but sharp public debate in the pages of the *Internationales Aerztliches Bulletin*. Fenichel had left Germany in 1933 and gone to Oslo, but in 1935 settled in Prague where he wrote occasional articles and reviews for the *IAeB*, which was the organ of émigré German socialist physicians headquartered in Prague. Fenichel was a member of that group which Russell Jacoby has labeled the "political Freudians," psychoanalysts on the left who decried the lack of critical consciousness within their discipline and who during these years were engaged in flight from fascism and resistance to it.[46] Fenichel's essay argues that books of applied psychoanalysis such as Edward Glover's *War, Sadism and Pacifism* (1933) wrongly assume that groups in history display the same neurotic dynamics as individuals, thus ignoring social and economic factors. For the Freudian Fenichel unconscious aggression is a given, the crucial matter being under what social and economic conditions it is unleashed.[47] For the Marxist Fenichel the vital issue is class conflict between the opposing interests of capital and labor.[48] Fenichel seconds Glover's recommendation that diplomats undergo psychoanalysis so that in a crisis sadistic impulses should be under control, but regards it as "grotesque" to envision a consequent "'recognition of the psychopathology of war'" leading to avoidance of war altogether.[49]

Glover responded to Fenichel's criticism in a subsequent issue of the *IAeB* by saying that Fenichel is attempting to use psychoanalysis "to pull socialism's chestnuts from the fire"[50] and that such attempts to use psychoanalysis as support for a political creed end up in falsifying psychoanalytic discoveries. While Fenichel is certainly right in pointing to the reductionism of Glover's thesis, in his uncritical reliance on a Marxist viewpoint he himself ignores or undervalues irrational elements in the genesis of war. But Fenichel's critique does cast doubt on the theoretical as well as practical utility of psychoanalysis in dealing with political events, even absent its founder's growing pessimism about the ability of rationality in general to affect the irrational and destructive in human affairs. Moreover, as Paul Roazen has argued, "Fenichel's clinical outlook became part of an oppressively standard orthodoxy" and was a function of Fenichel's own obsessionality, evident in his encyclopedic 1945 book *The Psychoanalytic Theory of Neurosis*.[51] This reminds us that one of the problems in solving human problems is that these problems must be solved by humans.

Perhaps Fenichel's colleague Siegfried Bernfeld offered a better because more modest model of the social utility of psychoanalysis. Bernfeld was active in progressive pedagogy and even founded an experimental school, wherein he hoped that both students and teachers might overcome the "oedipal problem behind inhibitions to authority" caused by society's "idealization of masculinity" and "repression of feminine identification."[52] Bernfeld was doubtful about the success of such a venture, since he rejected those who by repression of infantile destructive impulses idealized childhood. Yet he clung to the hope that the cultivation of youthful challenge to authority and the rise of women to positions of political power would at least mitigate social evils.

John Rittmeister gave his life for certain humanistic values. In 1937 he returned to his native Germany from Switzerland in order to work at the so-called Göring Institute. He was active in the communist resistance and was executed by the Gestapo in 1943. While in prison he kept a diary and on the last January 12 of his life he wrote about the ideals he saw embodied in psychoanalysis. Rittmeister cherished the critical rationalism of psychoanalysis as opposed to contemporary tendencies toward relativism and the excesses of subjectivity. While Jung celebrated the subjectivity and introversion Rittmeister found to be a threat to concern for others, Freud's teachings "in the ecumenical virtues of love" inspired in him some hope for humanity. For Rittmeister, Freud was in the tradition of the systematic doubt of Descartes which constituted "a humble and necessary acknowledgment of man's imperfection."[53]

Our century has witnessed the failure (and yet also the persistence) of political and social systems not based on sober and empathic insight into the lives of individuals: most obviously fascism, but also Leninism/Stalinism and unrestricted capitalism. While a psychoanalytic point of view can be supportive of a range of political positions from traditional conservatism to some varieties of radical leftism, its practice and growing institutionalization have often produced apolitical attitudes as well the "exhaustion of vitality" due to "status-preserving professionalism."[54] This latter tendency was evident in Zilboorg's 1939 essay on the enduring opposition to psychoanalysis. This "well-nigh invincible" opposition, he argues, stems from "narcissistic cathexes"[55] mobilized by the psychoanalytic challenge to free will and immortality. It is certainly true that Freud's thought, like that of Marx and Einstein, threatened humanity's recently acquired sense of mastery over the natural universe, but Zilboorg casts his argument primarily in professional terms rather than philosophical ones, giving pride of place in his essay to a critique of the "compulsive neurotic thinking about the cure of the mentally ill" characteristic of physicalist psychiatry.[56] This argument, while not without merit, is an ad hominem defense of psychoanalysis that to some extent belies Zilboorg's insistence that psychoanalysis at the time was still free of the ossifying effects of dogmatism and institutionalization.

Still, professionalism is a necessary and desirable component of the development and application of a system of thought, and no more so than in the realm of health and illness. It is in this sphere of the treatment of the individual patient that psychoanalysis makes its most tangible and significant contribution to the social and political environment. But, as we have seen, this contribution is limited by its individual and indirect approach. Moreover, the practice of psychoanalysis involves it in the affairs and interests of various institutions of society and state that to a greater or lesser degree compromise its commitment to the interests of the patient and to higher morality in general. And while specialized training refines treatment it also tends to effect an inordinate degree of what Kohut calls "tool-and-method pride"[57] in place of social and political awareness.[58] All these trends became manifest during the first four decades of the twentieth century. There is no simple solution to this problem, or perhaps no solution at all, but one must insist not only that psychoanalysts do their technical work well but that they ennoble as well as enrich the larger world by their thought, speech, and action beyond the couch, as it were. Psychoanalysts in particular have a special opportunity as well as a special responsibility to do this. The opportunity rests in the rich humanistic core of a discipline that values the individual and which today can serve as a universalistic antidote to renascent nationalisms. The responsibility lies in resisting the modern means of the manipulation of minds offered by the abuse of Freudian and post-Freudian psychological insights.[59]

In conclusion, we return to our case studies, because each represents a virtue important to the wise exercise of psychoanalysis. Freud offers the virtue of skepticism so important in a world of power-seekers and image-makers. All leaders are suspect because they are human. As George Orwell put it with respect to Gandhi: "Saints should always be judged guilty until they are proved innocent."[60] This was an updated version of Heine's acerbic commentary on the *Realpolitik* of the nineteenth century that would lead to the disasters of 1914 and 1939: "It is true that one must forgive one's enemies, but only after they have been hanged." Jones in his study of Ireland instructs us in the virtue of empathy, a vital complement to the less merciful psychoanalytic insistence on rationality.[61] And, finally, the careers of Fenichel, Bernfeld, and Rittmeister remind us of the virtue of commitment. All three virtues—skepticism, empathy, and commitment—comprise the actual and potential contribution of psychoanalysis to effective and compassionate engagement in the contemporary world. For even as we affirm that in the political and social maelstrom of modern Europe's "Time of Troubles" psychoanalysts were more acted upon than acting, we must conclude that they also were more sinned against than sinning.

Notes

1. "'Sur un rêve de plats jetés par la fenêtre': de la psychanalyse dans la société et la vie politique en Europe, 1900–1939," *Revue Internationale d'Histoire de la Psychanalyse* 5 (1992): 13–32. With permission of Presses Universitaires de France.
2. Virginia Woolf, "Modern Fiction," (1925) in idem, *The Common Reader* (London, 1929), p. 192.
3. Janice Haaken, "The Siegfried Bernfeld Conference: Uncovering the Psychoanalytic Political Unconscious," *American Journal of Psychoanalysis* 50 (1990): 289–304.
4. Paul Parin, "Warum die Psychoanalytiker so ungern zu brennenden Zeitproblemen Stellung nehmen," *Psyche* 23 (1978): 390–1.
5. N. J. Symons, "On Throwing Dishes from a Window in Dreams," *International Journal of Psycho-Analysis* 8:1 (1927): 69.
6. Heinz Kohut, "The Future of Psychoanalysis," in idem, *The Search for the Self: Selected Writings of Heinz Kohut, 1950–1978,* Paul Ornstein, ed. (New York, 1978), 2:684.
7. "Reports of the International Psycho-Analytical Association," *Bulletin of the International Psycho-Analytical Association* 9 (1928): 151–5.
8. Gregory Zilboorg, "The Fundamental Conflict with Psycho- Analysis," *International Journal of Psycho-Analysis* 20 (1939): 482.
9. Geoffrey Cocks, "The Nazis and C.G. Jung," in Arye Maidenbaum and Stephen A. Martin, eds., *Lingering Shadows: Jungians, Freudians, and Anti-Semitism,* (Boston, 1991), pp. 158–65.
10. David Joravsky, *Russian Psychology: A Critical History* (Oxford, 1989), pp. 230–9, 419–20.
11. "Reports of the International Psycho-Analytical Association," *Bulletin of the International Psycho-Analytical Association* 3 (1922): 513–20.
12. "Reports of the International Psycho-Analytical Association," *Bulletin of the International Psycho-Analytical Association* 6 (1925): 402.
13. Joravsky, *Russian Psychology,* p. 236.
14. Ibid., p. 237.
15. Susan Gross Solomon, "David and Goliath in Soviet Public Health: The Rivalry of Social Hygienists and Psychiatrists for Authority over the *Bytovoi* Alcoholic," *Soviet Studies* 41 (1989): 269.
16. Carl Müller-Braunschweig, "Psychoanalyse und Weltanschauung," *Reichswart,* October 22, 1933, pp. 2–3.
17. "The Psycho-Analytical Movement," *Bulletin of the International Psycho-Analytical Association* 4 (1923): 523.
18. "Bulletin of the International Psycho-Analytical Association," *International Journal of Psycho-Analysis* 5 (1924): 409.
19. Jan Goldstein, *Console and Classify: The French Psychiatric Profession in the Nineteenth Century* (Cambridge, 1987).
20. Alain de Mijolla, "Psychoanalysis in France (1893–1965)," trans. R. Hoffman (I.A.H.P. private document, 1986).
21. Ibid., p. 13; idem, "La Psychanalyse et les psychanalystes en France entre 1939 et 1945," *Revue Internationale d'Histoire de la Psychanalyse* 1 (1988): 167–

224; idem, "Documents inedits. Les psychanalystes en France durant l'Occupation allemande, Paris, Novembre 1943," *Revue Internationale d'Histoire de la Psychanalyse* 2 (1989): 463–76.

22. Harold Laski, in M. Howe, ed., *Holmes-Laski Letters: The Correspondence of Justice Holmes and Harold J. Laski, 1916–1935* (Cambridge, Massachusetts, 1953), p. 36.
23. Paul Roazen, *Encountering Freud: The Politics and Histories of Psychoanalysis* (New Brunswick, New Jersey, 1990), pp. 238–9.
24. Warren Boroson, "What Psychiatrists Say About Goldwater," *Fact* 1:5 (September/October, 1964): 24–6; *New York Times*, May 5, 1968, p. 62.
25. "Report of the Thirteenth International Psycho-Analytical Congress," *Bulletin of the International Psycho-Analytical Association* 15 (1934): 485.
26. Max Eitingon, "Report of the Berlin Psycho-Analytical Policlinic," *Bulletin of the International Psycho-Analytical Association* 4 (1923): 264.
27. Geoffrey Cocks, "The Professionalization of Psychotherapy in Germany, 1928–1949," in Geoffrey Cocks and Konrad H. Jarausch, eds., *German Professions, 1800–1950* (New York, 1990), pp. 308–28.
28. Clemens De Boor and Emma Moersch, "Stellungnahme zu P. Parins 'Kritischer Glosse'," *Psyche* 32 (1978): 400–402.
29. Parin, "Psychoanalytiker," pp. 386–7.
30. Carl E. Schorske, *Fin-de-Siecle Vienna: Politics and Culture* (New York, 1980), p. xxvii.
31. Roazen, *Encountering Freud*, pp. 43, 128.
32. Haaken, "Bernfeld," p. 301.
33. Alice Wexler, *Emma Goldman: An Intimate Life* (New York, 1984), p. 295.
34. Ibid., pp. 85, 189.
35. Gordon Patterson, "Freud's Rhetoric: Persuasion and History in the 1909 Clark Lectures," paper presented to the German Studies Association, Milwaukee, October 7, 1989.
36. Paul Roazen, *Freud and His Followers* (New York, 1975); William McGrath, *Freud's Discovery of Psychoanalysis: The Politics of Hysteria* (Ithaca, 1986).
37. Roazen, *Freud and His Followers*, pp. 342–5.
38. Sigmund Freud, *The Freud/Jung Letters: The Correspondence between Sigmund Freud and Carl Jung*, ed. William McGuire, trans. Ralph Manheim and R.F.C. Hull (Princeton, 1974), p. 145.
39. Vincent Brome, *Ernest Jones: Freud's Alter Ego* (London, 1982), p. 6.
40. Ernest Jones, *Free Associations: Memories of a Psycho-Analyst* (London, 1959), p. 12.
41. Roazen, *Freud and His Followers*, p. 348.
42. Ernest Jones, "The Island of Ireland: A Psycho-Analytical Contribution to Political Psychology," in idem, *Essays in Applied Psycho-Analysis* (London, 1923), p. 398.
43. Ibid., pp. 398, 399.
44. Ibid., pp. 401, 410.
45. Ibid., p. 410.
46. Russell Jacoby, *The Repression of Psychoanalysis: Otto Fenichel and the Political Freudians* (New York, 1983); Muriel Gardiner, *"Code Name Mary": Memoirs of an American Woman in the Austrian Underground* (New Haven, 1983).
47. Otto Fenichel, "Ueber Psychoanalyse, Krieg und Frieden," *Internationales Aerztliches Bulletin* 2 (1935): 33.
48. Ibid., pp. 33–34.
49. Ibid., p. 39.

50. Edward Glover and Otto Fenichel, "Ueber Psychoanalyse, Krieg und Frieden," *Internationales Aerztliches Bulletin* 2 (1935): 76–7.
51. Roazen, *Encountering Freud*, p. 125.
52. Haaken, "Bernfeld," p. 291.
53. Geoffrey Cocks, *Psychotherapy in the Third Reich: The Göring Institute* (New York, 1985), p. 67.
54. Kohut, "Future," p. 673.
55. Zilboorg, "Conflict," p. 492.
56. Ibid., pp. 481–2.
57. Paul Ornstein, "The Evolution of Heinz Kohut's Psychoanalytic Psychology of the Self," *The Search for the Self*, 1:85.
58. Parin, "Psychoanalytiker," p. 392.
59. Roazen, *Encountering Freud*, pp. 299–308.
60. George Orwell, "Reflections on Gandhi," (1949), in *George Orwell: The Collected Essays, Journals, and Letters*, S. Orwell and I. Angus, eds. (New York, 1968), 4:523.
61. Ornstein, "Evolution," p. 85.

5

Developmental Continuities in German Psychoanalysis and Psychotherapy since 1939[1]

Near the town of Winslow in the high desert of northern Arizona lies Barringer Crater. Four thousand feet wide and 570 feet deep, it was formed 50,000 years ago when a meteor slammed into the earth with an explosive force of 1.7 megatons of TNT. For anyone experiencing the impact, the sober recitation of scientific description and analysis might seem devoid of the shattering reality of the event. Such a disparity of perspective is evident in assessing the impact of National Socialism. The study of Hitler and the Nazis runs the risk of robbing the phenomenon of its impact as a massive irrational and destructive force and thus threatening to weaken our moral outrage over it. Just as it is an infrequent meteor that penetrates the protection offered by the earth's atmosphere, something as thoroughly reprehensible as Nazism marks in terms of its magnitude a rare eruption through the mantle of human civilization. For this reason our condemnation of the Nazis must be constantly restated. They are, as Camus reminded us, the brown and black plague of our age. At the same time, however, we must not allow moral fervor to cloud the clarity of historical analysis, for then we risk the loss of a more complete and useful understanding of the course and consequences of twentieth-century dictatorship.

Questions of personal and professional ethics have bulked large in the evolving history of psychoanalysis in the Third Reich. The pioneering research of such German scholars as Regine Lockot, Volker Friedrich, and Lüdger Hermanns, as well as the critiques by Dahmer, Lohmann and Rosenkötter, and Brainin and Kaminer have taught us much about the vicissitudes of morality among German psychoanalysts under Hitler. Such hard criticism of their psychoanalytic elders by the younger professional generation in West Germany represents a valuable Oedipal *Vergangenheitsbewältigung* in line with the turn of

German historical scholarship since the 1960s against repression of the past and toward a critical political and social history of modern Germany.

Such a critical history of psychoanalysis in Germany is a necessary and important thing, but one which needs to be expanded in three respects in order to achieve greater critical definition. First, the emphasis on individuals and their moral failings must be complemented by consideration of the structural context of institutions. Second, the history of psychoanalysis must be placed within the contexts of the history of medicine, psychiatry, psychotherapy, and psychology (the synoptic term here is "psychotherapy"). And, third, the leftist critical stance of some studies must be supplemented in such a way that elements of psychotherapy, and bourgeois society in general at the time, are not merely equated with National Socialism. Developments in this field had as much to do with persistent trends as with Nazism being simply the culmination or exemplification of such trends. The careful investigation of context is particularly important since history itself can get lost in the *allzumenschlich* emotions of contemporary political and professional argument, especially when the subject is one like Nazism that attracts and requires a high degree of moral condemnation. Moral outrage is therefore a necessary but not a sufficient condition for understanding Nazism.

Historian Martin Broszat has rightly called for a "historicization" of National Socialism so that objectivity can further contribute to an understanding of the period's complexity.[2] This is done not to provide opportunity for apologetics, but to direct intellectual and moral judgment even more accurately and proportionally in realms more removed from the direct exercise of evil in the Third Reich. Research into the history of psychotherapy in the Third Reich reveals that good and bad came out of its survival and development between 1933 and 1945. It is clear that the individuals involved did not operate at the level of the highest morality and that three factors overlapped to produce collaboration with the Hitler regime: (1) personal and professional susceptibility to Nazi views; (2) opportunism; and (3) structural conditions modifying and overcoming personal morality. To inquire after a complexity of motive is not to lift the burden of culpability from the shoulders of those who deserve to bear it, but rather to place questions of morality in the proper social, institutional, and historical contexts so as better to understand the Third Reich and its place in German, European, and Western history.

There existed among psychotherapists in the Third Reich some degrees of competent and morally defensible work occasioned by the incomplete Nazification of Germany, the degree of autonomy lent by "expertism," and the Nazi concern for human productivity. Given the degree of their professional autonomy, the psychotherapists, like many others, bear greater moral responsibility for acts undertaken and omitted. But moral blame in this case goes beyond the moral dereliction of individuals and toward the moral ambiguities of ideas, methods, and institutions. This fact leads us to the study of historical contexts that are no less disturbing—indeed, in the their extension of moral ambiguities outside the years 1933 to 1945 they are more disturbing—but also more complicated. If, as historian Dirk Blasius has argued, there were barriers placed by individual psychiatrists even in the way of the Nazi sterilization and extermination of "mental incurables,"[3] then the psychotherapeutic *treatment* of those Germans the Nazis regarded as racially valuable had to have been comprised of even greater moral and practical ambiguities. And since we are not dealing with the type of direct sadistic brutality toward those the Nazis regarded as racial enemies, such as that exercised by the Nazi concentration camp doctors described in Robert Lifton's recent book,[4] we must—historians and psychoanalysts together—contemplate and explicate motives and actions that were "overdetermined" out of a complex of special German traditions, features of modern industrial society, and general human failings.

This chapter attempts to provide a survey of the history of psychoanalysis and psychotherapy in Germany since 1939 by way of five interrelated topics: (1) the historiography of psychoanalysis and medicine; (2) psychoanalysis in the various contexts occasioned by the two world wars; (3) the domestic history of the Third Reich; (4) the place of the so-called Göring Institute in the health apparatus of the Nazi state; and (5) a concluding posing of fundamental questions about continuities in the history of psychotherapy in modern Germany.

The history of psychoanalysis and medicine has moved forward in three waves. The first, which persists to the present day, has been the product of practitioners and admirers who see an unbroken line of scientific progress and service to humankind. This type of Whig history has more recently been overtaken by a critical, often Marxist-informed, school of thought that emphasizes the socially self-serving dynamics of professionals and professions as well as the larger social phenomenon of the bourgeois sequestration and stigmatization of the mentally ill in the name of rational control and economic order. The third wave, while often building on the second, has stressed careful historical documentation and analysis of the social history of science, medicine, and the professions in general.

Most psychoanalysts have traditionally regarded their discipline as a science and have stressed discussions of the development of theory and practice and the individual contributions of pioneers and settlers. Three qualifications must be applied to any attempt at the history of the "science" of psychoanalysis, however. First, there is the ongoing debate over whether or in what sense psychoanalysis can be understood as a science at all. Second, even if psychoanalysis can be defined as a science, we must view it, like any science, in terms of a series of paradigms, not as an externally established set of "truths." And, third, complementing these internal dynamics of the field, we must place psychoanalysis at every stage in its history into its proper social and political contexts. It is this external dynamic upon which this essay concentrates. No science is more closely bound to society than medicine for the simple reason that doctors deal directly with people. And there is no field in medicine as intimately connected with human beings as members of society as those physicians and laypersons involved in the treatment of mental disorders of whatever nature or severity. This is so because in one way or another individual and social values and interests play a role on both sides of the psychotherapeutic relationship.

We must also keep in mind that psychoanalysis has to be studied in connection with the history of psychotherapy and psychology, which between roughly 1940 and 1980 culminated in a successful institutional challenge to a largely physicalist psychiatry within and without the medical profession. Thus at its broadest our task involves an examination of a new and vitally important aspect of the history of medicine in the twentieth century, a topic that has only recently attracted a great deal of scholarly attention from historians. Among others, Ute Frevert has shown how in the late nineteenth-century German society was "medicalized," that is, how social problems came to be viewed, and vitiated, as matters of individual hygiene and professional medical intervention, a process very much in the interest of the state and the medical profession.[5] Claudia Huerkamp has charted the struggles of German doctors in the nineteenth century to establish a market position within an evolving capitalist society, a historical development whose further unfolding Michael Kater has delineated up to 1945.[6] For psychiatry, Jan Goldstein has demonstrated how that discipline reflected and helped propagate the anticlerical politics of the Third French Republic.[7] For German psychiatry, Klaus Dörner has produced a critical view of the bourgeois sacrifice of the institutionally insane for the sake of a rational social order and a safe environment for business.[8] Hannah Decker and Regine Lockot have studied psychoanalysis in Germany, Decker on its variegated reception among physicians up to 1907 and Lockot on its coordination under National Socialism, while Ulfried Geuter and I have described the professionalization of psychology and psychotherapy, respectively, during the Nazi era.[9]

We are also learning a great deal about the impact of the Second World War on society. The history of psychoanalysis and psychotherapy during the war forms a necessary part of the expansion of our knowledge of the nature and effects of humanity's greatest conflict. A study of psychoanalysis in the world during the was is especially important since until recently its history in these years has been largely ignored, in contrast to the large number of accounts of psychoanalysis before, during, and after the First World War. The reasons for this disparity rest with the greater hagiographical potential of the history of psychoanalysis in the second decade of the century. Freud of course was still alive: just before the war he had defended the integrity of his conception of psychoanalysis by reading Adler and Jung out of the movement, and the years just after the war saw some of Freud's most trenchant theoretical and metaphysical work. The war itself spawned a dramatic failure of positivist psychiatry and some stunning confirmation of the validity and utility of the psychodynamic approach. Although both Freud and Karl Abraham perceptively worried about the dangers of the resultant popularity of their science, a concern literally, one might say, about its being "wrecked by success," treatments of this period generally give off the glow of first victories for a new science over what had seemed long odds. And even though psychoanalysis was some way from universal acceptance, its successes during this era laid the foundation for significant advances in the 1920s.

These successes, moreover, provided the potential for even greater development in the years just before and during the Second World War. We are just beginning to see how significant and widespread this development was, not only for psychoanalysis, but for psychotherapy and psychology in general. This history has been obscured, even repressed, since it seems initially lacking in drama and is filled with the ambiguities of cooptation into various levels of society and government. This contrasts with the inspiring earlier years of uncompromised discovery and struggle. The figure of Freud himself is missing, as he died twenty-two days after the outbreak of the war that seemed to confirm his dark musings between 1915 and 1930 on human aggression. His emigration from Austria in 1938 was the final act in the tragedy of an autonomous psychoanalytic movement in Central Europe, a tragedy that has, not surprisingly, preoccupied its chroniclers. From this point of view, there appears a caesura in the development of psychoanalysis in Europe and continuity only in the safe havens of the New World.

But the intrusion of psychology into medicine that was spearheaded by psychoanalysis could not be so easily turned back, especially with the outbreak of a war that would everywhere effect an unprecedented mobilization of medicine and psychology.[10] A war so disastrously directed against civilians called for service, emergency service that continued into the immediate postwar period. The work of the Hampstead Clinic in treating children displaced and orphaned by the Nazi air war against England is a notable example.[11] At the same time, however, such humanitarian efforts were accompanied by a further institutionalization of psychotherapy that called forth ethical ambiguities of theory and practice.

In Nazi Germany, of course, the case for the abuse is most easily made. This is so not only in terms of general violations of human rights and ethical standards, but also because of the overdetermined trend in the field itself toward the subordination of the individual patient to social norms. Under Hitler, this entailed potential sacrifice to constant fear of the police, to demands for high productivity, and to the dangers and stresses of war. And even if a given patient somehow did not suffer directly from any of these conditions, his or her successful treatment and adjustment to the social environment contributed to the efforts of a regime to visit suffering on other peoples. The unparalleled confluence of power and atrocity represented by National Socialism must not blind us, however, to the fact that in Germany, along with the special barbarity of Nazism, there obtained a number of the same structural conditions in the converging fields of psychology and medicine that existed elsewhere. Given the institutionalizing trends of the 1930s and 1940s, which we shall consider in more detail below, we should be surprised had there not been significant developments in psychotherapy in Germany, where work in the field had been highly developed before 1933. This is so even with the Nazi persecution of what they called "Jewish" psychoanalysis.

Earlier accounts, by ignoring the ethically problematical integration of psychoanalysis, psychotherapy, and psychology into the medical and social establishment during the World War II era, have not allowed us to see clearly the continuities of theory and practice that extend across the 1930s and 1940s down to the present day. Thus the survival of psychotherapy in Nazi-occupied Europe and its continuous, if conditional, development as a science and as a profession particularly in Germany compel us to consider even more carefully the inherent problems in the theory and practice of psychotherapy in society. As an extreme case, the history of psychotherapy in the Third Reich offers us not only a necessary historical perspective on the development of the field in Germany but also a revealing case study of the problematical aspects of the institutionalization of psychotherapy.

Russell Jacoby has recently argued that the transplantation of psychoanalysis from the cultural milieu of Vienna and Berlin to the more pragmatic cultural climate of America led psychoanalysis into becoming a staid means of social adjustment presided over by the medical profession instead of remaining a socially critical means of personal liberation.[12] But, aside from the fact that many European psychoanalysts were hardly as radical as those Jacoby portrays in their opposition to the American analytic trend, the same conformist medical, professional, and social conditions were extant in Europe. Since the Nazis did not sweep away, but rather exploited, much of the elite establishment in Germany, these traditions and trends not only persisted but were augmented by the Nazi emphasis on social unity and utility. The trend toward the professionalization of psychotherapy, after all, in the long run rested on the discipline's ability to achieve official status within the university system, the state medical bureaucracy, and the public and private insurance schemes by demonstrating its efficiency in helping society ameliorate the burden of psychological disorders. In the short run, however, the specific naivetés and enthusiasms of German culture joined with the zealous professional opportunism of non-Jewish psychotherapists under the leadership of Matthias Heinrich Göring to exploit with great success a Nazi regime hungry for experts to prepare its people for war.

In Nazi Germany professional conflict between psychotherapy and psychiatry and obedience to, and exploitation of, political authority were raised to new levels by, first, the unparalleled threat to science in general embodied in potential and actual Nazi interference and, second, the great professional opportunity proffered above all by the person of Göring. The history of this era is an excellent illustration of how ideas pass through institutions and how ideas themselves can be ethically ambiguous in terms of effect, especially in a field like psychotherapy that operates along the sensitive fault lines between individual and society. As in the United States, the practice of psychotherapy in Germany at this time was dominated by physicians. In 1938, for example, Göring himself observed that lay therapists should be trained[13] only so long as there were not enough doctors practicing psychotherapy. One of Freud's greatest fears, of course, was that doctors would take over psychoanalysis and try to reduce it to another physical science. Although in Germany the romantic heritage of psychotherapy in opposition to the prevailing positivistic psychiatry made this less of a danger, the communitarian bias of German romanticism, the opportunistic growth of lay therapy inside and outside the Göring Institute, and the conservative and often pro-Nazi stance of the medical profession still all served to bend medical psychology in the direction of service to social order and political authority.

That this problem was not restricted to Germany under the Nazis had been demonstrated in Sherry Turkle's study of the problems of the institutionalization of psychoanalysis in France. Turkle describes doctors as "a social group under the greatest possible pressure to emphasize the useful."[14] Doctors are also, it has been argued, especially susceptible to "generalizations of expertise" concerning moral and social issues.[15] This matter is of particular importance since any psychotherapist, lay or medical, occupies an especially crucial position between the individual and society. The psychotherapist has a significant degree of power over the patient and it is clear that the relationship, whether voluntary or involuntary, can be an effective means of preserving and enhancing social standards. While "the psychotherapeutic profession, on the whole, claims to be committed to the absolute priority of the interests of the individual patient,"[16] in practice the disentanglement of institutional claims on the provision, cost, and outcome of therapy, the attitudes of therapist and patient, and the prevailing social climate is well-nigh impossible.

Like recent work on the history of the Second World War, the study of psychotherapy in the Third Reich is itself part of a larger concern with the impact of National Socialism on German society. From the practitioners' side our knowledge has been significantly increased by research into the history of professions in Germany. This research has stressed the study of institutional dimensions as a corrective and a complement to the earlier and less critical tradition of intellectual and biographical studies. These recent works have centered on issues of interest, power, and conflict and, among other things, have demonstrated the continuities and complexities of professional development throughout the Third Reich.[17] The notion of some sort of generalized "Nazi culture" imposed unilaterally and uniformly from above has given way to an understanding of the more complicated historical dynamics of the interplay of institutions, individuals, and ideas even in Nazi society. As historian Konrad Jarausch has observed:

> The pervasiveness of the pattern of self-nazification amongst...professionals such as doctors...suggests that the social dynamic of National Socialism ought to be seen less as one irresistible force, than as the summation of countless individual and group struggles whose effects reinforced one another.[18]

These conclusions are in line with research into the domestic history of Germany under Hitler which shows that there were distinct limits to the regime's institutional transformation of society and that old elites, classes, and interest groups were able to make their own accommodations with the new regime.[19] Thus even in a dictatorship professional experts were able to preserve some of that prestige and autonomy which in democratic societies their expertise has guaranteed them.[20] Our evolving knowledge of the curious combination of chaos and constraint inside Nazi Germany suggests that there was room for individual and institutional maneuver and therefore greater opportunity for initiative from below in service to the bad, the indifferent, and even on occasion the good.

Psychotherapists in the Third Reich were in a particularly advantageous position to advance their professional interests. This was the case for a number of reasons, again chief among which was the presence among them of a cousin of Hitler's second-in-command, Hermann Göring. The result was summed up in an article in Joseph Goebbels's prestige paper, *Das Reich*, in 1944: "Psychotherapy...has made great strides in the last decade and in Germany has been visibly acknowledged by the state through the recent elevation of the German Institute for Psychological Research and Psychotherapy [in Berlin] to a Reich Institute in the Reich Research Council."[21]

But while we now know a great deal about the professional and institutional history of psychotherapy and psychoanalysis in the Third Reich, we still need to learn much more about the role of medicine and psychology in Nazi schemes for the social control of the German population and, more generally, the place of these disciplines in the life of society under Hitler, a life complementary to the death brought by the

Nazis to the enemies of the German racial community. Although imperfectly effected, Nazi social policies displayed a strong interest in the promotion—or at least the appearance of the promotion—of the welfare and productive energy of the German people. The regime's motives were mixed. Political pragmatism told them they must do something about the unemployment caused by the Great Depression in order to preempt any possibility of unrest or revolt on the part of the working class. Their racism prompted them to cultivate and exploit the allegedly superior racial qualities of "Aryans," especially in view of the inevitable racial struggle for survival against numerically superior biological inferiors. Finally, since the Nazis had inherited a modern industrial society they wished to gear up for war and extermination, they were confronted by the fact that "social security programs constitute a structural uniformity of modern societies, regardless of formal political system or ideological stance."[22] Although Nazi designs in this realm were somewhat limited by the chaotic "institutional Darwinism" of their bureaucracy, their guarantee of fat profits for big business, their substitution of comradely status for material benefits,[23] and their constant recourse to terror, especially against the working class, even into the war bureaucratic inertia caused planning in the realm of social insurance to go forward.[24]

How did the health sciences, in particular psychotherapy, fit into these conditions? While keeping in mind the often wide gaps between words and actions, between rhetoric and policy, and between intents and results, it appears that there were three basic components to the Nazi drive for the health of the "master race." First, Nazi physicians called for programs to promote healthful habits, public hygiene, preventive medicine, and rehabilitation. A dramatic and, in terms of its source, chilling example of this last ideal were the efforts of orthopedic surgeon Karl Gebhardt to propagandize the positive power of healthy thinking, or *Ausstreuen der Heilidee*.[25] Gebhardt, director of the SS sanitarium Hohenlychen and conductor of wartime experiments on concentration camp inmates, urged the use of psychological suggestion in the rehabilitation of patients whose productivity might otherwise be lost to society.[26]

The second component of the Nazi health campaign was a desire to reduce the expense to the state of health care, compensation, damages, and pensions. The psychotherapists at the Göring Institute repeatedly claimed that psychotherapy could quickly and cheaply return people to health and to work, saving public and private insurers large sums of money. Although psychotherapy never became part of the state health insurance scheme (or the university establishment) in the Third Reich, in 1943 the Göring Institute signed an agreement with an association of private health insurance carriers for white collar employees that in its implementation guidelines contained the following stipulation: "The admission of patients is to be handled with the greatest caution. Only socially and biologically valuable patients with positive prospects for a successful cure over the short term may be treated."[27] It is difficult to determine the precise proportion of racist rhetoric to racist conviction in this statement. What is clear, however, is the convergence of professional, financial, and political interests in the speedy dispatch of psychological disorders. These interests advanced the "neo-Freudian" trend within psychoanalysis itself toward shorter therapy at the expense of longer didactic analysis. The Luftwaffe tried psychoanalysis, but rejected it because the treatment's demand for readjustment of the patient's life was incompatible with the service's desire to return him to combat duty.[28] What unites these two examples with each other and with a universal trend in the history of psychotherapy in the twentieth century is the socially conditioned emphasis on effective function within the institutions of society, economy, and state.

The third component of the Nazi concern for the exploitable health of the populace included the related ideals of race, character, and will. These ideals encompassed the Nazi conviction that "Aryan" superiority was based on internal human qualities arising from sound biological stock and effective racial breeding. Nazi racism built upon an existing Social Darwinism in the medical profession and helped propel many German doctors, out of combinations of conviction and self-interest, to espouse the Nazi notion of health as a duty.[29] The Nazis, for example, charged the existing juvenile justice system with determining the fitness of an offender for psychological or psychiatric treatment; if there was little prospect for a successful readjustment more traditional and brutal methods would be applied.[30] Aside from the savage nonsense of their racial theory, the Nazis subverted any possible enhancement of the health of the German people by demands for high productivity, material sacrifice, and, finally, war.[31] Even their insistence on individual productivity tore at whatever contribution the ideal of a racial community might have made to any sense of psychological well-being within a supportive environment by creating an atmosphere of competitiveness and resultant stress and illness common to advanced capitalist societies.[32]

It is within this context of Nazi aims and the social realities of the Third Reich that the professional activities of psychotherapists in Germany must be placed. Psychotherapists by the nature of their work were not involved in complementary Nazi efforts to sterilize and exterminate those stigmatized as "mental incurables" and "useless eaters." Their capacities lay in the realms of medical care and the building of social and political conformity. Under Nazism the first capacity was defensible in terms of the Hippocratic oath though also hypocritical in practice since officially Jews were to be refused treatment and more generally objectionable in that medical care for citizens of the Reich meant cultivation of human resources for an evil and aggressive regime. The second capacity represented an inherently problematical feature of psychotherapy in modern society, but one especially dangerous under a dictatorship.

The extremes of moral ambiguity and moral cowardice in the practice of psychotherapy in Nazi Germany were reached where medicine and criminal law came into contact, for example with respect to homosexuals. The Nazis, expanding murderously upon existing laws against homosexuality and an almost universal social bias, regarded homosexuality as an instance of biological degeneracy and exterminated thousands of homosexuals.[33] The Göring Institute was centrally involved with the problem of homosexuality in society, the Nazi youth groups, and the German military during the Second World War. Psychotherapists lobbied for treatment of homosexuals instead of punishment and helped the Nazis try to deal with the chronic and embarrassing incidence of homosexual behavior in the Hitler Youth and the League of German Girls. In the case of the military, the psychotherapeutic point of view ran into greater scientific and political opposition. The Wehrmacht and the Waffen-SS adhered strictly to the criminal penalties called for under Article 175 of the penal code and in 1944 specifically excluded, save under certain circumstances, any resort to medical treatment as provided for under Article 51 of the code.[34] Psychoanalyst Felix Boehm participated in the deliberations that led to the complete criminalization of homosexuality in the army and that reflected a victory for Nazi hardliners, the exponents of total war, and the army psychiatrists who had always opposed andy therapeutic indulgence of sexual degenerates. Clearly the Göring Institute was now on record as supporting brutal Nazi wartime measures against homosexuals.

But the Nazis themselves were in fact of two minds about the problem of homosexuality. On the one hand, they endeavored to rid society of those individuals, including homosexuals, deemed unfit to be productive members of the *Volksgemeinschaft*. On the other hand, the Nazis wished to exploit as well as to punish, so the incidence of homosexual tendencies throughout the population, especially among youth, also suggested that reparative measures had to be undertaken. Göring and the psychotherapists were only too willing to seize this chance to prove the value of their discipline, particularly since it would demonstrate the superiority of psychotherapy over the "therapeutic nihilism" of established nosological psychiatry. The psychotherapists were supported by the Reich Criminal Police Office which on pragmatic grounds saw homosexuals falling into three categories: "treatable," "untreatable," and "one-time offenders." These categories had found their way into military guidelines by 1943. Those in the first classification were to be sent by the police into psychotherapy, those in the second category were to go to concentration camps, and those in the third category were to be assigned to "field punishment."[35] And in the Luftwaffe, where psychotherapists had some influence, the medical service continued in 1944, unlike the Wehrmacht psychiatrists, to declare congenital homosexuality to be treatable and those whose sexual perversion was the result of environmental factors to be curable.[36]

These bits and pieces of evidence are the starting point for a more exhaustive study of the role of psychotherapy, psychoanalysis, and psychology within the extent and limits of the Nazi use of medicine as a means of social control. Such a study will further clarify the developments in this field in the modern bureaucratic society of Germany. This will reveal continuities in the professional nature and social use of psychology in medicine in Germany before and after 1945, much of it ethically ambiguous, some of it decidedly objectionable, and a bit of it beyond reproach, but all of it not unrelated to important questions about human society in general in the twentieth century. At the same time, a study of the uses and effects of psychotherapy will tell us a great deal about the dynamics of society under the Nazi dictatorship.[37] This is especially important with respect to the Third Reich since we need to know much more about the psychological and social "middle ground" underneath the fanaticism, oppression, and opposition that has traditionally and rightly preoccupied historians of Nazi Germany. This "middle ground," after all, was where authoritarianism could stand and function through a mix of victimization, cultivation, adjustment, and coping. The charting of this ground, made possible by the incredible amount of documentation and testimony brought to us as a result of Nazism's huge impact on humanity and by the total defeat that transformed its offices into archives, is thus of great significance.

In conclusion, let us consider three fundamental questions about the history of psychoanalysis and psychotherapy in Germany since 1939, questions that must guide future research. The first is the question of the deformation of theory, practice, and personnel as a result of the depredations of the Nazi regime. It will not do, as Harald Schultz-Hencke did in advertising his own school of thought in the pages of *Les Temps Modernes* in 1949, merely to speak of the survival and protection of psychoanalysis.[38] Such defensive accounts by eyewitnesses and participants have continued to appear, in part in response to attacks on the older generation of analysts in Germany. While valuable in terms of basic information about the Nazi era, such accounts, aside from their defensive and obscurantist nature, are also usually characterized by loyalty to one faction or individual or another, thereby compromising in two distinct ways their value as historical analyses.[39] Such intradisciplinary crossfire makes it all the more necessary that comprehensive historical research be undertaken to supply the proper contexts.

The second question has to do with the extent to which the Nazis intentionally or inadvertently aggravated enduring trends in bourgeois society's use of psychotherapy as a means of oppressive social control and the extent to which they created anomalies that resulted in specific malformations of psychoanalysis, psychotherapy, and psychology in Germany before and after 1945. Linked to this question is that of the degree of professional and moral autonomy psychotherapists managed to retain under the Nazi dictatorship. Evidence suggests that, however extreme the conditions under which psychotherapy as a practice and as a profession operated in Nazi Germany, significant theoretical, practical, institutional, and professional continuities connect developments under Hitler to the preceding and succeeding developments in the field in Central Europe and the Western world as a whole.

A third fundamental question is that of the broader social and historical continuities of which psychotherapy is a part and to which study of its history can contribute. We have touched upon some of these questions, but let us briefly enumerate them since they also apply to the history of medicine and health care in general. How did medicine and psychotherapy contribute to demands for conformity, discipline, and performance? To what extent were aims in this direction effected over the life of the Nazi regime? To what extent did such ideas correspond to aims common among doctors in Germany before 1933? Were there differences in their acceptance and application among different medical specialists? Were there variations in theory and practice when applied to patients from different social classes? Were there variations according to malady? Were women treated differently than men? To what degree did these ideas and practices reflect social dynamics of a modern industrial society and not just those peculiar to Germany and to the Nazis?

The overarching social question is: What were the factors that allowed people to live and work under a regime such as that of Hitler's and to what degree do these factors inhabit society in better times? This is arguably *the* question of the twentieth century and a study of the uses and abuses of psychotherapy under Nazism can contribute much to our understanding of such crucial issues. Terror and fanaticism were the poles of this social phenomenon, but the fields around these poles were also charged with energies drawn from more general human institutions, habits, and responses. The institutionalization of psychoanalysis, psychotherapy, and psychology during the twentieth century in service to various professional and social ends has helped push work in this field primarily in the direction of short-term therapies that reflect the interest of the patient, therapists, and third party in adjustment to the social environment, slighting the search for self-knowledge on the part of the patient and scientific research on the part of the therapist. This trend carries with it moral ambiguities aggravated to varying distressing degrees under Nazism. This fact more than any other compels us not to ignore the developmental continuities of psychoanalysis and psychotherapy in Germany since 1939. If, as according to Freud, morality is self-evident, its achievement in the "iron cage" of institutions Max Weber in 1930 saw being constructed is anything but uncompromised.

Notes

1. "Continuités et développement de la psychanalyse et la psychothérapie en Allemagne depuis 1939," *Revue Internationale d'Histoire de la Psychanalyse* 1 (1988): 51–70. With permission of Presses Universitaires de France.
2. Martin Broszat, "Plädoyer für eine Historisierung des Nationalsozialismus," *Merkur* 39 (1985): 373–85.
3. Dirk Blasius, "Psychiatrischer Alltag im Nationalsozialismus," in Detlev Peukert and Jürgen Reulecke, eds., *Die Reihen fast geschlossen: Beiträge zur Geschichte des Alltags im Nationalsozialismus* (Wuppertal, 1981), pp. 367–80.
4. Robert Jay Lifton, *The Nazi Doctors: Medical Killing and the Psychology of Genocide* (New York, 1986).

5. Ute Frevert, "Professional Medicine and the Working Class in Germany," *Journal of Contemporary History* 20 (1985): 637–58.

6. Claudia Huerkamp, *Der Aufstieg der Ärzte im 19. Jahrhundert: Vom gelehrten Stand zum professionellen Experten: Das Beispiel Preussens* (Göttingen, 1985); Michael Kater, *Doctors Under Hitler* (Chapel Hill, 1989).

7. Jan Goldstein, "The Hysteria Diagnosis and the Politics of Anticlericalism in Late Nineteenth-Century France," *Journal of Modern History* 54 (1982): 209–39; idem, *Console and Classify: The French Psychiatric Profession in the Nineteenth Century* (New York, 1987).

8. Klaus Dörner, *Madmen and the Bourgeoisie: A Social History of Insanity and Psychiatry*, trans. Joachim Neugroschel and Jean Steinberg (Oxford, 1981).

9. Hannah S. Decker, *Freud in Germany: Revolution and Reaction in Science, 1893–1907* (New York, 1977); Regine Lockot, *Erinnern und Durcharbeiten. Zur Geschichte der Psychoanalyse und Psychotherapie im Nationalsozialismus* (Frankfurt, 1985); Ulfried Geuter, *Die Professionalization of Psychology in Nazi Germany*, trans. Richard J. Holmes (New York, 1992); and Geoffrey Cocks, *Psychotherapy in the Third Reich: The Göring Institute* (New York, 1985).

10. William Menninger, *Psychiatry in a Troubled World: Yesterday's War and Today's Challenge* (New York, 1948).

11. Dorothy Burlingham and Anna Freud, *War and Children* (New York, 1943).

12. Russell Jacoby, *The Repression of Psychoanalysis: Otto Fenichel and the Political Freudians* (New York, 1983).

13. Matthias Heinrich Göring to Franz Wirz, May 28, 1938, Kl. Erw. 762/3. Bundesarchiv, Coblenz.

14. Sherry Turkle, *Psychoanalytic Politics: Freud's French Revolution* (New York, 1978), p. 49.

15. Robert Veatch, "Scientific Expertise and Value Judgments: Generalization of Expertise," *Hastings Center Studies* 1:2 (1973): 29–40.

16. Louise Horowitz, "Whose Interests Should the Psychotherapist Represent?" in Raphael Stern et al., eds., *Science and Psychotherapy* (New York, 1977), p. 161.

17. Konrad H. Jarausch, *The Unfree Professions: German Lawyers, Teachers, and Engineers, 1900–1950* (New York, 1990).

18. Konrad H. Jarausch, "The Crisis of German Professions, 1918–1933," *Journal of Contemporary History* 20 (1985): 394.

19. Ian Kershaw, *The Nazi Dictatorship: Problems and Perspectives of Interpretation*, 2nd ed. (London, 1989).

20. Elliot Freidson, "The Changing Nature of Professional Control," *Annual Review of Sociology* 10 (1984): 1–20.

21. Heinrich Goitsch, "Heilwege für die erkrankte Seele," *Das Reich*, August 20, 1944, p. 20.

22. Philip. K. Armour and Richard. M. Coughlin, "Social Control and Social Security: Theory and Research on Capitalist and Communist Nations," *Social Science Quarterly* 66 (1985): 779.

23. Stephen Salter, "Class Harmony or Class Conflict? The Industrial Working Class and the National Socialist Regime, 1933–1945," in Jeremy Noakes, ed., *Government, Party and People in Nazi Germany* (Exeter, 1980), p. 83.

24. Marie-Luise Recker, *Nationalsozialistische Sozialpolitik im Zweiten Weltkrieg* (Munich, 1985).

25. Karl Gebhardt, "Erziehungsfragen im Behandlungsgang versicherungspflichtiger Kranker," *Deutsche medizinische Wochenschrift* 63 (1937): 737.

26. Karl Gebhardt, "Allgemeines zur Widerherstellungschirurgie," *Zentralblatt für Chirurgie* 63 (1936): 1570–6.

27. Matthias Heinrich Göring, Ausführungsbestimmungen, January 1, 1943, Kl. Erw. 762/4. Bundesarchiv, Coblenz.

28. Immo von Hattingberg, "Medical Care for Flying Personnel," in *German Aviation Medicine. World War II* (Washington, D.C., 1950), p. 1068.

29. Renate Jacke, "Medizin im Nationalsozialismus und ihr Widerschein in der Gegenwart," *Frankfurter Hefte* 38:3 (1983): 31–8.

30. Thomas DeWitt, "The Nazi Party and Social Welfare, 1919–39," Ph.D. dissertation, University of Virginia, 1972.

31. Tim Mason, *Sozialpolitik im Dritten Reich. Arbeiterklasse und Volksgemeinschaft* (Opladen, 1978), pp. 314–15.

32. Kershaw, *Nazi Dictatorship*, pp. 147–8.

33. "Widernatürliche Unzucht ist todeswürdig," *Das Schwarze Korps*, May 22, 1935, p. 8.

34. Begutachtung von Strafsachen wegen widernatürlicher Unzucht, December 15, 1944, H20/474. Bundesarchiv-Militärarchiv, Freiburg.

35. Der Chef des Oberkommandos der Wehrmacht, Richtlinien für die Behandlung von Strafsachen wegen widernatürlicher Unzucht, May 19, 1943, H20/474. Bundesarchiv-Militärarchiv, Freiburg.

36. Sanitätsinspekteur der Luftwaffe, Anweisung für Truppenärzte zur Beurteilung gleichgeschlechtlicher Handlungen vom 7.6.1944, H20/474. Bundesarchiv-Militärarchiv, Freiburg.

37. Blasius, "Psychiatrischer Alltag," p. 467.

38. Harald Schultz-Hencke, "La Psychothérapie et la Psychanalyse en Allemagne," *Les Temps Modernes* 5 (1949): 526–37.

39. Walter Bräutigam, "Rückblick auf das Jahr 1942. Betrachtungen eines psychoanalytischen Ausbildungskandidaten des Berliner Instituts der Kriegsjahre," *Psyche* 38 (1984): 905–14.

6

The Curve of Heinz Kohut's Life[1]

The curve of psychoanalyst Heinz Kohut's life began in Vienna on May 3, 1913 and ended in Chicago on October 8, 1981. The conception of the course of human life as a curve was his own. It reflects not only the essence of the "psychology of the self" Kohut developed during the last decade of his life, but Kohut's life experience as a whole. In 1978 he wrote that the "concept of a nuclear self...has, from the beginning, a destiny, a potential life curve,"[2] by which Kohut meant that the course of life is not a hostage to childhood conflicts, as Freud had argued, but a coherent expression of the experience of a self.

Kohut's last paper was edited and delivered posthumously by his son on the occasion of the fiftieth anniversary celebration of the founding of the Chicago Institute for Psychoanalysis on November 7, 1981. It was entitled "Introspection, Empathy, and the Semicircle of Mental Health." The first half of this title referred to the paper Kohut had presented for the twenty-fifth anniversary of the Institute, while the second half of the title was inspired by the post-Homeric story of Odysseus and his infant son Telemachus. Odysseus is reluctant to leave his young wife and son for the war against Troy and so feigns mental illness by sowing his field with salt. But one of the delegates of the Greek state, suspecting a trick, throws Telemachus in front of the plow. Odysseus immediately makes a semicircle around the baby and thus demonstrates his mental health by saving his son's life.[3] Kohut sets this story against Sophocles' Oedipus, the doomed figure who inspired Freud's view of human development. For Kohut the story of Odysseus is symbolic of "that joyful awareness of the human self as being temporal, of having an unrolling destiny: a preparatory beginning, a flourishing middle, and a retrospective end; a fitting symbol of the fact that healthy man experiences, and with the deepest joy, the next generation as an extension of his own self."[4]

The image and shape of a curve embrace Kohut's critique not only of Freud's notion of "the child as father to the man," but also of the Western tradition of what in a letter to a colleague in 1978 he called "fearless self-sufficiency."[5] While sharing the psychoanalytic view of the importance of the psychodynamics of early life, Kohut came to see childhood as something other than a rock of Prometheus—or, perhaps better, Procrustean bed—to which the adult is bound. Rather, childhood was a time when a properly empathic parental environment could mobilize the child's potential psychological strengths. Kohut thus rejected the biological aspect of psychoanalysis that sees human life as a struggle between sexual and aggressive drives and the social environment. For Kohut psychoanalysis was a pure psychology dealing with the experiential rather than with the biological. Moreover, Kohut argued that psychoanalysis had imbibed a peculiarly modern Western ideal of independence while self psychology had shown the ongoing importance of human relationships in the development of character. Kohut's curve therefore expresses nurture and enclosure within as well as across generations—this in contrast to a lonely trajectory of attempted escape from the gravity of origins.

While much has been published on Kohut's theories and while Kohut himself has offered glimpses of his life in his own writings, he always remained a very private person. The letters contained in his collected correspondence thus offer a more detailed and nuanced look at his life and career than has ever been possible before. That Kohut embraced Freud in his own way is a reflection of the life that emerges in these letters. Even though he was born in Freud's Vienna, Kohut was a child of the twentieth century just as surely as Freud, born in 1856, was a child of the nineteenth. Kohut admired such contemporaneous musicians as Arnold Schoenberg, Anton von Webern, and Alban Berg; writers like Thomas Mann, Robert Musil, Eugene O'Neill, Franz Kafka, Ezra Pound, and James Joyce; and artists such as Pablo Picasso, all of whom "were active in depicting the broken-up self and its artistic recreation."[6] And Kohut's view of empathy as a means to knowledge also reflected a modern appreciation of the interdependence of observer and observed, while Freud maintained a nineteenth-century faith in the classical "distinction between observer and observed."[7] It is as instructive as it is ironic that the year Kohut was born, 1913, was the year in which Freud wrote "On Narcissism."[8] Fifty years later and a hemisphere away Kohut was to make his most decisive contributions to traditional psychoanalysis on the subject of narcissism and then use that subject as a point of departure for his own psychology of the self.

But it was Kohut's early years in Vienna that provided the basic emotional and intellectual stimulation for his creative and scientific work in psychoanalysis, on narcissism, and toward self psychology. These years also embodied a point of departure in the literal as well as the metaphorical sense. For both Freud and Kohut were forced to leave Vienna as a consequence of Nazi Germany's annexation of Austria in 1938 and their departure within six months of each other would also come to symbolize both Kohut's moving toward and moving away from (or, as Kohut himself might put it, beyond) Freud. While Freud left Vienna in June 1938 for exile and death in England, Kohut escaped to England in March 1939 on his way to the United States. Like Freud, he started with neurology, but, also like Freud, changed to psychiatry on his way to becoming a psychoanalyst. For Kohut, the transplantation of psychoanalysis into the United States that had begun in the 1920s and had accelerated in the 1930s was to provide a solid basis not only for a career as a psychoanalyst but for the construction of his own version of the discipline. American psychoanalysis comprised a strong trend toward ego psychology first pioneered by Freud himself (and his daughter Anna) as well as an insistence on the medical control of psychoanalysis against which Kohut, following Freud, would rebel.

Vienna in 1913 was a city of established culture and incipient crisis. It was a city associated with the work of composers such as Schoenberg and Gustav Mahler, writers like Hugo von Hofmannstahl and Arthur Schnitzler, artists such as Gustav Klimt and Oskar Kokoschka—and, of course, Sigmund Freud, who in 1900 published *The Interpretation of Dreams*, the first great work of a new science of the mind called psychoanalysis. But, particularly after 1900, representative government in the Austro-Hungarian Empire had degenerated into imperial bureaucratic authoritarianism while a newly virulent brand of mass politics was beginning to crystallize around charismatic figures like the anti-Semitic mayor of Vienna, Karl Lueger.[9] The Empire as a whole, moreover, was beginning to come apart as a result of ethnic and nationalist agitation. Within a year a crisis with Serbia over the recently annexed Austrian province of Bosnia-Herzogovina would explode into war.

It was into such an environment that Heinz Kohut was born in May 1913, the same month a "rough beast"[10] named Adolf Hitler left Vienna and slouched towards Munich on a path that would lead back to the Austrian capital twenty-five years later and end Kohut's years in his homeland. Felix Kohut, Heinz's father, was in the paper business (Fa. Bellak & Kohut) and was also an accomplished amateur pianist. His mother, Else (née Lampl) was also musical, blessed with a fine singing voice. Music thus became an important part of Heinz Kohut's life. Heinz took piano lessons as a boy and cultivated an educated taste in music ranging from German classical composers to jazzman Louis Armstrong. His first published psychoanalytic paper, which appeared in 1950 and was co-authored by musicologist and old friend Siegmund Levarie was "On the Enjoyment of Listening to Music."[11] The Kohut family was solidly upper middle class and both Felix and Else vacationed in Italy and Switzerland. During Kohut's childhood, the family lived in an apartment in the Alsergrund district and then moved to a big house at Paradiesgasse 47 in Grinzing, a village within the Döbling district north of the city center.

The First World War took Felix Kohut away from home and brought the paper business under increasing government and military control.[12] For the next five years Heinz and his mother also had to endure at least some of the hardships that ensued from a long war of attrition and the Allied blockade of Germany and Austria. It seems that it was during this period that Kohut's character was formed most decisively and in such a way as to give both form and content to his subsequent contributions to psychoanalytic thought.

The most revealing account of Kohut's early years is most probably contained in his famous case study, "The Two Analyses of Mr. Z." It is likely that this essay describes Kohut's training analysis with Ruth Eissler in the 1940s and a subsequent self-analysis in the 1960s. Kohut never told anyone that he was (or was not) Mr. Z., but both his wife and son became convinced that this was the case, and since publication of the case several of Kohut's colleagues and friends have intuited this relationship. The dominant parental figure in "The Two Analyses of Mr. Z." is the mother, whose controlling behavior and paranoia breed insecurity and self-doubt in her son. Kohut, in published recollections of his childhood, dwells on the absence of his father rather than on the presence of his mother. But the absence of the father would more than likely only have aggravated the intrusive presence of the mother and thus intensified the wish to have the father at home. And, following psychoanalytic reasoning, what is unmentioned is just as—if not more— significant as what is mentioned: Kohut was able to treat the absence of the father publicly; the early influence of his mother he was not. That Kohut waited until 1979 to publish "The Two Analyses of Mr. Z." would seem to demonstrate the insecure personal status of what he regarded as the seminal case for self psychology.[13]

An examination of the case study in fact reveals only lightly camouflaged events in Kohut's life. In the second analysis, in fact a self-analysis probably facilitated by a mental crisis late in Else Kohut's life, the image of Kohut's mother is of a possessive, domineering, and seductive woman who "emotionally enslaved those around her and stifled their independent existence."[14] Else also displayed paranoid tendencies that further oppressed Heinz and the gentle, easygoing Felix. Mr. Z., who has "the face of a dreamer and a thinker,"[15] is, like Kohut, an only child. His father is a successful business executive who is away from the family early in the son's life. He returns, as Felix did from the First World War, when the boy is five years old. But the father remains distant, driven to other women in "flight from the mother."[16] Unlike Odysseus with Telemachus, "the father had tried to save himself, and in doing so had sacrificed his son."[17]

Although the boy's first two years were happy ones, the nurture his mother provided her infant son became increasingly disruptive of his autonomous development. She regularly examined his feces. Later, she systematically inspected his skin for blemishes and popped any offending blackheads. She subjected him to constant criticism, something to which Kohut would remain sensitive all his life.[18] When Mr. Z. got his own room she would not allow him to close the door. His masturbatory fantasies, commencing around the time his father returned from the war, were masochistic ones of being controlled by women. Most often they adopted a slave motif drawn from *Uncle Tom's Cabin*, which Kohut's mother had read aloud to him when he was a child.

Both the mother and the father contributed to a sense in Mr. Z. of his being denied value as a person: she by treating him as an object and as a part of herself; he by deserting him. Nor did his father's return satisfy Mr. Z.'s psychological needs: "I was deprived of a young, vigorous father," Kohut told an interviewer in 1978. "He was replaced by an old man, a grandfather, and that was not the same."[19] Significantly, this observation also reflects the denigration of the father by the mother described in "Mr. Z."

Though until 1921 Heinz was indulged as the only child in the Lampl clan, after the war his parents' busy business and social life isolated him. He was also sent away on summer vacations in Austria, France, Switzerland, and Germany, although his mother often accompanied him. He later recalled to a friend that he once became ill while staying with friends and neither his father nor his mother visited him. Kohut was diverted early on not only by hiking, scouting, boxing, and soccer, but also by stories of space travel and an adolescent secret society.[20] Another story, repeated in "Mr. Z.,"[21] was a skiing trip he took with his father. Heinz was disappointed to sense what was an occasion for closeness between father and son was also an opportunity for the father to meet his mistress.

Kohut also had an intense and intellectually stimulating relationship with a young tutor, Ernst Morawetz, who, it seems, is represented by the young counselor with whom Mr. Z. had one or two homosexual encounters. Together with Morawetz, Kohut immersed himself in the world of museums, music, and the works of Kant, Nietzsche, and Schopenhauer. He was the beneficiary of a classical education ("eight years of Latin and six years of Greek"[22]) in Vienna, but he also spent a couple of summers at boarding schools in Switzerland and France. This aggravated the isolation he felt from his parents: "Royalty was around, but that did not make up for an essential deep loneliness. I would get postcards from my father from one end of Europe and from my mother at the other end."[23] Even when the family was together, the distance between parents and son remained great: Two days after his sixty-seventh birthday and in the midst of difficulties stemming from the Chicago Institute's attitude toward his challenge to psychoanalytic orthodoxy, he wrote on May 5, 1980, to colleague Arnold Goldberg and underlined the "*emptiness*" of the birthday parties he had as a child.

As a result, Kohut idealized his tutor and many of his teachers in school—in particular a high school history and geography teacher, Ignaz Purkarthofer[24]—and spent a great deal of time with his uncle, Hans Lampl, who became like a father to him. When Kohut returned to Vienna for the first time in 1957, he made a point of visiting Lampl, who was ill and would die soon afterward.[25] As early as grade school, Kohut recalled many years later, he had developed an interest in medicine, an interest Kohut says his artistically inclined father could not appreciate. It was not until Heinz was in medical school that his father, who died of leukemia in 1937 at the age of fifty, came to understand and value his son's work.

Kohut in the meantime had become the quintessential young Viennese intellectual, frequenting the coffee houses that were centers for discussion and debate. Many of these discussions were with his best friend Siegmund, whom he had met in 1924 and with whom he would tour Paris and Brittany in the summer of 1929. Döbling itself was famous for its cultural salons and the Döblinger Gymnasium, where Kohut received his classical education, was one of the secondary schools that trained students for entry into the university.[26]

Kohut passed his graduation examinations (*Matura*) at the Döblinger Gymnasium in 1932. He went on to study medicine at the University of Vienna; he also interned for a year at hospitals in Paris. Kohut, like many Viennese intellectuals, had for some time been interested in psychoanalysis and began his own analysis in the 1930s, first briefly with Walter Marseilles and then with August Aichhorn. He received his medical degree in November 1938, but in March of that year Nazi Germany had annexed Austria. As for so many others, this represented a personal disaster for Kohut. Although the Kohuts were not religious, they were legally members of the Jewish Community (*Israelitische Kultusgemeinde Wien*) and thus their "racial" background was Jewish.[27] Kohut could not remain in Austria.

In a sense, Kohut left Vienna twice. On the afternoon of June 4, 1938, acting on a tip from Aichhorn, he went to the train station in Vienna to witness the departure of Freud into exile. With this event, he recalled many years later, "I had the feeling of a crumbling universe."[28] Kohut could certainly empathize with Freud and surely could see himself leaving Vienna under similar circumstances in the near future. Moreover, his friend Siegmund emigrated in July.

But first there was the matter of his medical exams. The Nazis initially threatened the immediate expulsion of all Jewish university students. But in June it was decreed that those in their last year could take their oral exams.[29] In early October Kohut was notified that he would have to take eight examinations within a period of four weeks starting immediately; he finished on October 26.[30] Then in early November Kohut and his mother had to hide during the anti-Semitic riots that began on November 9 during "the night of broken glass." What before had been demoralizing and threatening had now become dangerous: When the night before Kohut had written Siegmund, in a letter that was resumed only on November 16, about the "crazy act in Paris," he parenthesized ominously that in Vienna that evening there had been both an earthquake and an eclipse of the moon. Moving from their exposed single dwelling in Grinzing the Kohuts spent "crystal night" with Siegmund's parents at their apartment and then a few nights elsewhere with non-Jewish friends until the terror abated. Josef Löwenherz was the leader of the Jewish Community and his wife, Sophie, felt that the apartment would not long be safe.

It was Löwenherz who, together with Kohut's uncle Hans operating in England and in Switzerland, procured Kohut a transit visa for England in February of 1939.[31] Until then Kohut was able to get a tedious clerical job in the Rothschildspital, the hospital of the Jewish Community, under the official protection of Quaker Pastor Frank van Gheel

Gildemeester and Rabbi Benjamin Murmelstein.[32] So the near future Kohut had been anxiously anticipating ever since Freud's departure eight months before arrived only in March 1939 when he led a group of Jews by train through Germany and thence to freedom in England. He was a placed in the Kitchener Camp at Richborough near Sandwich, Kent, where he worked in the first aid station.[33] He caught pneumonia, however, and was allowed to stay with his uncle Hans in London; Hans Lampl, director of the Austrian paper firm Leykam-Josefsthal A.G., had emigrated to England in 1938.[34] Kohut's stay in England was contingent on his receiving a visa to enter the United States; this he secured through an affidavit signed by the Chicago business partner of his friend Siegmund's uncle. At the end of February 1940 Kohut sailed for the United States across an Atlantic Ocean now prowled by German submarines. He settled in Chicago where Siegmund, who was teaching and conducting at the University of Chicago, lived.

The legacy for Kohut of his years in Vienna was twofold. Although he did not speak German at home out of a desire to become an American, he preserved a strong love for his homeland. He once recalled with genuine pleasure an occasion during a visit to Amsterdam when "my old Viennese began to come bubbling out." To be sure, there remained some ambivalence in Kohut about this. Almost all of his relatives had died in Nazi concentration camps. He spoke of his "playing with psychological fire" in returning to Vienna for the first time in 1957; and as late as 1970 he was telling colleague Margaret Mahler that she was "brave to have accepted a scientific assignment in Vienna," adding that he had "so far declined all such invitations."[35] But when friend Henry von Witzleben commented that Kohut resisted using German,[36] he responded that it was only when he could "speak and think German" that he felt really content and how wonderful it was to be in Austria and to hear people speaking "normally." Kohut conceded that his friend must have detected something in his letter that he had in the meantime forgotten. But late in his life he responded to contacts from Gymnasium friends who had learned of his fame and was looking forward to a reunion with them in May 1982 on the fiftieth anniversary of their graduation.[37] Kohut was also very pleased in 1977 to be honored with membership in the Austrian Academy of Sciences and even more pleased at receiving the Austrian Cross of Honor for Science and Art that same year.[38] And late in life he expressed privately a particular nostalgia for Germany, a view in keeping with his paternal grandfather's greater German (*grossdeutsch*) predilections.

The second aspect of the legacy of Kohut's Vienna years consisted of his lifelong concern with the human capacity and need for empathy. This concern was part of an intellectual commitment common in Europe to psychoanalysis as a broad humanistic discipline rather than simply a medical one. Such a view would conflict with the American emphasis on medical training for psychoanalysts but also exploit powerful postwar trends in America and elsewhere toward supplementing (or even replacing) the biology of drives with a psychology of intentions and social interactions. Empathy for Kohut was a matter of nurture ("was one fully accepted by one's parents or not?"[39]), but it was also an intellectual tool, a means to knowledge, an idea Kohut acquired from Immanuel Kant's idea that one cannot separate what one knows from how one comes to know it. The essence of reality is unknowable, Kant argued, therefore, Kohut argued ("because I was from earliest childhood on emotionally prepared for this insight"[40]), only introspection and empathy can reveal the inner life of human beings. Self psychology would therefore be an experiential psychology.

Kohut's own childhood and adolescent experiences with parents who were distant, coupled with his innate brilliance and the intellectual atmosphere of Vienna, were later to sensitize him to patients suffering from narcissistic disorders who were the psychological casualties of modern families in which there is insufficient nurturing of the infant's and child's sense of self-worth and self-confidence: "Parents are away a lot. Daddies are not around, or they don't feel any pride in themselves. Children feel abandoned and depressed."[41] Such children become "narcissistic personalities," who, like Kohut himself, crave attention and affirmation. Kohut's "disinclination to talk about particular chapters of my early life" was an indication of the pain he felt over his experiences, a pain certainly deepened by the Nazi annexation of Austria, an event that seemed to Kohut to justify the paranoia of his mother that was the psychological complement to her desire to control those around her. All his life Heinz had struggled with the question of who was crazy, he or his mother: now the arrival of the Nazis appeared to have confirmed her suspicions of the outside world. As his old friend Charles Kligerman recalled at the memorial service for Kohut in Chicago in 1981: "The rise of Hitler and the destruction of the idealized Viennese world in which he had become *persona non grata* were tremendous blows to his self-esteem."[42] These feelings were aggravated by the fact that Kohut, raised in a nonreligious and assimilated family environment, regarded himself as Austrian rather than Jewish. He would later tell his son that, unlike the Jews, he was not able to comprehend why he had to leave Austria, since in spite of his Jewish ancestry he did not have a Jewish identity. As he put it in 1980, "all of a sudden, these bullies came along who claimed they were the real Germans and I was all of a sudden a foreigner and didn't belong."[43]

Kohut was at first able to obtain only a low-paying internship at the small Roseland Hospital in Chicago. He later claimed to have learned English primarily through reading the works of Lewis Carroll, but he had received some tutoring in the language in Vienna in 1938 as well as some instruction in it in the transit camp during 1939.[44] He received his Illinois medical license in August 1941 and became a resident in neurology at the University of Chicago Hospitals the same year. By 1944, however, he had begun to make the turn from the temporary professional haven of neurology, the study of the nervous system and its diseases, to psychiatry, the study and treatment of mental disorders, by becoming an instructor in that discipline as well.[45] He received his board certification in neurology in 1946 and in psychiatry in 1949. From 1947 to 1950 he was an assistant professor of psychiatry at the University of Chicago School of Medicine. In the fall of 1946 Kohut had begun training at the Chicago Institute for Psychoanalysis, from which he graduated in 1950. He became a member of the institute in 1953. He had gained United States citizenship near the end of the war in 1945 and had married an institute social worker, Betty Meyer, in Milwaukee in 1948.[46]

Kohut's mother had remained in Austria until February 1940 before moving to the United States via Italy. After arriving in Chicago in March she, in characteristically fearless fashion, opened a small notions store named "De Else" on 47th Street. After her son left Vienna, she not surprisingly kept to herself; Aichhorn reported to Kohut in 1939 that she had not responded to his many invitations to visit.[47] Presumably in response to a Nazi decree of February 21, 1939, which required Jews to hand over all gold, platinum, silver, precious stones, and pearls,[48] Else had taken some of the family's valuables to the Dorotheum, the state-owned auction house and pawnbrokerage. Twenty-one years later the Kohuts applied for and received a restitution payment from the Austrian government.[49] In escaping Vienna, she also had to sell the family's home at a loss and to abandon her very successful stationery store on the Währingerstrasse. Soon after the war Aichhorn, to whom Kohut was sending food, books, and even coal, wrote that he had run into the man who was now living in the Kohuts' house and he had given Aichhorn the distinct impression of feeling somewhat guilty about how he had come to own the property.[50]

During the 1950s Kohut rapidly established himself as a major force at the Institute for Psychoanalysis. He quickly became a training analyst, one of the elite who analyze students and supervise their analyses of patients. He participated in the recasting of the curriculum and taught the core theory sequence "in a manner," according to Kligerman, "that set the standard for every subsequent teacher."[51] Kohut's brilliance allowed him to teach extemporaneously; in the theory course there was no syllabus—in his own words, he "taught off-the-cuff and different each time."[52] He received high marks from the students; on one occasion the only criticism, not surprising given the depth and breadth of his knowledge and his need to be the center of attention, was that he was much more effective as a lecturer than as a discussion leader.[53] This brilliance and self-confidence could also on occasion manifest itself as a self-righteous dismissal of opposing points of view and what he regarded as inadequate or irrelevant formulations. Kohut always took great pride in his erudition. Finally, he also had a thriving clinical practice that provided much of what he liked to call the "experience-near" material with which he would construct his later "experience-distant" theories on narcissism and the self.

Kohut also rapidly gained professional stature on the national level. These were the boom years for psychoanalysis, particularly in the United States, where the numerous refugees from Europe and the American wartime mobilization of psychological services had promoted unprecedented growth in the field. Kohut became a member of the editorial board of the *Journal of the American Psychoanalytic Association* in 1955 and spoke out on the issue of factional infighting within and among psychoanalytic institutes. He also established close relationships with, among others, prominent fellow Viennese colleagues Kurt Eissler, Heinz Hartmann, and Marianne Kris. His reputation was further enhanced by ventures in "applied psychoanalysis," most significantly a paper on Thomas Mann's novella *Death in Venice*.

Most important during these years, however, was the fact that Kohut had begun to think critically about psychoanalytic theory and practice. He was typical of the time in that he adhered to a psychoanalytic ego psychology that stressed the ego's autonomy from, as well as its mediation between, internal drives and external environment. But he was concerned about the Freudian mixing of biology and psychology.[54] This early concern would eventually find expression in his psychology of the self as an insistence on psychoanalysis as a pure psychology devoted to the study of human experience *by means of* human experience. A drive, an ego, or an id cannot be experienced, but a self can, Kohut would argue.

Kohut's first major statement on the experiential basis of psychoanalytic knowledge came in a paper read at the Twenty-Fifth Anniversary Meeting of the Chicago Institute in November, 1957. Kohut claimed that the inner life of human beings can be observed only "through introspection in ourselves, and through empathy (i.e., vicarious introspection) in others."[55] Kohut acknowledged limits to such introspection and retained in this paper a belief in the primal nature of the sexual and aggressive drives. This paper was published in 1959 and had a mixed reception: praise for its careful clarification of the investigative method special to psychoanalysis, criticism for being "lopsided" and arguing for the obvious.[56] Its significance for Kohut's work as a whole, however, is that it argued for what was unique about psychoanalysis and against attempts either to reduce psychoanalysis to biology by emphasizing the drives or by diluting it into sociology by stressing what ego psychologist Heinz Hartmann called "adaptation" to external conditions.[57] Within the curve set by his own life experience this essay would form the basis for a thoroughgoing critique of psychoanalytic theory and practice.

The first five years of the new decade, however, were chiefly ones of involvement in the national politics of psychoanalysis, while the latter half of the decade was to see Kohut's growing participation in the international affairs of the discipline followed by a decisive break. This break, and the experiences that immediately preceded it, would help bring Kohut's earlier work to fruition in the 1970s. During 1963 and 1964 he was president of the Chicago Psychoanalytic Society and then was president of the American Psychoanalytic Association from May 1964 to May 1965. The APA had around 1100 members, the great majority of whom were physicians, who were seeing roughly 11,000 patients a year. It was at this time that Kohut became known to many as "Mr. Psychoanalysis," loyally and publicly asserting that his discipline's "scientific aspects are outstanding and that it is primarily a biological science."[58] In his inaugural address in Los Angeles Kohut emphasized the importance of scientific advances for greater understanding of human psychology in the long term as opposed to the limited therapeutic gains psychoanalysts could hope to make given the small numbers of analysts and analysands. He also stressed the need to combat "our worst disease, an excessive tendency toward dissension."[59] But Kohut was in fact not a defender of the status quo in American psychoanalysis. In his valedictory as president in New York the following year, Kohut highlighted controversies over the place of child psychology in the APA and the issue of the training of nonmedical analysts.[60] In both of these areas Kohut backed unsuccessful efforts to expand the boundaries of the discipline.

The insights Kohut was gaining through his ongoing clinical work were reinforced by his organizational experiences during these years. At the time and later he maintained that by observing himself and others in the administration of psychoanalysis he learned a great deal about inflated pride and narcissistic wounds.[61] He also commented that he must have fled into administration in the first place to escape tension over his growing sense of challenging psychoanalytic orthodoxy in his clinical practice and writing.[62] During this time Kohut's seminal contributions on the subject of narcissism were contained in three papers: "Forms and Transformations of Narcissism" (1966); "The Psychoanalytic Treatment of Narcissistic Personality Disorders" (1968); and "Thoughts on Narcissism and Narcissistic Rage" (1972). These contributions to psychoanalytic theory and practice would gradually evolve into the psychology of the self that Kohut would work out most significantly in three books during the ensuing decade, *The Analysis of the Self* (1971), *The Restoration of the Self* (1977), and *How Does Analysis Cure?* (1984).

Kohut argued that his clinical experience and that of many others had shown that the traditional psychoanalytic emphasis on sexual and aggressive drives and conflicts was no longer adequate to explain and treat many psychoanalytic patients. He had discovered three types of narcissistic transferences: mirroring, twinship, and idealizing. Transference is the process by which the person of the analyst becomes the embodiment of the patient's parents or early care-givers. These emotions then are available for recognition and analysis, for "working through" by the patient. Kohut argued that common patient objections to psychoanalytic interpretations he encountered in his practice were not just resistances to dealing with repressed unconscious material, as traditional theory held, but were often symptoms of a narcissistic disorder stemming from early emotional deficits. Kohut maintained that contemporary family structure had created a psychological environment of loneliness in place of the close Victorian family atmosphere of supercharged sexual tension. In 1981, for example, Kohut spoke of the poor rich people's children who I now treat, who grew up on the wealthy North Shore, whose parents were always unapproachable. They were playing bridge, going out. There was nobody but hired help, but you could never get at them.[63]

For Freud and most psychoanalysts the child is a bundle of drives coming into conflict with civilized restraints. This culminates in the Oedipus conflict whereby the child is to renounce desire for the parent of the opposite sex and reorient himself or herself eventually to normal genital sexuality with adult partners outside of the family. The universal phenomenon of neurosis, psychoanalysts believe, is the result of the imperfect resolution of this fundamental conflict. Kohut, in part drawing upon a post-Freudian tradition of psychoanalytic thought and practice that emphasizes the pre-oedipal forging of relationships between young children and their parents, primarily the mother, ultimately developed the idea of the "self" as a substitute for the mechanistic Freudian structure of id, ego, and superego. Kohut also rejected the "Kleinian" view of the psyche as determined by inborn sexual and aggressive drives channeled by the infant's relations with objects in the first months and years of life. Melanie Klein, D. W. Winnicott, and Margaret Mahler, following Freud, were typical of the prevailing psychoanalytic view that narcissism was an impediment to proper emotional relationships with others.[64] According to Kohut, however, narcissism *per se* is not pathological and has a line of development from archaic to mature separate from the development of object relations. The self develops in interaction with the environment throughout life by means of the creation of "selfobjects," other people who in the child's early years are experienced as part of the self. Ultimately, Kohut conceived of the self as "bipolar." One pole comprises the self's need to be affirmed ("mirrored") by the parents.[65] The other pole consists of ideals originating from identification with idealized early care-givers. The mature self, the product of empathic parenting, has an affirmative yet realistic sense of its own capabilities and limitations. The immature self is brittle and hollow, anxiously seeking validation from external sources.

One signal indication of Kohut's own validation in the science and profession of psychoanalysis during these years was his growing relationship with Anna Freud. Freud's youngest daughter had established herself at the Hampstead Clinic in London as an expert in working with children and was the author of the influential *The Ego and the Mechanisms of Defense* (1936). Kohut's correspondence with her began in 1963; she was a guest in the Kohut home during a visit to Chicago in December 1966;[66] and during 1968 and 1969 she was one of those who urged Kohut to allow his name to be placed in nomination for President of the International Psycho-Analytical Association. Anna Freud shared Kohut's critical Old World view of the domination of psychoanalysis by the medical profession in America as well as of the various groups "pulling away from analysis"; and she viewed Kohut as one of the few genuinely creative minds among the world's psychoanalysts. For his part, Kohut (not, to be sure, unlike other psychoanalysts) displayed great deference toward "Miss Freud" (it was not until 1975 that he would begin a letter to her as "Dear Anna Freud"), and in his correspondence with her he took the opportunity to be exceptionally harsh in his criticism of Anna Freud's bitter rival Melanie Klein. However, by 1978 at the latest Anna Freud had concluded that Kohut "had become antipsychoanalytic."[67] While there are no traces of conflict or even of significant disagreement anywhere in their correspondence, their contact diminished steadily after 1969 and became almost completely confined to personal, social, and organizational matters. This would seem to indicate a widening scientific divergence, although in 1972 she did write an appreciative note to him about how helpful his essay of that year on narcissistic rage had been in her thinking about one of her patients.[68]

Kohut's bid for the presidency of the IPA was preempted by events and on February 10, 1969, he expressed great disappointment to Anna Freud over this. He also wrote that day in the same vein to another supporter, his former training analyst Ruth Eissler:

> But much as I dreaded the humdrum of an administrative job, the emotional hardships of being the leader of a heterogeneous group, and especially the imprisonment by work which I do not enjoy, once I had made up my mind to undertake the job if it were offered, the emotional situation changed. Plans were beginning to form in me: about programs, about organizational moves, about addresses to be given—and to turn away from them now is not easy. But, as I wrote to Miss Freud, after one disturbed night I am again sleeping soundly and the waves of resentment and hurt pride which overtook me for a day or two have receded.

Along with feelings of disappointment and rejection—as well as any narcissistic injury that may have helped further spur Kohut's creative turn from psychoanalytic orthodoxy during the ensuing decade—there was a significant amount of genuine relief. Kohut had always been ambivalent about holding office because it interfered with his teaching, practicing, and, most important, his writing. In 1969 he was finishing the manuscript of his first book, *The Analysis of the Self*, which would appear in 1971. Most crucially, however, it was also during this time that Kohut went through his period of self-analysis reworking the training analysis he had undergone with Ruth Eissler. The self-analysis coincided with a crisis in the life of his mother Else, who began to suffer from "a set of circumscribed paranoid delusions."[69] She would subsequently suffer a stroke and die in 1972 at the age of eighty-one. Shortly before her death she would embrace the Catholicism in which she had been confirmed as a little girl and would be buried in a Catholic cemetery.[70] His mother's mental difficulties reactivated old conflicts in Kohut that he claimed led directly not only to greater self-understanding and happiness but to what he considered the psychoanalytic breakthrough represented by self psychology. The famously difficult prose of *The Analysis of the Self* may well reflect the personal and professional conflicts Kohut had to work through during these years.

The self-analysis as reported in "Mr. Z." focuses on the struggle of the patient's self to "disentangle itself from the noxious self-object, to delimit itself, to grow, to become independent."[71] This represents a change from the first analysis which in classic psychoanalytic fashion concentrates on the oedipal dynamics of a strong tie to the mother and the resultant ambivalent attitudes toward the rival father. The conclusion of the first analysis in "Mr. Z." is that the patient's narcissism is a defense against oedipal wishes. The second analysis, however, validates the patient's perception of the mother's psychopathological intrusiveness and paranoia and appreciates his need to establish psychological autonomy. It must be said that there would seem to be a middle position in which oedipal dynamics and maternal disorder are not mutually exclusive. Be that as it may, for Kohut his mother's crisis revealed once and for all the pathological features of her personality and established the correctness of the latter analysis and relieved him of much of his doubt about himself. In a very deep sense, Kohut had spent much of his life worrying about who was crazy—himself or his mother. Now he believed he knew.

By the time *The Analysis of the Self* was published, Kohut would have another reason to husband his time and energy in order to continue his writing. In the fall of 1971 he was diagnosed with lymphatic cancer. Intruding as it did on Kohut's new-found happiness this was an especially bitter blow and one that would force him from then on to decline invitations to give lectures, hold seminars, and receive awards.[72] Although his cancer entered a long period of remission, Kohut had to suffer a great deal during the last decade of his life. In January 1979 he underwent a coronary bypass operation and endured a long convalescence as a result of a series of complications.[73] These sequelae included labyrinthitis which Kohut with characteristic wit described as "an inner ear problem that makes me feel seasick without the compensation of ocean breezes."[74] And in late 1980 he fell ill with a life-threatening pneumonia following upon the rigors of a self psychology conference in Boston.

The absolute priority Kohut gave to his profession and to his creative work meant that the exhaustion that came with illness and age caused him to have to give up even more of the social life he cherished.[75] This was not easy for him to do; as he told *People Magazine* in 1979, "I'm no ascetic."[76] His narcissistic personality demanded attention and affirmation by others, as witnessed by an almost childlike joy in the telling of stories, the presentation of ideas, the exhibition of skills, and the bestowal of honors. Although his was hardly a life of unbroken happiness, Kohut was full of humor, charm, and playfulness. He could laugh at himself and display a vital *joie de vivre*, as evidenced by his closing a letter to a young German colleague with this observation in anticipation of his annual vacation: "There seems to be a serious water shortage in California, but who cares? The California wines are getting better and better."[77] Although he worked during his vacations in the village of Carmel-by-the-Sea, he also looked forward eagerly every year to the rejuvenation he could find in the slower pace and scenic beauty there. Nowhere else was he happier.

The last decade of Kohut's life constituted a creative burst that brought with it both fulfillment and frustration. *The Analysis of the Self* generated both praise and criticism, but it attempted to integrate a "narrower" concept of the self into the traditional psychoanalytic model of the mind. *The Restoration of the Self*, published six years later, would establish "a self psychology in the broader sense"[78] wherein the "bipolar self" formed the basis of the entire personality. These works attracted a significant number of serious and devoted adherents in Chicago, throughout the United States, and abroad. But alongside came three forms of the "misunderstanding" of his work that so upset and frustrated Kohut: criticism, cultism, and popularization. Given the comprehensive and synthetic nature of *The Analysis of the Self* (not to mention its difficulty), Kohut came under fire for allegedly having merely restated in his own words the work of many other predecessors; in one instance he came close to being charged with plagiarism in the pages of the *IJP*.[79] At the same time, Kohut's ideas and person began to attract the type of attention and support he, displaying at least some of the elitism common among psychoanalysts, feared might lead to cultism. This danger was compounded, he believed, by the potential and actual popularization of his ideas in the United States as a result of the cultural movement surrounding "the new narcissism." Although Kohut said that lay people often understood his ideas better than many of his professional colleagues, his ideas on narcissism were also popularly misunderstood; as he wrote concerning an "erroneous impression" of his work in *Newsweek* in 1978, "I do not share in the prevailing pejorative outlook on narcissism." But he also recognized that his own emphasis on empathy and human contact as well as his visibility as a figurehead, effectiveness as a speaker, and desire for attention heightened this danger.[81] He summed up his feelings in this regard in a letter to his son and daughter-in-law on November 30, 1978:

> My professional position is peculiar. I get buffeted around by nasty rejections and warmest praise—I could do with less of both but must admit that I am sometimes quite upset about it all.

Although in 1973 Kohut could write that "my ideas have led me into new regions,"[82] in 1978 he would still maintain that "what we are doing is in the very center of psychoanalysis."[83] But by 1978 very many psychoanalysts, while acknowledging in particular the importance of Kohut's ideas on narcissism, judged Kohut's theories as being outside the pale of the discipline. By this time Kohut had dethroned (but not banished) the Oedipus complex. The oedipal *phase* was ubiquitous, as was the oedipal *conflict*, but this, Kohut thought, did not make such conflict normal. Such conflict was determined not by biology but by parental response to the child's growing assertiveness and affection. As Kohut sees it, classical analysis deals essentially with "Guilty Man," while self psychology concerns itself more with "Tragic Man," the former stressing pathology, conflict, and failure, and the latter with some qualification emphasizing growth, adjustment, and success. As he wrote to a colleague in 1981:

> What you said about the difference between classical analysis and self psychology, "in classical analysis we end up with what was and what is, while in self psychology we end up with what might have been, and what can be," is very nice to read and I think—I hope—that it is true.[84]

In this, to return to the ancient image of "the semicircle of mental health," Kohut is counterpoising a liberal tradition of "striving, resourceful man" as represented by the "modernist" Greek playwright Euripides against the idea of the "sacrificial he-goat" as dramatized by the conservative Sophocles in *Oedipus Rex*.[85]

Kohut was no radical, much less a utopian. Politically he remained liberal and socially conscious, at one point, for instance, contributing to a fund to help Hungarian colleagues suffering under government oppression.[86] Neither was he philosophically or scientifically naive. He retained a strong Central European tradition of skepticism, intellectual rigor, and historical consciousness. All his life he continued to be influenced by the works of Kafka, seeing in them an expressive rendering of modern anxiety and anomie. He found the shallow and self-indulgent narcissism of the "me-decade" disturbing, especially in terms of parental neglect of children.[87] He ultimately thought psychoanalyst Erik Erikson's theories of identity formation deficient because they describe the adolescent and early adult surface rather than the childhood depths of the personality and because they "are really value judgments disguised in scientific terms."[88] Unlike Freud, he believed religion, together with art and science, to be "one of the three great cultural selfobjects of man."[89] He associated himself with Unitarianism and felt it was particularly important for his son to have an appreciation for religion. But he was not interested in the unworldly perfection of heavenly salvation—as he once put it in musical terms he borrowed from Siegmund Levarie:

> Great music is not just a perfect chord. Great music is always a deviation into dissonance and a complex way of coming back again to the consonance. This is what drives music through the tunes and harmonies until it finally rests or alludes again at the rest of balance. And so we are spurred on by the necessary shortcomings of that early grace, if you want to use the religious term, of acceptance and perfect mirroring, perfect calmness as we were uplifted, and the perfectly graspable alter-ego environment of other human beings. Which child grows up in a perfect milieu? Some scars, some trauma, some shortcomings belong to life.[90]

In short, Kohut remained suspended between a European and an American view of life—not pure pessimism versus pure optimism, to be sure—but rather a deep understanding for human problems as well as for human potentials. This is the reason the title for *The Restoration of the Self* embodies lines from Eugene O'Neill's play *The Great God Brown* (1926): "Man is born broken. He lives by mending. The grace of God is glue."

Together with close Chicago colleagues such as Ernest Wolf, Arnold Goldberg, Michael Basch, and Paul and Marian Tolpin, as well as Paul and Anna Ornstein of Cincinnati, Kohut was involved in attempts to institutionalize the training and practice of psychoanalytic self psychology in Chicago. As early as 1976 the Curriculum Committee of the Institute had "agreed to the desirability of giving the students an overall picture of the analytic scene in the first year, including the psychology of the self."[91] Actual training in self psychology first took the form of Saturday workshops and then the establishment of postgraduate courses, and finally the setting up of a popular curricular track.[92] Although Kohut himself progressively tended to perceive rejection of his work, interest in self psychology manifested itself to varying degrees at institutes around the country and around the world.[93] Various of Kohut's works were translated into German, Italian, French, Spanish, Portuguese, Swedish, and Japanese, while in the United States self psychology was promoted most effectively by annual conferences. The initial conference in Chicago in 1978 drew 450 participants, the second in Los Angeles attracted 600, and the third in Boston saw 950 attend.[94]

Generally, Kohut's work was most popular among younger analysts for whom his emphasis on empathy fit their postwar cultural and educational experiences. And even though the psychoanalytic establishment in the United States managed to limit severely the number of nonmedical candidates, there was longstanding and continuous pressure from within and without the psychoanalytic community for expansion of the discipline's popular and practical base that culminated in a successful class-action lawsuit in 1989. One example of Kohut's appeal along such lines is the argument for self psychology as supportive of feminism. While it is the case that the psychoanalytic movement has for a long time been more open to contributions by women than the fields of medicine and psychiatry in general, Freud's theories have long been criticized for their cultural bias against women. But the move in psychoanalysis toward an emphasis on the pre-oedipal relationship with the mother, work pioneered, among others, by Melanie Klein and Anna Freud, has undercut much of this traditional fixation on the male as the norm in psychoanalysis. And with the opening of psychoanalytic ranks in 1989 to nonmedical practitioners, many of whom are women, a significant part of the current agenda in psychoanalysis involves work on and by women. Although Kohut himself built his theories largely on experience with male patients and retained a psychoanalytic emphasis on sexuality, self psychology appears to be compatible with feminist values in three respects: aside from its pre-(or supra-)oedipal orientation, "it separates value acquisition from an oedipal superego that is based on castration anxiety; and it places a special value on empathy."[95] Moreover, the whole idea of the self and the realization of its potentials offers a model that emphasizes common human psychological and social options rather than biologically based gender differences.

Kohut's influence also spread because of the interest in his work not only in fields allied to psychoanalysis such as social work, pastoral counseling, and various psychotherapies, but in the social sciences and humanities in general. While psychoanalysis had traditionally influenced fields outside medicine and psychology, Kohut's work seemed more applicable to a whole range of "nonpathological" human phenomena. While this interdisciplinary trend has ebbed organizationally somewhat since Kohut's death, it was particularly pronounced in the field of history during the last years of his life. For some time a number of historians had been using psychoanalytic perspectives in their work. Kohut himself was very interested in history and in the contribution his ideas could make to understanding individuals and groups in the past. He was especially concerned with the leaders and the led in the charismatic mass movements of the twentieth century, the most fateful of which had affected him and his family directly.[96] His son, after graduating as a research psychoanalyst from the Cincinnati Psychoanalytic Institute, became a historian and Kohut took special pleasure and pride in participating with him in a psychohistory conference in 1980.

Matters in Kohut's own field during these years, however, were less than serene. Criticism of Kohut's theories ran broad and deep within the psychoanalytic community. Kohut himself not only complained about being misconstrued and misunderstood which—given the sophistication of his thinking and the inevitable difficulties in formulating new ideas—should not have been a surprise, but he was particularly pained by what he felt were personal attacks and snubs from many of his colleagues. While some friendships survived professional disagreement, others did not. One particularly painful case of the latter involved John Gedo, an early admirer of Kohut's work whom Kohut once regarded as "one of the finest minds of the younger generation in psychoanalysis."[97]

Perhaps what Kohut regarded as the cruelest blow came in the spring of 1978. At that time a number of his colleagues at the Chicago Institute (and elsewhere) were afraid that he and his followers were planning to split off. Perhaps more as a result of personal resentments and envy than of concern over the possibility of a secession, Kohut was subsequently not reelected to the Institute's governing body, the Psychoanalytic Education Council.[98] As with the earlier rebuff in seeking the IPA presidency, Kohut was happy not to have to bother with such official duties, especially since he more than ever was committed to research as well as being increasingly weakened by illness. He was also entering that stage of career when official capacities are as a matter of course laid aside: in 1981 he became inactive as a supervising analyst and became training analyst emeritus.[99] But this rejection hurt terribly and although he was reelected to the Council for a three-year term in 1980, the original defeat was emblematic of the problems in general Kohut encountered as a result of going his own way in psychoanalytic theory and practice.[100] Even his presentation scheduled for the fiftieth anniversary of the Institute in November, 1981, was problematic. Originally, Kohut's lecture for this occasion was to be given the status of an "Academic Lecture," but then this status was rescinded; as a result, Kohut insisted on arrangements that he felt would assure a proper forum and reception for his paper. In the event, Kohut died of congestive heart failure almost a month to the day before the celebration and his son Tom edited and read the paper for him.

As a final demonstration of the fruitful intertwining of Kohut's life and work, we must return to the theme of empathy within and across generations. Kohut was passionately concerned with the promise represented by youth for the interdependence of human beings within and across generations. His praise for President Kennedy after the assassination and his note to Mrs. Kennedy both struck the theme of youth, the former by recalling Robert Frost as "the old youthful poet" at Kennedy's inauguration and the latter by dedicating the eulogy to Kennedy's son. Kohut's enthusiasm for Arkansas Senator J. William Fulbright was based largely on Fulbright's juxtaposition of the idealism of youthful protestors against the war in Vietnam with the aged cynicism of the war's political and military sponsors.[101] Although Tom recalls that his father at first supported American policy in Southeast Asia, the fact that his own son actively opposed and resisted the war strengthened this idealistic orientation.

Even though Kohut was frequently apart from his family due to travel and work, he cultivated an especially warm relationship with his son and wrote him frequent and loving letters over the last twenty years of his life. Kohut dedicated *The Restoration of the Self* to "G and his generation," that is, to Tom (middle name August, or, familiarly, "Gustl," given in honor of August Aichhorn). Tom might have represented for his father both Telemachus and Odysseus ("the first would-be draft evader in literature"[102]), not only the son but also a father who, unlike Odysseus and Kohut's own father, did not go off to war. The leitmotif here is the preservation of empathic relations, although, sadly, Kohut's dedication to the scientific elaboration of such relations had to claim much of the time he could otherwise have devoted to his own family. Finally, for Tom to become an historian and write a book using in part his father's theories to analyze the psychological basis for the mass appeal Emperor Wilhelm II exercised in leading Germany into war in 1914 describes circles upon circles in the Kohut family history.[103]

Young colleagues like John Gedo, Tilmann Moser, and Arnold Goldberg, among many others, were typical of Kohut's appeal to the youth of his profession to challenge their elders. In 1973 he placed this appeal in the context of the first opera he had ever seen, Richard Wagner's *Die Meistersinger von Nürnberg* (1867). Kohut's father had taken him to see this opera, the reason why Kohut would in turn take his son to see it. Kohut interprets the opera as a lesson in the importance of graceful aging and in the perils for the psychoanalytic community of "tool-and-method pride." What Kohut means by "tool-and-method pride" is the tendency for specialists to exalt means over ends and to ignore or disparage "the creative rebel" in their ranks. Because he felt some conflict over challenging psychoanalytic orthodoxy, conflict reflected in the density of his prose during these years, Kohut does not issue a call to arms, rather he emphasizes the words of hero Hans Sachs in *Die Meistersinger*: "Do not hold the masters in contempt, but [sic] do revere their art!"[104] For while Kohut saw himself as a pioneer with the emotional disposition and cognitive ability "to look at things as if I were seeing them for the first time," he disliked polemics and personal confrontations.

Orthodox psychoanalysts would tend to see in this dual wish to challenge authority yet avoid confrontation an oedipal symptomatology aggravated by the early omnipresence and domination of the mother and the absence of the father during the first five years of life.[105] From this perspective, Kohut's emphasis upon narcissism and the self—as well as his recollection of the distance of *both* his parents—are defense mechanisms against an unresolved Oedipus complex. Such psychodynamics would also have caused resistance to the findings of his training analysis with Ruth Eissler. On the other hand, as Kohut himself put it in his critique of the classical conception of the Oedipus complex:

> Is it not the most significant dynamic-genetic feature of the Oedipus story that Oedipus was a rejected child?...The fact is that Oedipus was not wanted by his parents and that he was put out into the cold by them.[106]

Criticisms of Kohut's theories abound, and the influence of his ideas among psychoanalysts remain severely restricted. There are arguments about whether self psychology can replace the orthodox psychoanalytic paradigm or can be integrated into it, whether narcissistic disorders represent a significant percentage of psychoanalytic cases, the extent to which the "self" itself is an abstraction rather than an experience, and the like. It is not clear what the future holds for the development and influence of Kohut's ideas. But the story of Kohut's life and career reveals the close and fruitful link between the personal and the scientific inherent in the subject matter and method of psychoanalysis. In Kohut we see the conjunction of a special set of early life experiences, an innate brilliance and creativity, and, within the cultural milieu of *fin-de-siècle* Vienna, the unique intellectual and emotional stimulation of psychoanalysis. The curve of Heinz Kohut's life would bear all these lineaments toward new worlds across space, time, and thought.

Notes

1. "Introduction," in Heinz Kohut, *The Curve of Life: Correspondence of Heinz Kohut, 1923–1981*, Geoffrey Cocks, ed. (Chicago, 1994), pp. 1–31. c 1994 by the University of Chicago.
2. Heinz Kohut, *The Search for the Self: Selected Writings of Heinz Kohut*, Paul Ornstein, ed. (Chicago, 1991), 4:594.
3. *Search*, 4:562. Kohut wrongly ascribes this story to Homer. See also Kohut to Chicago Institute librarian Glenn Miller, April 9, 1980. Copies of the professional correspondence cited in this essay are from the Chicago Institute for Psychoanalysis.
4. Ibid., 4:563.
5. Ibid., 4:572.
6. Ibid., 3:331. See also below, April 7, 1977; and March 24, 1981; on Musil, see Kohut to Siegmund Levarie, September 19, 1938.
7. Paul H. Ornstein, "The Unfolding and Completion of Heinz Kohut's Paradigm of Psychoanalysis," in *Search*, 3:10.
8. Peter Gay, *Freud: A Life for Our Time* (New York, 1988), p. 338; "On Narcissism" was published in 1914.
9. Carl E. Schorske, *Fin-de-Siècle Vienna: Politics and Culture* (New York, 1980), pp. 116–80; and see Kohut to Siegmund Levarie, February 21, 1980.
10. William Butler Yeats, "The Second Coming" (1919), *The Collected Poems of W. B. Yeats* (New York, 1956), p. 185.
12. *Search*, (1978) 1:135–58. This was Siegmund Löwenherz who upon arrival in the United States in 1938 Hebraized his name to Levarie (both names meaning "lion heart").
13. David Mitrany, *The Effect of the War in Southeastern Europe* (New Haven, 1936), pp. 83–84, 86, 101, 122.
14. *International Journal of Psycho-Analysis* 60 (1979): 3–27; *Search*, 4:395–446. There is no mention of the case in Kohut's correspondence before 1979 and from then on only scant reference. The case also appears in a revised German

translation of Kohut's *The Restoration of the Self* (New York, 1977). *Die Heilung des Selbst*, trans. Elke vom Scheidt (Frankfurt a. M., 1979), in place of "From the Analysis of Mr. X."; see Kohut to Anita Eckstaedt, October 11, 1975; February 10, 1976; and March 26, 1977; see also discussions of the case beginning in 1978 in Arnold Goldberg, ed., *Advances in Self Psychology* (New York, 1980), pp. 449, 450, 552–3, 511, 513.

15. *Search*, 4:417; see also Kohut, *How Does Analysis Cure?* (Chicago, 1984), pp. 16–17, 148–9; and the similar cases described in *Search*, 3:295, 297–8; and Kohut, *The Analysis of the Self* (New York, 1971), pp. 81–2, 146–7. The radical Emma Goldman (1869–1940) also viewed the "woman as mother...[as] 'the greatest deterrent influence' in the life of her children, treating them as her own possession and robbing her offspring of any independence." Alice Wexler, *Emma Goldman in America* (Boston, 1986), p. 195.

15. *Search*, 4:396.

16. Ibid., 4:417.

17. Ibid.

18. See, for example, Lutz Rosenkötter to Kohut, October 13, 1980.

19. *People*, February 20, 1979, p. 61.

20. *Search*, 2:661; Kohut, *Self Psychology and the Humanities*, Charles B. Strozier, ed. (New York, 1985), p. 24.

21. *Search*, 4:433–6.

22. Kohut to Marquis Biographical Library Society, July 1, 1972.

23. Mark Perlberg, "A New Mirror for Narcissus," *Human Behavior*, February 1977, p. 21.

24. *Search*, 2:771–72. Kohut dedicated his last book, *How Does Analysis Cure?* (1984) to Morawetz and Purkarthofer, but misspells the latter's name.

25. *Search*, 2:663–64; Kohut to Stephan Stewart, October 16, 1957.

26. Steven Beller, *Vienna and the Jews: A Cultural History, 1867–1938* (Cambridge, 1989), pp. 40–53.

27. Kohut himself never made much at all of his Jewish background, although he did once take the opportunity to attend a United Nations Security Council debate on Palestine. See Kohut to August Aichhorn, May 29, 1948. According to Walter Lampl, the Kohut family did not observe the Sabbath, but they did reserve seats at the temple in the Ninth District near Liechtenstein Park. On Yom Kippur, "Felix, observing Jewish religious law and customs, would walk from Paradiesgasse some three miles to attend services. Else would drive her car to the temple's vicinity and walk from there." Walter Lampl, personal communication, March 10, 1993.

28. Susan Quinn, "Oedipus Vs. Narcissus," *New York Times Magazine*, November 9, 1980, p. 120. See also Mitchell G. Ash, "Central European Emigré Psychologists and Psychoanalysts in the United Kingdom," in Julius Carlebach et al., *Second Chance: Two Centuries of German-speaking Jews in the United Kingdom* (Tübingen, 1991), pp. 101–20; and VA K 139. Österreichisches Staatsarchiv, Vienna.

29. Norman Bentwich, "The Destruction of the Jewish Community in Austria 1938–1942," in Josef Fraenkel, ed., *The Jews of Austria: Essays on their Life, History and Destruction* (London, 1967), p. 470.

30. Kohut to Siegmund Levarie, October 5 and 26, 1938. Kohut's Jewish professors were replaced for the exams by Nazi professors.

31. Kohut to Siegmund Levarie, February 14 and June 28, 1939. The elder Löwenherz stayed in Vienna until the end of the war as head of the Jewish Community; see Raul Hilberg, *The Destruction of the European Jews* (Chicago, 1961), p. 292.

32. Kohut to Siegmund Levarie, December 12, 1938; Bentwich, p. 469; and Herbert Rosenkranz, "The Anschluss and the Tragedy of Austrian Jewry 1938–1945," in *The Jews of Austria*, pp. 479–526.

33. On the Kitchener Camp, see Ronald Stent, "Jewish Refugee Organizations," in *Second Chance*, pp. 591–93.

34. Lampl resumed his post as director from 1947–50; see also Kohut to August Aichhorn, February 2, 1947. On Kohut in London, see Kohut to Siegmund Levarie, October 27, 1939.

35. Kohut to Mahler, May 23, 1970.

36. von Witzleben to Kohut, February 23, 1963; Kohut's reply is undated and his original letter to von Witzleben is missing.

37. Walter Neudörfer to Kohut, June 15, 1981.

38. As he wrote to Hertha Firnberg, Austrian Federal Minister for Science and Research, on November 7, 1977: "[T]he values of the Austria that I had known seemed again to come alive and a wound I thought could never heal seemed finally to close." Kohut was also named to honorary membership in the Österreichische Studiengesellschaft für Kinderpsychiatrie: see Kohut to Lore Watzka, July 2, 1976; and Wolfgang Huber, *Psychoanalyse in Österreich seit 1933* (Vienna, 1977), pp. 122, 203.

39. Perlberg, "A New Mirror for Narcissus," p. 18.

40. *Search*, 4:447–48; see also ibid., 4:551–52.

41. *People*, p. 61.

42. Charles Kligerman, "Memorial for Heinz Kohut, M.D., October 31, 1981," *Annual of Psychoanalysis* 12–13 (1985): 12.

43. Quinn, "Oedipus Vs. Narcissus," p. 124. As Betty Kohut has recalled, this recent experience sharpened Kohut's concern over the rabid anti-communism of the postwar years in the United States. Among his letters is an address by University of Chicago Chancellor Robert Maynard Hutchins concerning investigations of communist influence at the school: The University of Chicago Senate, "Annual Report of the Chancellor (Investigation by State Legislature)," May 6, 1949, pp. 1–3.

44. Kohut to Siegmund Levarie, June 25, 1939; Kohut wrote two letters to Levarie in excellent English on September 3 and October 13, 1939. Kohut wanted to serve in the military but only as a doctor. Levarie also was not a citizen, but served in the Pacific from 1945 to 1946: see Kohut to Levarie, March 12, 1945.

45. In 1969 Kohut would resign from the Chicago Neurological Society; Kohut to Joel Brunlik, November 14, 1969. But he remained a lecturer in the University of Chicago Department of Psychiatry from 1958 to 1981; and in 1979 was named an honorary member of the Michael Reese Hospital and Medical Center Department of Psychiatry.

46. See Kohut to August Aichhorn, December 28, 1948; in this letter Kohut reports their great good fortune in finding an apartment in the midst of a severe housing shortage. Before the war Betty Kohut had gone to Vienna to be analyzed and had taken a seminar for pedagogues from Aichhorn; see Kohut to Aichhorn, May 18, 1949.

47. Aichhorn to Kohut, July 23, 1939; this letter was written from Budapest.

48. "Dritte Anordnung auf Grund der Verordnung über die Anmeldung des Vermögens von Juden. Vom 21. Februar 1939," *Reichsgesetzblatt* (1939) I:282.

49. Edward K. Fliegel to Kohut, December 19, 1960; and VA 17.666, VA 37.820, HF-Abg.F. 679, HF-NHF I: Österreichisches Staatsarchiv. The Dorotheum auction house was the place where most of the officially "aryanized" goods from Vienna were brought. See Robert B. Knight, "Restitution and Legitimacy in Post-War Austria," *Leo Baeck Institute Yearbook* 36 (1991): 413–41.

50. Aichhorn to Kohut, November 19, 1946; see also Aichhorn to Kohut, February 19, 1947. After the war the house and Else's store were placed under the trusteeship of an aunt who had survived the war. Else's Citroen C6 automobile was also confiscated; see Verzeichnis über das Vermögen von Juden, July 12, 1938, p. 3, VA K 71/34. Österreichisches Staatsarchiv, Vienna.

51. Kligerman, "Memorial for Heinz Kohut," p. 11.

52. Kohut to Eli Zaretsky, February 14, 1980.

53. Institute for Psychoanalysis Teaching Evaluation, n.d.; see also Janice Norton to Kohut, May 31, 1961; and Ana Marquinez-Castellanos to Kohut, April 9, 1979. While Kohut's written style is often (but not always) dense and complex, his spoken style (reflected in published extemporaneous remarks) is "simple and lyric": Paul Tolpin to Anders Richter, November 28, 1979.

54. Paul H. Ornstein, "The Evolution of Heinz Kohut's Psychoanalytic Psychology of the Self," in *Search* 1:25.

55. *Search*, 1:206.

56. "Journal of the A. Psa. A. re Introspection and Empathy," n.d.

57. *Search*, 3:97, note 3.

58. Emma Harrison, "Analysis Appeals to the Educated," *New York Times*, May 2, 1964, p. 29; see also Kohut, "On the Occasion of Heinz Hartmann's Seventieth Birthday," November 4, 1964, p. 2.

59. *Search*, 1:392.

60. *Search*, 1:395–404. On non-medical training, see *Journal of the American Psychoanalytic Association* 17 (1969): 645.

61. *Search*, 2:772; Kohut, *The Kohut Seminars on Self Psychology and Psychotherapy with Adolescents and Young Adults*, Miriam Elson, ed. (New York, 1987), pp. 31–32.

62. Kohut, *How Does Analysis Cure?*, pp. 87–8.

63. Dr. Robert L. Randall, "First Meeting with Heinz Kohut, M.D., March 22, 1981," p. 5. Such characters inhabit the Chicago novels of Sara Paretsky.

64. Paul H. Ornstein, "From Narcissism to Ego Psychology to Self Psychology," in Joseph Sandler et al., eds., *Freud's "On Narcissism: An Introduction"* (New Haven, 1991), p. 179.

65. Douglas Detrick, "Self Psychology and the Empathic Environment," *The Humanist* 41 (May/June 1981): 28. Polarity was one of the two principles of nature, according to Kohut's beloved Goethe, the other being increase.

66. See Heinz Kohut, "Notes concerning Anna Freud in Chicago; December 1966," December, 1966.

67. Elisabeth Young-Bruehl, *Anna Freud: A Biography* (New York, 1988), p. 440.

68. Anna Freud to Kohut, June 21, 1972.

69. *Search*, 4:412. Since Else's emigration to America, there had always been tensions between her and her son and his wife.

70. Kohut gave a memorial speech at his mother's funeral, but unlike the similar addresses he gave for August Aichhorn, Max Gitelson, and his mother-in-law, Doris Meyer, no copy of the memorial to his mother exists in the correspondence.

71. *Search*, 4:416.

72. Kohut to Frederick Hacker, December 7, 1971; and to Anna Freud, December 25, 1971. See also Kohut to George Pollock, November 14, 1971. In the 1950s Kohut had stopped smoking and started running a mile or more a day; he also played tennis regularly and as a result lost a great deal of weight. See Kligerman, "Memorial for Heinz Kohut," p. 14; and Kohut to Ignazio Matte-Blanco, August 21, 1969.

73. See Kohut to Douglas Levin, June 23, 1979; and to Nathaniel London, July 17, 1979. Ironically, when Kohut was searching unsuccessfully for a letter by Ger-

man heart specialist Karl Friedrich von Wenkebach as a present for his cardiologist he inquired at the same Dorotheum auction house to which his mother had been forced to take the family's valuables in 1939. See Kohut to Dorotheum, December 22, 1980; and for a sunny appraisal, John Dornberg, "Vienna's Dorotheum," *Smithsonian* 21:9 (December, 1990): 110–20.

74. Kohut to Ursula Mahlendorf, October 28, 1979.
75. Kligerman, "Memorial for Heinz Kohut," p. 14.
76. *People*, p. 61. Kohut expressed his reaction to the very brief article that emerged from the time-consuming photographing and interviewing in a letter of February 23, 1979, to his son and daughter-in-law: "What an anticlimax!"
77. Kohut to Tilmann Moser, March 23, 1977; see also a parody that, according to Siegmund Levarie, Kohut enjoyed immensely: Donald Barthelme, "Conversations with Goethe," *New Yorker*, October 20, 1980, p. 49.
78. Ornstein, "Heinz Kohut's Paradigm of Psychoanalysis," p. 2.
79. See also Kohut, *The Restoration of the Self* (New York, 1977), pp. xix–xx. According to the editor and proprietor of the papers of psychoanalyst Erich Siemenauer of Berlin, Siemenauer was privately bitter over what he felt was Kohut's usurping of his position as a pioneer in the research on narcissism. Ludger Hermanns, personal communication, January 21, 1992.
80. *Search*, 4:569; and *Newsweek*, February 27, 1978, p. 11.
81. Kohut to Jerome Oremland, October 9, 1977; to Victor Monke, October 22, 1979; and to University of California, Berkeley, January 22, 1980. Kohut was not interested in writing for the general public: see Kohut to Sydelle Kramer, May 21, 1979. But he was interviewed regularly and once gave a television speech in Italy; Lyda Gairinger to Kohut, October 14, 1969.
82. Kohut to Siegmund Levarie, May 5, 1973.
83. Kohut to Nathaniel London, October 4, 1978.
84. Kohut to Roger Petti, February 17, 1981.
85. *Search*, 4:561.
86. Kohut to Barbara Lantos, May 25, 1955; see also Kohut to Senator Everett Dirksen, June 18, 1968.
87. Lois Timnick, "Rift Threatens Freudian Theory," *Los Angeles Times*, October 27, 1979, p. 2.
88. Kohut, *The Kohut Seminars*, p. 224. As was the case with American object relations specialist Otto Kernberg, Kohut was not in touch with Erikson, although Erikson did attend a session at a self psychology conference; see Anna Ornstein to Kohut, January 31, 1979.
89. Randall, "First Meeting With Heinz Kohut," p. 7.
90. Robert L. Randall, "Second Meeting With Heinz Kohut, M.D.," April 12, 1981, p. 8.
91. Institute for Psychoanalysis, Curriculum Committee, January 13, 1976, p. 1. At this meeting Kohut emphasized that he was now more interested in writing than in teaching and that younger colleagues would have to take the lead in this realm (pp. 2, 3).
92. Ernest Wolf to Heinz Walter, April 15, 1981; see also Kohut to Wolf, July 7, 1978; and to Joris Duytschaever, June 2, 1979.
93. See, for example, Philadelphia Psychoanalytic Institute to Kohut, February 15, 1980; Franco Paparo to Kohut, n.d.; and Tilmann Moser to Kohut, October 25, 1970.
94. Kohut to Fernando Cesarman, March 13, 1981. These conferences have taken place ever since. Kohut's last was the fourth at Berkeley, California in 1981;

the editor's note in *Search*, 4:525, incorrectly identifies this conference as the fifth.

95. Judith Kegan Gardiner, "Self Psychology as Feminist Theory," *Signs* 12 (1987): 767; see also *Search*, 2:783–92; and Arnold Goldberg to Edward Jones, October 1, 1980.

96. See Charles B. Strozier, "Introduction," in *Self Psychology and the Humanities*, pp. xxvii–xxx.

97. Kohut to Selma Kramer, June 13, 1972. See also John E. Gedo, "To Heinz Kohut: On His 60th Birthday," *Annual of Psychoanalysis* 3 (1975): 313–24.

98. George Pollock to Kohut, June 9, 1978. There was outrage expressed over this: see Kay Field to Kohut, June 19, 1978; and Debbie Cardon to Kohut, June 20, 1978.

99. George Pollock to Kohut, July 14, 1981. Faculty emeritus status would follow at age seventy.

100. George Pollock to Kohut, May 29, 1980. Kohut was also subsequently named to Life Membership in the Chicago Psychoanalytic Society; Robert Leider to Kohut, March 9, 1981.

101. On Kohut's own description of his "characteristic.... adolescent idealism," see *Search*, 2:661.

102. *Search*, 4:562.

103. Thomas A. Kohut, *Wilhelm II and the Germans: A Study in Leadership* (New York, 1991).

104. *Search*, 2:691. Siegmund Levarie points out that this line should read: "and do revere their art!" (*und ehrt mir Ihre Kunst*). Kohut's substitution of "but" could be interpreted as an expression of unconscious aggression since that conjunction makes sense with "Hold the masters in contempt." Kohut also manifested a lifelong Germanic and Enlightenment respect for reason, order, authority, and documentation. See his (also narcissistic) concern about CME (Continuing Medical Education) credits for the 1979 UCLA Self Psychology Conference: Kohut to Shulamite Ash, December 20, 1979; and February 14, 1980.

105. Historian Peter Loewenberg has analyzed the drastic political consequences in Germany among less stable and more afflicted individuals of the oedipal dynamics of the conjunction of wartime absence of fathers, malnutrition, and military defeat in "The Psychohistorical Origins of the Nazi Youth Cohort," *American Historical Review* 76 (1971): 1457–1502.

106. *Search*, 4:564; for Kohut's responses to criticism of "The Two Analyses of Mr. Z.," see *Search*, 4:514–20, 570, 573–4, 688–90; and Kohut, *How Does Analysis Cure?*, pp. 84–91.

Part III

Medicine

7

Health, Medicine, and Illness
in Modern Germany[1]

The Third Reich is a black hole in German history. Like hypothetical black holes in space, it draws everything towards itself. At the edges of black holes massive gravitational forces slow time to a stop. Anything falling toward a black hole, therefore, would appear to an observer to fall forever. Similarly, since 1945 historians of Germany have found themselves gripped by the gravity of teleology. The pull exerted by the Third Reich has often led, in the words of Richard Evans, to a view of modern German history "from Hitler to Bismarck."[2] While it was not the aim of the German Historical Institute conference on "Medicine in 19th and 20th-Century Germany: Ethics, Politics, and Law," from which the papers in this volume stem, to detail the already well-documented medical crimes of the Nazis,[3] it was the central purpose of the conference to place the medical crimes and collaborations of the National Socialist era into their larger German and Western contexts. In so doing, the papers, comments, and discussions attempted to pull the history of the Third Reich back into the history of Germany, Europe, and the West, rendering it less of a black entity unto itself than a part of other, broader constellations characterized as much by differentiation as by the historiographical problem of teleology. This very task and result, of course, only underscores the reach and press on German history of the dark gravity of the Third Reich. But the heavy presence of Hitler's Germany also constitutes a vital opportunity for historians—and humanity—to confront the lessons of the German past for the sake of the human present. The weight of moral gravity takes over from that of teleology. This is especially the case with the history of medicine. Questions of health and illness are universal. What is more, the modern history of medicine in the West reaches deeply and broadly into society and culture as well as across national and temporal boundaries. The history of medicine—particularly in regard to the Third Reich—also raises monumental moral questions concerning modern human dispositions of the quality and quantity of life and death. Such lessons and questions have relatively rarely been confronted by physicians themselves. This reticence has been particularly marked at the highest—and oldest—levels of the German medical establishment with respect to the history of their profession between 1933 and 1945. That the German Historical Institute brought together physicians as well as historians from Germany, North America, and Great Britain was especially salutary in helping to counter inertia of this kind. Again like a black hole, the Third Reich has often held light itself in its grip.

Parallel to the problem of teleology in German history lies the historical problem of continuity and discontinuity between the history of the Third Reich and the history of modern Germany as a whole. How does Nazi Germany fit into the history of the Germans and of the German nation? Before, during, and even after the Second World War, this question elicited some rather crude answers. Some charged that Nazism was the inevitable outcome of German society, culture, character, and history. Others contented themselves with the striking though most often shallowly conceived conundrum of the land of Goethe, Beethoven— and Hitler. Still others in the West, deeply influenced by the cold war, equated German National Socialism with Soviet Marxism as manifestations of the uniquely modern form of rule of totalitarianism. Conservative and apologist Germans seized upon this interpretation, among others, to argue that Nazism was an accident in German history occasioned by modern secular revolutionary impulses in Europe. On the other hand, various Marxist models saw European fascism in general as symptomatic of the mortal crisis of late monopoly capitalism.

The predominant postwar paradigm among historians in the West, however, was the liberal idea of the German *Sonderweg* ("special path"). This was the thesis that, unlike France and Britain, Germany during the nineteenth century had not undergone a socially, politically, and economically modernizing bourgeois revolution; this failure allowed pre-industrial feudal elites to lead the country down a uniquely German authoritarian path to Hitler.[4] The issue of the power of the Prussian-German state in particular, therefore, has an important dual quality: not only the matter of government intervention unique in degree and kind to Germany but the *type* of government and the interests of its masters. Since the 1960s, however, historians have generated new varieties of sophisticated questions and answers about the nature of the

Third Reich, its place in the history of Germany, and the course of modern German history as a whole. Many of these findings have come about as a result of work in other periods and aspects of the history of modern Germany. In particular, the study of the various stations and conditions of the modern industrial society Germany had become by the onset of the twentieth century has provided great insight into significant developments up to and through the Third Reich. Arguments over the impact of modernization have therefore been especially important in evaluating the course and consequences of German history in the era of the two World Wars. The "Bielefeld School" used social science methods to refine the *Sonderweg* model of the uniquely German authoritarian divergence from the evolution of modern democracy in the West.[5] Neo-Marxist approaches have been most persistent in posing the questions of the degree to which Germany had in fact undergone a transformation into a bourgeois state and society, the degree to which as a result "feudal" elites were in fact in control, and thus the extent to which it was in fact political and economic liberalism itself that was responsible for the conditions that led to the rise of the Nazis.[6]

Ongoing research into the social, economic, and political complexities of modern German history has significantly qualified both the *Sonderweg* approach and that of its critics. In the history of medicine, issues such as the professionalization of doctors, the "medicalization" of society, the role of the state in medical professionalization, health, and public hygiene, the political battles over health insurance, the relationships between medicine and Nazism before and after 1945, the rise of eugenic thinking, and the places of women and patients all engage the question of the respective roles of a unique German past and of a general Western pattern of development.[7] The various complex functions within the "polycracy" of a somewhat chaotic Nazi party and state, it has been argued,[8] created a continuity of such established systems. Moreover, distinctly modern technical capacities in medicine—as elsewhere—were required by Nazi policy as well as preserved by Nazi political disorder. Medicine and public health in modern Germany in particular have been the subject of critical study for their role in furthering economic, political, and military demands for social productivity (*Leistung*) through the "practical utility" of various prophylactic policies and therapeutic methods.[9] Closer to the black core of Nazi ideology and policy—the singularity, to extend our astrophysical metaphor, of its biological racism and the resultant Holocaust—discontinuity takes on greater, though not exclusive, importance. In all of this, as in other specialized fields of German history, historians of medicine have had to consider the relative importance, particularly with regard to the rise of Nazism, of various traditional junctures: To what extent have longstanding German political, social, and cultural characteristics antedating the nineteenth century played a role? What is the relevance of the founding of a Germany dominated by Prussia in 1871? Or was it more the series of disastrous events after 1914 and 1918 that constituted the more decisive elements?

The history of medicine in general has gone through distinct stages of evolution. In the nineteenth century it displayed a Whiggish orientation that celebrated the advance of enlightened and progressive forces of science and humanitarianism against an ancien regime of obscurantism and persecution. Such histories were in line with the bourgeois ethos of the age, highlighting heroic men clearing away ignorance and helping impose the rational order of freedom upon a chaotic and superstitious society. In the course of the twentieth century, Marxist thought, similarly preoccupied with progress, gradually turned some historians to the history of the proletariat. This tendency, ghettoized politically—and then also geographically during the cold war—eventually contributed to a growing historical interest in social history in reaction to the traditional emphasis upon the ideas and activities of political leaders and cultural elites. Much of the initial interest of historians of Europe centered on the working class, the most numerous class of modern urban industrial society.[11] In the realm of health and illness, research demonstrated the close tie between disease and social class, living conditions, and occupational environment.[12] During the 1950s this historical school was dogmatized in East Germany and ignored in West Germany; it grew in the Federal Republic during the 1960s and was partially suppressed there in the 1970s; increasing academic exchange on the subject across the intra-German border characterized the 1980s; and unification brought even fuller collaboration but also some evaluation and weeding out of Marxist-Leninist historians in the former Democratic Republic.

Increased interest in the history of the middle classes[13] has spurred further work in the history of medicine. Some of this recent research arose from structuralist critiques of the ethos of bourgeois "social control" seen to be manifested in nineteenth-century medicine and in Whiggish accounts of it. Much of the work has concerned itself with the medical profession and in particular the process of its professionalization during the late nineteenth and early twentieth centuries. The subject of professionalization was pioneered by sociologists in the 1930s and 1940s. This early work, however, merely validated "the normative claims of professionals and...linked [them] to the advancement of modernization."[14] Beginning in the 1960s, more critical studies concentrated on the powerful organized self-interest manifested among the professions.[15] Historians of the German professions have highlighted the differences—in particular the greater role of the state in professionalization—as well as the similarities to the Anglo-American model. Historians of Germany have also had to examine the whys and ways of the involvement of professionals with Nazism and the Third Reich, an issue particularly acute in the case of medicine.[16]

Doctors in Germany and Europe during the nineteenth century moved from rather artless dependence upon rich clients toward autonomy based on some degree of specialized knowledge, standardized training, and the growing demand for medical services.[17] The medical profession was also especially affected after 1871 by the social policy of Imperial Germany. Free trade sentiment, particularly among liberal Berlin physicians, had resulted in 1869 in medicine being legally designated by the North German Confederation as a trade rather than as a profession. This allowed doctors to practice almost without any restrictions, but also allowed unlicensed medical practitioners, or "quacks" (*Kurpfuscher*), the same freedom. Many doctors did not welcome this competition and objected as well on scientific grounds to the end of sanctions against quackery. In any case, Bismarck's policy of attempting to disarm Social Democracy through the introduction of state health insurance in 1883 changed the ground upon which doctors in Germany operated. The growth in the number of medical practitioners and "the constant expansion of the medical insurance system had the effect of...making competition keener."[18] An open conflict, unique in kind and degree to Germany, erupted between ever more professionally organized physicians—using union tactics such as boycotts, lockouts, and strikes—and the insurance companies. This, coupled with most doctors' political aversion to increasing socialist control over the *Krankenkassen* system, laid the basis for further rightward radicalization among physicians after 1918.

The growth of the medical profession and of the state health bureaucracy grew into—as well as over—more general social dynamics involving health and illness. The "modernization" of Germany, whatever—like "tradition"—its roughness as a measure, brought with it a "medicalization" of society, that is, "the extension of rational, scientific values in medicine to a wide range of social activities."[19] The growing power and prestige of doctors, and of science in general, tended dangerously to convince many of them—and much of the public—of their expertise in a wide range of social, political, and philosophical matters.[20] But this process was not uniform, unidirectional, or unproblematic, confined to the professional aims of doctors, the ideals of social reformers, or the political and economic aims of elites. Doctors themselves were divided along political and intradisciplinary lines. And the health care system in Germany as a whole, whatever its ultimate or inherent failings, was also possessed of features with contemporary comparative policy implications.[21]

But health and illness in general are matters of complex social influences. The most obvious trend of the nineteenth century was the increase in morbidity—the suffering and dying from chronic illnesses spawned by living and working conditions—over the earlier predominant mortality crises of plagues and epidemics. In Imperial Germany morbidity figures reflected significant short-term social inequality but were revealing not only of the effects of maldistribution of wealth but also of values and attitudes.[22] While people from all social classes and regions sought medical care, there was also resistance and recourse to alternative therapies. In the nineteenth century this stemmed not only from the persistence of traditions and mentalities but also from the fact of medicine's inability to treat and cure most illnesses. In the twentieth century, even though medical therapy eventually made great strides and patient reliance on doctors (and drugs) grew, individuals and groups found reasons to remain skeptical or opposed to modern scientific medicine and the burgeoning state medical bureaucracy.[23] Many, if not most, German doctors subscribed to the notion that "*Der Patient bleibt stumm.*" But the words of George Bernard Shaw in the preface to his play *The Doctor's Dilemma* (1906) applied to Germany as well as to Britain and the West in general:

> The doctor may lay down the law despotically enough to the patient at points where the patient's mind is simply blank; but when the patient has a prejudice the doctor must either keep it in countenance or lose his patient.

There was some basis, for example, for one of the justifications offered by German industry for its preference for its own factory doctors over the free choice of doctors under the state health insurance scheme. Industrialists argued, among other things, that "inexperienced doctors could be fooled by patients and would indulge them because they feared losing them to competition."[24]

Some historians have argued that hygienic values were imposed by ruling elites for purposes of social control. Others maintain that such values more often simply percolate downward[25]—or even upward or at least around—randomly. It is certainly the case, as Richard Evans has shown in his study of cholera in nineteenth-century Hamburg, that powerful economic, social, and political interests could influence or even determine medical policies as well as privilege scientific theories compatible with these interests.[26] And institutions such as hospitals and movements such as that for social hygiene can be locations for the slippery slopes leading from progressive treatment to repressive mistreatment. This perspective has been particularly useful in the subfield of the history of psychiatry since mental illness was regarded as a direct threat to the moral and behavioral order prescribed for modern society.[27] In Germany at the end of the nineteenth century what at the time was labelled "Imperial German psychiatry" displayed an authoritarianism that—somewhat ironically—admitted the ability only to classify rather than treat or cure mental illness.[28] In both medicine and psychiatry in Germany, these ambiguities culminated in the outright evil of exterminatory Nazi eugenics. But even with the atrocious instance of National Socialism, the history of medical treatment as a whole in the Third Reich cannot be reduced to the victimization of patients. Many dominant values and attitudes were internalized by the general population. Even (or especially) under the oppression and exhortation howled out by the Third Reich there were also widespread instances of what sociologist Michel de Certeau has labeled "antidiscipline" created by the "polytheism of scattered practices."[29] Nazi biopolitics made such responses particularly common in matters of health and illness since even in the best of times medical personnel regularly intrude more deeply into people's lives than other official and professional entities.[30]

The history of medicine in Germany has also had to address the sad and ultimately tragic phenomenon of anti-Semitism, specifically the fate of Jewish physicians and patients in the Third Reich.[31] Anti-Semitism among German physicians had been aggravated by a surplus of young doctors waiting to get into the national health insurance system during the Great Depression. The large numbers of Jewish doctors in metropolitan areas such as Berlin, Frankfurt, and Hamburg made them easy scapegoats. In the late nineteenth century Jews had been shunted into less attractive medical specialties such as dermatology and internal medicine which were now more highly developed and in greater demand. Moreover, Jews had long been widely caricatured as obsessed with money and sex, as well as being associated with mental and physical illness.[32] University medical faculties were closed to Jews unless they converted. And while Jewish physicians for the first time received field commissions during the First World War, "[t]he prejudice that no Jew could fit the Prussian ideal of martial masculinity was difficult to dispel."[33] This observation reminds one, among other things, of Fritz Stern's judgment distinguishing Germany in this regard—as in others—from the rest of Europe: "In Germany there was no Dreyfus Affair because there was no Dreyfus."[34]

The study of prejudice and racism in the history of medicine in Germany also provides a link to recent methodological discussions concerning the relative value of linguistic and social science modes of explanation in history. Postmodernism, poststructuralism, and deconstruction have all challenged "the core premises of the Enlightenment project of emancipation—i.e., abstract universalism, the unitary subject, and the (intelligible) social totality."[35] These movements—sometimes known collectively as "the linguistic turn"—argue that "knowledge" is an imposition of the powerful in the absence of any stable meaning "beyond the text." But postmodernist, poststructuralist, and deconstructionist thought all privilege the critical investigator at the expense of theory and subject matter; in this paradigm, it seems, everything but the work of the investigator is subject to the distorting volatility and fullness of language. While the historian must not be naive about knowledge as a function of power, he or she also must not cynically abandon the search for what knowledge can be gained through painstaking thought and research. At the same time, however, the historian must be aware of both the inevitability and—within limits—the utility of retrodiction (the historian's subjective and objective experience) and likewise the uses and limits of theory. And when it comes to National Socialism, how can the historian not know—and not judge—the Nazis through their recorded words and deeds as anything but definitively and irredeemably evil?

But the questioning of the power behind received and created "knowledge" has bolstered an appreciation for different "voices" previously written out of history by the Western "authoritarianism of truth-seeking." While none of the essays in this volume adopts a postmodern approach to its material, much of the subject matter of the essays consists of the "voices" of the previously ignored, undervalued, and victimized: the sick, the mentally ill, the handicapped, women, and ethnic and religious minorities. More generally, the rich and varied subject matter of the history of health and medicine introduce new phenomena into—and new ways of seeing old phenomena in—German history. This increase in the variety of subject matter is a modest but appropriate way of "deconstructing" received truths and categories in German history by way of testing, modifying, enriching, or even confirming them. And the universal human quality of most of the subject matter of the history of medicine easily carries the historian across the many regional boundaries of political, cultural, and (too often) Prussian "Germany." Finally, while recognizing specific German historical contexts, this material has also been consistently comparative, taking the historian across the borders of Germany and back again. This can contribute to what Michael Geyer has deconstructively argued should be on the agenda for historians of Germany: the recognition of the "fragility and permeability of all (and not just the German) national constructions."[36] Geyer maintains that the noisy quests for national unity in the nineteenth century, especially those in Central Europe, were in fact frantic attempts to flee from the "internal heterogeneity of nations" in search of "fictions of...autonomy for the nation and hegemony for Europe."[37]

The ten essays in this volume discuss vital major aspects of the history of medicine in Germany during the nineteenth and twentieth centuries. The essays are arranged in a generally chronological order with essays more or less grouped around shared subject matter: Johanna Bleker and Alfons Labisch both deal with the effects on patient groups of the institutional policy of hospitals and the government, respectively; Richard Evans analyzes the varieties of Social Darwinist thought in Germany before 1930; Charles McClelland and Geoffrey Cocks treat different aspects of the professionalization of medicine; Heinz-Peter Schmiedebach, Paul Lerner, and Gisela Bock all discuss problematic and fateful aspects of the history of psychiatry; and Atina Grossmann and Michael Kater deal in different ways with issues of continuity in the history of medicine in Germany before 1933 and after 1945.

Johanna Bleker's study of hospitals in various regions of Germany in the fifty years before the country's first unification under Prussia argues that hospitals had a number of reasons for being and were not simply a function of the advance of medicine. Hospitals were one means of dealing with the social and economic problems brought by the new migratory labor required by the growth of manufacturing. Hospitals brought advantages and disadvantages to doctors, who were divided over their desirability. The advantages included greater technical capacities and control of patients; among the disadvantages were low pay. The latter was a common phenomenon in Europe in the early nineteenth century, as expressed in the words of Tertius Lydgate, the idealistic young doctor in George Eliot's *Middlemarch* (1873), a novel of England in the 1830s:

> "The highest object to me is my profession, and I had identified the Hospital with the best use I can at present make of my profession. But the best use is not always the same with monetary success. Everything which has made the Hospital unpopular has helped with other causes—I think they are all connected with my professional zeal—to make me unpopular as a practitioner. I get chiefly patients who can't pay me. I should like them best, if I had nobody to pay on my own side."

Lydgate's ambivalent attitude toward the hospital in the fictional town of Middlemarch also suggests Bleker's challenge to the traditional view that hospitals in the nineteenth century were simply places of contagion and oppression that patients avoided. Bleker offers evidence that hospitals more often were sought-after oases from a dangerous life and not just loci for the victimization of helpless patients. Her study is therefore typical of a "third wave" of research in the history of medicine that draws from the "social control" critique of the Whiggish first wave while qualifying or contesting the second wave critique through extensive documentation.[38]

Like Bleker, Alfons Labisch emphasizes the importance of the bourgeoisie's desire to control the newly mobilized industrial and commerical labor force, but the chief concern of his essay is the "political patriarchalism" embodied in Bismarck's health insurance legislation. And while Bleker concentrates more on the dynamics of patients' responses to the policies imposed upon—and created around—them, Labisch focuses on the aims and methods of governmental policymakers. Labisch argues that Bismarck's policy was a peculiarly mercantilist one arising from his *Junker* loyalties and designed to tie the workers to the state instead of to the Social Democratic party or their employers. This was an effort, Labisch says, at "forming society by politics." One discerns in this analysis an emphasis upon traditional Prussian forms and attitudes that would seem to argue for the uniqueness of the German experience under Bismarck. The question is how decisive a role the reactionary aims and institutions of Bismarckian political and social policy played in the evolution of an increasingly industrialized state and society before 1914. At the very least, one can draw instructive contrasts to the history of medicine in other countries. It is clear, for example, that doctors in Germany were in the position of having to face (and exploit) an established state policy in the realm of health care, while elsewhere in Europe and in the United States, the state had to confront independently mobilized physicians advancing and securing their interests and control over the medicalization of society.

Richard Evans' essay on the historiography of Social Darwinism in Germany underlines the relatively recent mainstream consensus among historians that Social Darwinism was from its origins in the late nineteenth century a politically and philosophically variegated phenomenon. According to this view, the radical and racist varieties of Social Darwinism that presaged and animated the Nazis were in the minority and were only a part of a "transition from evolutionism to selectionism, from left to right, in the 1890s." Evans critiques various versions of and challenges to this consensus, arguing that the most important issue is why the authoritarian and racist variety won out; for Evans, this eventual if temporary ascendancy was due to more than just the consequences of Nazi political victory in 1933. Until 1914 varieties of Social Darwinist thinking persisted among Social Democrats, Pan-Germans, and the emergent "racial hygienists." This last group had a major effect on what Evans calls "the welfarist discourse" before World War I. But, according to Evans, it took the slaughter of the war and the crises of the 1920s and 1930s to radicalize theory and practice along selectionist lines. More generally, Evans sees German history as much more than a prologomena to Hitler even in one of the realms of the history of ideas and of professional and public discouse often most closely identified with the roots of Nazi ideology.

Charles McClelland analyzes the professionalization of doctors in Germany during the first thirty years of the twentieth century. McClelland argues that there was no specifically German "fatal flaw" in this process. Rather, corporatist characteristics inherent in the structure of modern professions combined with a series of economic disruptions and political reverses after the First World War to make National Socialism an attractive political option for many doctors. McClelland labels this process "interrupted professionalization" and not evidence for the inevitable evils of professionalization *per se* and also not peculiar to the German experience of it. This interpretation differs from that of Konrad Jarausch who sees a problematic "neo-corporatist" strain of professionalization across all the professions in Germany. This arose, according to Jarausch, out of a more general tradition of illiberalism and a bourgeois shift from liberalism to nationalism during the German Empire.[39] Michael Kater, on the other hand, has emphasized discrete qualities of the culture and history of modern Germany by concentrating on certain characteristics, such as political conservatism, anti-Semitism, militarism, and male chauvinism, which he argues were common among German doctors. When combined with the military disaster that befell the German Empire in the First World War and the economic and political crises that bedeviled the Weimar Republic after the war, these attitudes made many doctors receptive to the prejudices of the Nazis as well as to their promises.[40]

Heinz-Peter Schmiedebach investigates the social place of the mental patient as determined by the interests both of the state and of psychiatrists. Psychiatry was a creation of the nineteenth century: Johann Christian Reil of Halle coined the term "psychiatry" in 1808. Schmiedebach examines "the social construction of mental illness through psychiatry and the asylum. The great theoretical and practical divide among German psychiatrists in the nineteenth century was between "mentalists," who argued for psychological causation and treatment, and "somaticists," who believed that mental illness was physical in origin. Schmiedebach shows, however, that both sides shared a conservative moral view of their patients. The mentalists wished to create "self-discipline" in their charges while the somaticists imposed a "patriarchal philanthropism." In addition, Schmiedebach maintains, psychiatrists became ever more tractable when it came to government priorities, chiefly because of concern for their professional fortunes. The "therapeutic activism" of mid-century was gradually replaced by official insistence upon social order in the face of the growing urban masses and as a result of "therapeutic nihilism" among psychiatrists.[41] By the turn of the century, according to Schmiedebach, psychiatry was being significantly influenced by eugenic thought and the dual concern of the state over the cost of housing the mentally ill and cultivating the maximum number of men for labor and war. These trends culminated in the mass starvation of mental patients in German asyla during the First World War.[42] And while more beneficent policies made headway under the Weimar Republic, these measures were doomed by the Great Depression. There was also a tragically ironic effect of distinguishing the curable from the incurable: for the latter, sterilization was an increasingly attractive alternative to psychiatrists and bureaucrats even before 1933.[43]

Paul Lerner focuses on the treatment of war neuroses during the First World War. While army psychiatrists were initially overwhelmed by the number and nature of what was at first called "shell shock," a variety of relatively effective treatment modalities were quickly developed and deployed. The traditional somaticist point of view insisted that these disorders were organic. But the psychogenic school of thought, which had been gaining adherents since the turn of the century, predominated over the course of the war. This was due largely to the efficacy of its various methods in returning soldiers to battle and reducing the pension obligations of the government. Lerner documents a significant degree of differentiation among psychiatrists in the first two decades of the twentieth century. While there were complaints about the brutality of some of the methods, in particular Kaufmann's electrotherapy, the "therapeutic turn" of the war years laid the basis for a psychiatric reform movement during the 1920s. These reforms were of course cut short by economic and poltical catastrophe at the end of the decade, but Lerner also documents the social ambiguities of psychiatric therapies in and of themselves as agents both of healing and of control.

Gisela Bock seeks to place Nazi forced sterilization and "euthanasia" policies in the overall context of German history. In so doing, she offers a nuanced examination of the imporatant historiographical issues. Some scholars see Nazi race hygiene as part of a process of modernization and rationalization; others view it in terms not of the outgrowth of modernization but of a crisis within it. Bock also weighs the arguments for the importance of ideas ("intentionalist") versus structure ("functionalist") in the implementation of Nazi racial policy. Finally, she considers the question of the historical origins of this policy: Early or late nineteenth century? The First World War? Or 1933? Bock argues that the crucial transitions occurred with the First World War and the Nazi assumption of power in 1933. Although she notes the fact that most of the agents of "euthanasia" under National Socialism came from the ranks of "progressive" doctors, Bock argues that Nazi policies can be more effectively viewed in ethical terms than in the terms of modernization, a theme taken up in conference discussions about the lack of ethics instruction in German medical education past and present. According to Bock, there are distinct continuities in this history but also distinct discontinuities. The crucial issues for Bock are: (1) the Nazi introduction of compulsion into the realm of social engineering; and (2) individual decisions one way or the other when it came to crossing ethical boundaries in the treatment of other human beings as "valuable" or as "unworthy."

My own essay attempts to place the actions of the doctors tried at Nuremberg for medical crimes into the larger contexts of German and Western history before and after 1945. I argue that much of what motivated the doctors who carried out experiments on concentration camp inmates during the Second World War arose from various conditions set by the social place of medicine in modern Germany and the West. The Nuremberg Doctors' Trial is significant not simply as a further revelation of Nazi atrocities, of the successes and failures of international justice, or of the moral choices made or not made by doctors in Germany and, subsequently, by doctors in service to other nations at other times. The trial tells us a great deal about the historical contexts and structures of the history of medicine in modern German society and the West. And it also offers us a chance to reevaluate the place of German history in the history of the West. I attempt to show that an evolving corporate ethic peculiarly strong in Germany and especially evident among professionals was aggravated by Nazi policies and the military exigencies of the Second World War. The medicalization of German society during the twentieth century advanced but also complicated the position of doctors, patients, and the public health system. These complications were worsened by a series of genuine and perceived health crises as a result of military, political, and economic crisis after 1914. The Nazis in turn intensified official and popular concern with matters of actual and "racial" health while their policies of mobilization and war further aggravated problems of health and illness among almost all segments of the population.

The final two essays also extend their analysis into the years after 1945. Atina Grossmann discusses the history of abortion in Germany from the late Weimar period through the Third Reich and the immediate postwar years and into the era of the two German republics. She shows that there has been significant continuity in German public policy concerning abortion, in particular a tendency to see abortion not in terms of individual (women's) rights but rather in terms of social and economic conditions or of individual "fitness." Attempts by feminists and communists in the late Weimar period to change the law criminalizing most abortions were defeated and the Nazi government toughened the law against abortions for "Aryans" while advocating and even compelling abortions for women of "inferior" quality. In 1945 both the government of the collapsing Third Reich and postwar Allied administrations suspended the law to allow abortions for women who had been raped by Red Army soldiers. In the Soviet zone, reform of the law was pursued, although the underlying rationale of collective welfare prepared the way for the recriminalization of abortion in 1950. In 1972 the Democratic Republic relegalized abortion while also increasing pro-natalist benefits. Abortion remained illegal in the Federal Republic and reunification has left the issue a source of both compromise and conflict, with doctors continuing to play a major role in an ambiguous legal environment.

Michael Kater closes the volume with a detailed examination of the so-called Sewering scandal of 1993. Like many of the preceding studies, Kater's essay documents a continuity of personnel across traditional divides, in this case the oft-presumed chasm of 1945. And while Nazi racial policies were abandoned, Kater also shows that the conservative political and social culture of the Federal Republic permitted and even encouraged the persistence of provincialism and old prejudices as well as perpetrating a blindness to the moral lessons of the immediate past and a concomitant tolerance—and even indulgence—of former Nazis. Recent research in the history of medicine in Germany—such as that presented at the German Historical Institute conference—has documented the major role played by doctors in all realms of the Third Reich. This knowledge renders the longstanding unwillingness of the German medical profession in particular to examine critically its own past that much more regrettable and reprehensible.

At the end of this book, therefore, we return to its beginning. The reticence of the German medical profession to acknowledge deeply troubling dimensions to its past testifies to the morally and intellectually darkening gravity of the Third Reich in German history. Against such inertia, historians like those whose work is contained in this volume must continue to bring to bear the weight of concerned and effective scholarship.

Notes

1. "Introduction," in Manfred Berg and Geoffrey Cocks, eds., *Medicine and Public Health and Medical Care in 19th and 20th Century Germany* (Cambridge, 1996). Reprinted with permission of Cambridge University Press.
2. Richard J. Evans, "From Hitler to Bismarck: 'Third Reich' and Kaiserreich in Recent Historiography," *Historical Journal* 26 (1983): 485–97, 999–1020.
3. See, among others, Alexander Mitscherlich and Fred Mielke, *Wissenschaft ohne Menschlichkeit: Medizinische und Eugenische Irrwege unter Diktatur, Burokratie und Krieg* (Heidelberg, 1949); Alice Platen-Hallermund, *Die Tötung Geisteskranker in Deutschland* (Frankfurt am Main, 1948); Robert Jay Lifton, *The Nazi Doctors: Medicalized Killing and the Psychology of Genocide* (New York, 1986); and Robert N. Proctor, *Racial Hygiene: Medicine Under the Nazis* (Cambridge, Mass., 1988).

4. Ralf Dahrendorf, *Society and Democracy in Germany* (Garden City, 1967); Jürgen Kocka, "Ursachen des Nationalsozialismus," *Aus Politik und Zeitgeschichte*, June 21, 1980, pp. 9–13.

5. Hans-Ulrich Wehler, *Das deutsche Kaiserreich 1871–1918* (Göttingen, 1973).

6. Geoff Eley, "What Produces Fascism: Pre-Industrial Traditions or A Crisis of the Capitalist State?" in idem, *From Unification to Nazism: Reinterpreting the German Past* (Boston, 1986), pp. 254–82; David Blackbourn and Geoff Eley, *The Peculiarities of Germany History: Bourgeois Society and Politics in Nineteenth-Century Germany* (New York, 1984).

7. On comparative policy implications, see Donald W. Light and Alexander Schuller, eds., *Political Values and Health Care: The German Experience*, MIT Press Series on the Humanistic and Social Dimensions of Medicine, 4 (Cambridge, Mass., 1986).

8. Peter Hüttenberger, "Nationalsozialistische Polykratie," *Geschichte und Gesellschaft* 2 (1976): 417–42.

9. Michael Hubenstorf, "'Aber es kommt mir doch so vor, als obs Sie dabei nichts verloren hätten.' Zum Exodus von Wissenschaftlern aus den staatlichen Forschungsinstituten Berlins im Bereich des öffentlichen Gesundheitswesens," in Wolfram Fischer et al., eds., *Exodus von Wissenschaften aus Berlin: Fragestellungen—Ergebnisse—Desiderate; Entwicklungen vor und nach 1933*, Akademie der Wissenschaften zu Berlin Forschungsbericht 7 (Berlin, 1994), pp. 368–9, 448; Alfons Labisch, *Homo Hygienicus: Gesundheit und Medizin in der Neuzeit* (Frankfurt, 1992), p. 133.

10. Marxist historiography was no less a bourgeois heir of the Enlightenment in its preoccupation with progress. The only difference was that while liberals saw the bourgeoisie as a means to the future through its ongoing success, Marxists saw the bourgeoisie as a means to the future through its ultimate failure.

11. For an early classic example of the genre, see E.P. Thompson, *The Making of the English Working Class* (New York, 1964).

12. Dirk Blasius, "Geschichte und Krankheit: Sozialgeschichtliche Perspektiven der Medizingeschichte," *Geschichte und Gesellschaft* 2 (1976): 386–415.

13. See, for example, Peter Gay, *The Bourgeois Experience: Victoria to Freud*, 4 vols. (New York, 1984–96).

14. Konrad Jarausch, "The German Professions in History and Theory," in Geoffrey Cocks and Jarausch, eds., *German Professions, 1800–1950* (New York, 1990), pp. 9–10.

15. See, for example, Margaret S. Larson, *The Rise of Professionalism* (Berkeley, 1977); and Paul Starr, *The Social Transformation of American Medicine* (New York, 1982).

16. Claudia Huerkamp, "The Making of the Modern Medical Profession, 1800–1914: Prussian Doctors in the Nineteenth Century," in *German Professions*, pp. 66–84.

17. Claudia Huerkamp, *Der Aufstieg der Ärzte im 19. Jahrhundert. Vom gelehrten Stand zum professionellen Experten: Das Beispiel Preussens* (Göttingen, 1985).

18. Charles E. McClelland, *The German Experience of Professionalization: Modern Learned Professions and Their Organizations from the Early Nineteenth Century to the Hitler Era* (Cambridge, 1991), p. 86.

19. Paul Weindling, "Medicine and Modernization: The Social History of German Health and Medicine," *History of Science* 24 (1986): 277.

20. See, for example, Eric J. Engstrom, "Emil Kraepelin and Public Affairs in Wilhelmine Germany," *History of Psychiatry* 2 (1991): 111–32; cf. Robert M. Veatch, "Scientific Expertise and Value Judgments: The Generalization of

Expertise," *Hastings Center Studies* 1:2 (1973): 20–40; and Max Weber, "Wissenschaft als Beruf" (1918), in idem, *Gesammelte Aufsätze zur Wissenschaftslehre* (Tübingen, 1922), pp. 524–55.

21. See, for example, Jane Caplan, *Government without Administration: State and Civil Service in Weimar and Nazi and Nazi Germany* (New York, 1988).

22. Reinhard Spree, *Health and Social Class in Imperial Germany: A Social History of Mortality, Morbidity and Inequality*, trans. Stuart McKinnon and John Halliday (Oxford, 1988).

23. Edward Shorter, *Bedside Manners: The Troubled History of Doctors and Patients* (New York, 1985); for the effects among former soldiers, for example, see Robert Weldon Whalen, *Bitter Wounds: German Victims of the Great War, 1914–1939* (Ithaca, 1984); and Jame M. Diehl, *The Thanks of the Fatherland: German Veterans after the Second World War* (Ithaca, 1993).

24. Martin H. Geyer, *Die Reichsknappschaft: Versicherungsreform und Sozialpolitik im Bergbau 1900–1945* (Munich, 1987), p. 239.

25. Norbert Elias, *The Civilizing Process*, trans. Edmund Jephcott (New York, 1978).

26. Richard J. Evans, *Death in Hamburg: Society and Politics in the Cholera Years, 1830–1910* (Oxford, 1987).

27. Klaus Doerner, *Madmen and the Bourgeoisie: A Social History of Insanity and Psychiatry*, trans. Joachim Neugroschel and Jean Steinberg (Oxford, 1981); Michel Foucault, *Madness and Civilization: A History of Insanity in the Age of Reason*, trans. Richard Howard (New York, 1965); Roy Porter and Mark Micale, "Reflections on Psychiatry and Its Histories," in idem, eds., *Discovering the History of Psychiatry* (New York, 1994), pp. 3–36.

28. Hannah S. Decker, *Freud in Germany: Revolution and Reaction in Science, 1893–1907* (New York, 1977), pp. 50–53.

29. Michel de Certeau, *The Practice of Everyday Life*, trans. Steven Rendall (Berkeley, 1984), p. 47; see also Richard J. Evans, "In Pursuit of the Untertanengeist: Crime, Law and Social Order in German History," in idem, *Rethinking German History* (London, 1987), pp. 156–87.

30. Geoffrey Cocks, "Partners and Pariahs: Jews and Medicine in Modern German Society, " *Leo Baeck Institute Yearbook* 36 (1991): pp. 191–206; see also Fridolf Kudlien, "Bilanz und Ausblick," in Johanna Bleker and Norbert Jachertz, eds., *Medizin im "Dritten Reich"*, 2nd ed. (Cologne, 1993), pp. 222–8; and Geoffrey Cocks, *Psychotherapy in the Third Reich: The Göring Institute* (New York, 1985).

31. Michael H. Kater, "Unresolved Questions of German Medicine and Medical History in the Past and Present," *Central European History* 25 (1992): pp. 407–23.

32. Sander L. Gilman, "Jews and Mental Illness: Medical Metaphors, Anti-Semitism, and the Jewish Response," *Journal of the History of the Behavioral Sciences* 20 (1984): 150.

33. Kater, "Unresolved Questions," p. 414.

34. Fritz Stern, "The Burden of Success: Reflections on German Jewry," in idem, *Dreams and Delusions: The Drama of German History* (New York, 1987), p. 108.

35. Jane Caplan, "Postmodernism, Poststructuralism, and Deconstruction: Notes for Historians," *Central European History* 22 (1989): p. 201.

36. Michael Geyer, "Historical Fictions of Autonomy and the Europeanization of National History," *Central European History* 22 (1989): p. 341.

37. Ibid., pp. 316, 341, 317.

38. For another example of this type of research, see W.F. Bynum et al., eds., *The Anatomy of Madness: Essays in the History of Psychiatry*, 2 vols. (London, 1985).

39. Konrad H. Jarausch, *The Unfree Professions: German Lawyers, Teachers, and Engineers, 1900–1950* (New York, 1990), pp. 22–4, 220–1.
40. Michael H. Kater, *Doctors Under Hitler* (Chapel Hill, 1989).
41. Bernd Walter, "Fürsorgepflicht und Heilungsanspruch: Die Überforderung der Anstalt? (1870–1930)", in Franz-Werner Kersting et al., eds., *Nach Hadamar: Zum Verhältnis von Psychiatrie und Gesellschaft im 20. Jahrhundert* (Paderborn, 1993), pp. 66–97.
42. Approximately 40,000 mental patients starved to death under the Vichy government in France during World War II; see Max Lafont, *L'Extermination douce* (Nantes, 1987). On the German case in the First World War, see Hans-Ludwig Siemen, *Die Menschen blieben auf der Strecke…Psychiatrie zwischen Reform und Nationalsozialismus* (Gütersloh, 1987), pp. 29–30. More research needs to be done to determine the extent to which the starvation of German mental patients in World War I was motivated out of eugenic considerations or was the "logical" extension of general popular privation to the asyla.
43. Hans-Ludwig Siemen, "Die Reformpsychiatrie der Weimarer Republik: Subjektive Ansprüche und die Macht des Faktischen," in *Nach Hadamar*, pp. 98–108.

8

Partners and Pariahs:
Jews and Medicine in Modern
German Society[1]

On October 2, 1936, a headline in an English newspaper announced: "Hitler Needs Jewish Doctors." The short article underneath claimed that there was such a shortage of doctors in Germany that the Nazi regime was offering an "amnesty" to émigré Jewish physicians who would return for training with the army medical corps.[2] As we shall see, this particular report and others like it in the foreign press before and during the war were surely far from accurate. Jews did continue to play a role in German medicine even after 1933, primarily of course as victims of a longstanding cultural bias raised to deadly virulence by the newer racism of the Nazis. But the place and image of Jews in German medicine even in the Third Reich was also determined by historical factors that had helped shape the reality of Jewish and non-Jewish doctors and patients in Germany during the late nineteenth and early twentieth centuries. Chief among these factors were the professionalization of medicine and the evolving social dynamics of illness and health. Actual attempts by agencies in Nazi Germany to exploit Jewish medical expertise, efforts fabricated, exaggerated, and distorted abroad between 1936 and 1944, thus assume importance not as meaningful modifications of Nazi policy nor of diminution of the historical significance of German anti-Semitism but as part of the ongoing social history of medicine in Germany, a history in which Jews had served as partners as well as pariahs.

Almost half a century before, on January 12, 1881, pathologist and medical reformer Rudolf Virchow spoke to a gathering of liberal politicians in Berlin on the dangers to Germany posed by the growing anti-Semitic movements of the day. In spite of what he saw as the gravity of the situation, Virchow closed his address on an optimistic note: "I have spoken candidly and have, I think, caused as little damage as possible, just like a doctor in examining a wound. But I believe a thorough examination is vital and will bear fruit."[3] This speech was reprinted in 1936 in the *Internationales Aerztliches Bulletin*, the journal of German socialist physicians exiled to Prague, as part of that organization's attempts to combat the Nazi regime by revealing the atrocities and absurdities of the Third Reich's medical and health policies.[4] Of course the editors of the *IAeB* could not know what we know about the ultimate result of the Nazi campaign against the Jews. The Holocaust justly and inevitably throws a deep shadow across any history of the Jews in the lands of Central Europe during the last two centuries, but in so doing poses problems of teleology for historians. As Michael Ignatieff has put it, "In no field of historical study does one wish more fervently that historians could write history blind to the future."[5] This is a problem generally for historians of modern Germany, creating a view of German history, in the words of Richard Evans, "From Hitler to Bismarck."[6] While such a view is fruitful in terms of exploring certain of the continuities in German history, it also characterizes the problem of teleology created by the shattering impact of the Nazi era. And finally, as Henry Friedlander has recently observed, the special need for commemoration of the victims of Nazi genocide threatens in some instances to become a substitute for rigorous historical investigation of the subject.[7]

When it comes to the subject of anti-Semitism and the medical profession in Germany, one finds the optimism of Virchow ultimately unfounded. An investigation into the history of anti-Semitism in the German medical profession from the late 1800s to 1945 does not, however, reveal a simple augmentation of undifferentiated prejudice but rather a set of complex dynamics congruent with the view of German history won by the most recent studies in the history of German society both before and after 1933. Certain crucial "peculiarities" of German history also persisted within the ranks of doctors. Thus while this history instructs us in the "illiberal" features of liberalism (in the case of medicine the consequences of "interventionism" in social problems), it also reminds us of the effects of the special tradition of "illiberalism" in Germany. As Fritz Stern has put it in the case of anti-Semitism in the German officer corps, "In Germany there was no Dreyfus Affair because there was no Dreyfus."[8] Moreover, the history of anti-Semitism in the medical profession is not only a history of the nature, degree, and incidence of a widely held prejudice, but it is also the history of

Jews and their involvement in the medical profession in Germany as doctors, patients, and fellow citizens or, after 1933, noncitizens. In turn, any account of the members of the medical profession must be placed in the context of the social history of health and illness. This is especially the case, as we shall see, with the Third Reich, not only because the 1930s and 1940s were decades of crucial change in the social place of medicine, health, and illness in Germany and elsewhere but also because of both the charged absence and presence of Jews in this context as reality and as image, both Nazi and otherwise.

While anti-Semitism has been a consistent feature of Western civilization, its ferocity has ebbed and flowed. It was particularly strong in Europe between 1880 and 1945 due to a number of conditions, chief among which was the force of nationalism and which in Germany assumed a reactionary *völkisch* cast. The change prompted the Jewish ophthalmologist Julius Hirschberg, who was born in Potsdam in 1843, to recall from a twentieth-century vantage point his youth as a time "when anti-Semitism had not yet been invented."[9] Whatever discrimination Jews had faced before the late nineteenth century that revealed the cultural majoritarian bias of the emancipation effected during the Enlightenment, the first half of the new century in particular was to manifest a pervasiveness of discrimination and virulence of hatred against the Jews perhaps unparalleled in all of history. That this development was accompanied and to a significant degree accelerated by unprecedented Jewish assimilation and success in many fields, especially in Germany, is a particularly important factor to keep in mind when studying anti-Semitism in the professions.

To characterize this period as one of increased anti-Semitic prejudice is not to say that the anti-Semitic attitudes and policies of the Nazis were the logical, much less inevitable, outcome of this trend. Recent research has revealed the great variety of approaches to the "Jewish problem" in Germany, views falling basically into three groupings, those favoring assimilation, those advocating segregation, and those espousing expulsion. Although there is division over the question of a fundamental dichotomy between the traditional Christian bias of the majority and that of the racist minority or whether there were more complex connections across the borders of the three basic groupings, there is now widespread agreement that anti-Semitism in Germany was a complex phenomenon not reducible to the notion of it as a "rehearsal for destruction."[10] As Peter Gay has put it in terms of Theodor Fontane's description of German cultural attitudes toward Jews, "evidence was...mixed: favorable in large part, ominous in small details."[11] At the same time, however, one of course cannot argue that previous bias was unrelated to the versions of anti-Semitism displayed by Hitler and the Nazis.[12] Indeed, the very pervasiveness and variety of anti-Semitic attitudes among the German populace would allow for acquiescence in or indifference to, if not wholehearted support for, the anti-Semitic policies of the Nazis, especially since the Nazis were adept at presenting vague and flexible promises that appealed to the complaints and ambitions of a wide variety of individuals across the social and political spectrum. And the crises after 1914 served to shake up the already somewhat murky waters of German social morality, tragically depositing the sediment at the top.

Not only was anti-Semitism socially pervasive as well as variable in its origins and forms, it was always coupled with other concerns or discontents specific to the individual or group involved. Its occasion and virulence was also situational, as with the search for scapegoats during hard times or, as in the case of the opportunistic psychotherapists who in 1933 emphasized their alleged independence from "Jewish" psychoanalysis in the face of attacks from rival psychiatrists, manipulated[13] for protection or advantage. The professions in general were an important arena for these attitudes, since it was during the late nineteenth and early twentieth centuries that professions emerged alongside class and caste as powerful elements in a modernizing German society and economy. And Jews played a particularly important role in this realm, especially in the "free professions" such as law and medicine that, unlike the traditional Christian strongholds of the officer corps, the high judiciary, and the bureaucracy, were open to Jews. Like the English Dissenter and the French Protestant, the German Jew "filled the functions which society abandoned to him."[14] The same principle applied to the concentration of Jews in medical specialties such as dermatology and internal medicine that grew in technical sophistication and thus in importance and came to be in increasing demand in the urban centers of Germany.[15]

Although the number of Jews entering the medical profession declined at the end of the nineteenth century and their advancement on university medical faculties remained hindered, Jews were overrepresented in medicine by a factor of ten: in 1933 Jews of Mosaic faith constituted 0.76 percent of the Reich population, about 10 percent of the physicians in Germany, and between 30 and 40 percent of the doctors in Berlin.[17] After the First World War, doctors faced a series of "very specific dislocations,"[18] including an oversupply of medical students, the lack of state acknowledgment as a profession, and the depredations of "socialized medicine" seen by many doctors as oppressive, inefficient, politicized, and leftist. Jews tended to be prominent in the health insurance (*Krankenkasse*) system and in socialist politics in general due to their general commitment to social justice, their predominantly urban location, and, once again, the function of a type of *Lückentheorie* in terms of social and professional opportunity.[19] Thus Jews tended to become both specific and general targets of disaffected doctors caught in changing social, economic, and political conditions. One fateful result of all of this was the membership after 1933 of as many as 45 percent of all physicians in the Nazi party.[20] This is one instance of what Fritz Stern has called the German Jews' "burden of success."

But the German medical profession was susceptible to the blandishments of the Nazis for other reasons as well, reasons that, if anything, were even more fateful, especially for Jewish doctors and Jews in general, in terms of the policies of the Third Reich. The most dangerous trend within medicine and the biological sciences in Germany and the West as a whole during this era was that of "biologism," the certainty that human problems could be definitively solved by the application of ruthless biological principles.[21] Social Darwinism and the eugenics movement were symptoms of a way of thinking that was strengthened in Germany by the *völkisch* movement. Coupled with the growing technical sophistication, influence, and power of the scientific professions and the tendency of doctors in particular to engage in "the generalization of expertise,"[22] this trend aggravated the tendency of professionalism to exalt expertise at the expense of ethics. This, according to Rainer Baum, is "the nature of modern sin, the withdrawal of moral concerns from public roles in our lives."[23] Moreover, there was a long tradition in Europe of associating Jews in particular with both healing and illness.[24] Psychiatry was especially prone to the vague categorizations that cultivated prejudice,[25] although it resembled medicine in general in its emphasis on the relatively "quick fix" of individual treatment instead of the more complex gradualism of social reform. With the "medicalization" of society in the late nineteenth century, doctors became "a social group under the greatest possible pressure to emphasize the useful."[26] This technical orientation toward the problems and responsibilities of the individual was attractive to political forces of both left and right committed to crash programs in the spirit of the "culture of impatience."[27] Finally, as Susan Sontag has argued, during the nineteenth century disease became a powerful metaphor for the "unnatural,"[28] which in the twentieth century combined with racial anti-Semitism to produce an especially noxious pattern of thought and action. One has only to look at the disease imagery that oozes over the pages of *Mein Kampf* to appreciate the danger inherent in this turn.

We do not yet have detailed studies of the relative incidence of anti-Semitism within the various branches of medicine or of the relevant mixes of religious, regional, generational, or social and economic backgrounds among doctors. We also do not know with precision the differences in attitudes between city and countryside. While collaboration and competition with the many Jewish medical practitioners in the large cities, especially Berlin, could in general lead either to resentment or admiration, rural provincialism and ethnocentrism were probably aggravated as the spread of the transportation and media networks in Germany generated impressions, even in advance of the propaganda of the Nazis, of urban life as corrupt, debilitating, and embodied in the figure of the Jew.[29] Case studies will go some way toward filling this gap, since anti-Semitism varied within a shared cultural context in nature, degree, and function from individual to individual, as, for example, Peter Loewenberg has shown in his psychohistorical analysis of Heinrich Himmler.[30]

What a majority of German physicians displayed at the advent of the Third Reich, however, was ambition, a fear of deprofessionalization as a result of the economic and political woes of Weimar, and a specifically strong German tradition of illiberalism. This last element, combined with the powerful force of a German nationalism characterized by a bellicosity born of particularist doubt and geopolitical anxiety, had for a long time torn at the liberal qualities associated with professional culture and had produced the "unpolitical" disdain for representative government[31] that accompanied their very real political activity on the level of their own professional interests. These motives played an important role in the activities of doctors under National Socialism, since, as recent research has shown, *Gleichschaltung* was very often a process of "self-nazification" pursuant to advantage or protection within a polycentric power system.[32] Thus anti-Semitism was one element among many determining the attitudes and actions of physicians in Nazi Germany. It was an important element, however, since there is evidence to suggest that denunciations of Jews, while common throughout the social spectrum, were most common among the members of the new middle classes and especially those groups of ambitious people with much to lose and much to gain.[34]

Since the record of doctors in abandoning and persecuting their Jewish colleagues and patients is a well known and dismal one and the involvement of doctors in the euthanasia program and the Final Solution has become increasingly well understood, it is my purpose here to concentrate on a specific issue in an area of life in the Third Reich where factors other than murderous intent played important roles. Although this subject matter is minor when compared to the role of doctors in tolerating and effecting the Nazi policy of genocide against the Jews, it is not simply a matter of recording exceptions and anomalies, such as the odd case of risky patient loyalty to a Jewish physician[35] or I.G. Farben's use of the name of a famous Jewish medical researcher, Paul Ehrlich, in its advertising abroad.[36] Rather my concern is with what may have been attempts on the part of a number of agencies between 1936 and 1944 to employ Jewish physicians, both full Jews and so-called *Mischlinge*, to treat German soldiers and civilians and the possible part such a policy might have played in the shaping of both the image and reality of the Jewish physician in the context of the larger social history of health and illness in Nazi Germany.

Although by September 1938 all doctors who were full Jews or Mosaic half-Jews had been decertified, the army in particular continued to worry about the shortage of physicians in the event of war. As we have seen, there was at least one foreign report of this as early as 1936. Just after the outbreak of the war the *Manchester Guardian* reported that Jewish doctors had already been drafted into the German army and that the appeal for Jewish doctors, in particular specialists, to return had been renewed.[37] While these particular reports may reflect a distorting concern over the prewar influx of Jewish physicians into Great Britain,[38] there is documentary evidence from at least one German source for the Wehrmacht's worries. According to surgeon Siegfried Ostrowski, who worked until 1939 at the Jewish Hospital in Berlin, around the time of the Munich crisis in 1938 army medical officials were discussing the return of Jewish physicians to civilian duty to replace doctors called up for military service and, if necessary, even the drafting of Jewish doctors into the army.[39]

It is not far-fetched to give some credence, therefore, to renewed reports from abroad in 1942 that the German military again was wrestling with the worsening consequences of a shortage of medical specialists among whom Jews had been numerous.[40] It was also reported that an ill-defined demand of the Army Chief of Medical Personnel to Reich Health Leader Leonardo Conti for the "release and deployment" of Jewish doctors was effected by Conti for civilian hospitals,[41] although it is not at all clear who was to be released from where. In 1944 the United States Office of Strategic Services reported that "Jewish nurses and doctors...have been accepted by official health organizations"[42] and Conti himself was apparently the source for the self-serving postwar claim in the United States Strategic Bombing Survey report on German wartime medical services that "by 1943 all physicians of 50 per cent Jewish ancestry were reinstated to full medical practice, and in the summer of 1944 when the air raid casualties increased in alarming proportions all physicians of 100 per cent Jewish ancestry were reinstated to full medical practice."[43] Even though Conti had a long record of vehement anti-Semitism,[44] he also in his career occasionally displayed a frame of mind that marked him off from some of the more volatile of his Nazi brethren. We do not know what Conti thought of the Final Solution (he committed suicide at Nuremberg) and the pressures of the war in his realm might have compelled him to seek some sort of systematic employment of Jewish physicians. In any case, as Michael Kater has suggested, these policies could have issued in mid-1942 from Hitler's new plenipotentiary for health, Karl Brandt.[45] Although such actions would not have had to have been based on legal exceptions to the 1938 decree expanding the Reich Citizenship Law to prohibit the practice of medicine by Jews on non-Jews,[46] it is the case that decrees in 1939, 1940, and 1941 implementing and amending the Reichsärzteordnung of 1935 allowed for the possibility of exceptions that *could* have been used to readmit Jews, at least Mosaic half-Jews, to practice on non-Jews.[47] Some *mischling* doctors of the second degree had already been drafted into the army.[48]

But is it likely that full Jews were readmitted to practice, as Conti claimed? It seems extremely unlikely, although, according to Raul Hilberg, in some cities in Hungary in 1944 Jewish doctors were exempt from deportation because of domestic need and foreign pressure.[49] In Germany Jewish doctors, designated as *Krankenbehandler*, and nurses who treated Jews were protected only until August of 1942.[50] Thus Conti's claim for 1944 could only have involved full Jews in mixed marriages since all other full Jews had already been deported. Although in the occupied territories the army regularly fought with the SS over Jewish workers,[51] by 1944 the SS was ruthlessly exploiting Jewish medical labor in the camps and so for practical as well as ideological reasons would have not been willing to part with them. Only when the camps were abandoned with the German retreat did some Jewish doctors end up in Germany treating slave laborers.[52] In any case, it is likely that Hitler would have stopped any such program cold.[53] We know only of the occasional accidental exceptions: Christopher Browning has told of a Jewish doctor deported to Poland from Stettin in 1940 who worked throughout the war as a physician and who after 1942 would only have been treating Germans or Poles.[54]

Official exceptions were made by Conti for *Mischlinge*.[55] (It was due to the shortage of doctors that Conti in 1942 opposed the plan of the Reich Interior Ministry's Stuckart to sterilize all first degree *Mischlinge*.[56]) As early as June 1941 the Reich Education Ministry was scouring university clinics for doctors who could serve the civilian population at large in an emergency capacity. The need was so great, the Ministry averred, that even *jüdische Mischlinge* and *jüdisch versippte* physicians (related by marriage) were needed for emergency service.[57] Although the university archive consulted reveals none of the results of this query,[58] we do know that the Nazi regime was faced with a desperate shortage of doctors, especially on the home front. This was of course a problem that only worsened as the war intensified both at the front and over the cities of Germany. The basically misogynist Nazi regime was even compelled to allow women to become doctors in order to replace the Jews who had been forced out of the profession and the "Aryan" doctors who had been drafted into the military. When, for example, in 1944 the Gestapo was rounding up conspirators in the wake of the July 20 attempt on Hitler's life, three of the four von Bredow daughters were arrested, but not Marguerite, who was a doctor in a hospital.[59] And when psychoanalyst Horst Eberhard Richter landed in a Berlin military hospital in late 1942 after contracting postdiptherial polyneuritis on the Eastern front, he was attended by a young half-Jewish physician.[60]

Even had this practice been more extensive than it apparently was, it would have little historical meaning in terms of overall Nazi racial policy. It is not as policy that this phenomenon is potentially important, but as part of a broader social history of illness in the Third Reich. Doctors in Germany found themselves in the middle of significant social change, being courted and challenged both from above and below. During the Third Reich "Aryan" physicians confronted both the promise of professionalization, as embodied in the 1935 decree recognizing medicine as a profession rather than as a trade, but also the concomitant "deprofessionalization" resulting from the imposition of political control, the deterioration of educational standards, and the perversion of professional ethics.[61] At the same time, the modern trend toward physician monopoly of health care and dominance over the patient was both advanced and challenged from below in Germany between 1933 and 1945, especially as a result of wartime exigencies. The increasing importance of doctors was most evident in the demand for prescription drugs, a demand that as early as 1936 was described by an alarmed city medical director from Oberhausen as an *Arzneihunger*.[62] The regime sought to encourage prescriptions to heighten productivity, especially of those stimulants one pharmacologist rather boldly labeled "the chemical whip."[63] On the other hand, by 1941 the SS Security Service was complaining about the deleterious effects of the flood of advertising (*Reklameflut*) issuing from the drug companies.[64] But the use of the large number of drugs coming onto the market for the first time in the 1930s tended as well to decentralize medical care by often reducing increasingly overworked doctors to conduits for prescriptions. The difficult living conditions brought on by the war, the increasing political surveillance of doctors and patients, and the shortages of both doctors and drugs only encouraged the treatment or endurance of illnesses without recourse to a physician.

This pattern of behavior was especially common under a wartime regime characterized by a mix of coercion and chaos. People, within the limits imposed by the nature of their situation and their government, were often left to their own devices in dealing with the difficulties of life under National Socialism. Recent research has suggested that the Nazis failed to create the type of solidarism displayed by their propaganda, but that the propaganda itself permeated the society, "remaining as an insistent background noise to daily life."[65] The result was an exercise in what the sociologist de Certeau has called "antidiscipline" or "subversion." This was not a process of conscious political choice but rather the active transformation of the conditions of life by means of the "polytheism of scattered practices"[66] against the imposition of systems by the powerful. And while patriotic support for Hitler and the regime remained strong throughout German society, such personal preservative "strategies" add a further dimension to the delineation by Martin Broszat of the ascending categories of popular *Opposition*, *Resistenz*, and *Widerstand* to the Nazi dictatorship and are, as de Certeau himself argues, particularly relevant in the more general social realm of health and illness where professionalized medicine intruded more deeply and regularly into people's lives than other professions, thus occasioning greater popular reaction. For example, the more the Nazis required doctors' attestations for work absences and supplemental rations, the more people made use of such documents.[67] A somewhat atypical yet illustrative instance of this type of "coping" was Heinrich Böll's regular exploitation, with the help of the family doctor, of a sinus infection to avoid onerous Nazi youth group activities.[68] While it would be easy to overstate the effects of these actions, they also cannot be ignored, especially in an age of popular political assertion extending from South Africa to eastern Germany.

What role did Jewish doctors play in this history? At present the answer to this question consists almost entirely of further questions. How did Germans react to Jewish doctors? How did Jewish physicians balance personal survival, hatred for the regime and its soldiers and citizens, and observance of the Hippocratic oath? Were restrictions imposed, such as a ban on the recruitment of women or treatment of the opposite sex? And, especially in the case of *Mischlinge*, to what extent would patients have been officially or perceptually aware of the "racial" difference?

Since the presence of Jews after 1938 was in any case limited, it also makes sense to speak more generally of the presence of an absence. This was particularly the case in terms of the shortages of qualified doctors, especially those left over for the civilian population. Doctors tended toward the old and exhausted or, especially in the hospitals, the young and inexperienced, prompting a scramble by factories and agencies to secure their own doctors and drug supplies.[69] Despite widespread anti-Semitism aggravated by Nazi propaganda, individual Jewish doctors certainly must have been missed by patients and colleagues, especially since Jewish physicians remained an important part of German life even between 1933 and 1938. In the case of specialists the loss of Jewish practitioners often simply could not be borne: even Nazi leaders relied on them.[70] Just as importantly, members of the lower classes of society, to whatever degree they thought of it in these terms, suffered from the absence of the many Jewish doctors who staffed the clinics run by the state health insurance system, a system that the Nazis purged of its most dedicated functionaries, plundered to pay for rearmament, and restructured to "encourage" people to stay well and on the job. An extreme example of the price paid for Nazi policy came from the SS Security Service itself. On August 4, 1941 it reported that in Banat, the German enclave in the Balkans, a possible health catastrophe loomed because, unlike the Jewish doctors who had treated the uninsured poor for free, non-Jewish doctors demanded payment.[71]

The image of the Jewish doctor in the minds of Germans during the Third Reich is even more difficult to assess. Resentment against Jewish doctors could have been strengthened by the growing dissatisfaction over the impersonality of "modern" medicine, a trend that accelerated after the war in all the nations of the West.[72] At the same time, it was of course non-Jewish doctors who became the focus for popular discontent in Germany after 1933, which might have undercut traditional and Nazi-inspired stereotypes about Jewish doctors. And while people groused about medical treatment, they continued to flock to physicians so that badly needed treatment by a Jewish doctor might well have created trust in any number of individual instances. The war, however, most probably brought with it an intensification of the Nazi image of "the Jew" as a source of contagion from the East. This image built upon earlier prejudices against the *Ostjuden* who had come in large numbers to Central Europe during the nineteenth century.[73] The perceived threat to an increasingly bourgeois society preoccupied with high standards of personal hygiene was revived by the growing danger of the incidence and spread of diseases like typhus brought in from the East by POWs, slave laborers, and German soldiers.[74] Unlike the First World War, epidemics did not occur. But this fear, added to the other difficulties brought on by the war, rather than creating a sense of shared—though incomparable—suffering, probably tended to harden people's attitudes toward outsiders in general. And the particular association between Jews and disease promoted by Nazi film and print would have been strengthened by any knowledge or rumor of the increasingly high incidence of disease actually visited upon the Jews by the Nazis in the ghettos and camps.[75]

Even before the war the Nazis had created a general anxiety in the populace about the social consequences of ill health and especially about hereditary illness. The law designed to prevent the reproduction of so-called "degenerates" spawned what the Reich Interior Ministry called "an almost psychotic fear"[76] among the people, a fear heightened by the wartime program to kill off mental patients.[77] The war of course sharpened concerns about physical and mental well-being, feelings made more brittle not only by Nazi claims for the vigor of the "master race," but also by ongoing physical ailments, often aggravated by Nazi youth group activities, traceable to the First World War, the inflation of 1923, and the Depression.[78] And while some Nazi officials argued that employment of severely wounded soldiers would be an inspiring example of heroism, some army medical officers worried that such a policy would have a depressing effect on the populace.[79] Damage to the "secret narcissistic illusion of intactness"[80] occasioned by injury or illness often leads to feelings of rage against the outside world. It is possible that this reaction was generalized among Germans and that it helped increase animosity against the image of Jews and Jewish doctors. In any case, the ferocity of the fighting in the East and its hastening approach toward the homeland would (*pace* Hillgruber's notion of a "heroic" struggle) have increased the general xenophobia of the population. The Wehrmacht itself had from the beginning fought a different war in the East than it did in the West: whereas Jewish prisoners of war in the West generally "enjoyed relative immunity,"[81] in the East (where the rules of the Geneva Convention were not observed) the army cooperated with the SS by identifying and handing over Jewish POWs.[82]

Although professional and occupational groups could serve as sanctuaries for Jewish members, as was the case with bureaucrats in the Reich Interior Ministry,[83] the medical profession proved to be no safe haven for Jews. The bulk of German physicians turned against or away from their Jewish colleagues (and patients) out of ambition, prejudice, and fear, while many of them served prominently in the Nazis' war against the Jews of Europe. German Jews likewise found little effective help among the populace as a whole after 1933. The Germans by and large responded to the persecution of Jews with favor, indifference, or at best resignation. The image of the Jewish doctor in particular remained colored in the minds of many Germans by ancient associations with mystery and disease. And this image was intensified by Nazi propaganda and the real and imagined threats to physical well-being occasioned by the war. Any deployment of Jewish physicians would by and large have served to mitigate this prejudice, but the extent of such contact between Jewish doctors and "Aryan" patients is still uncertain.

Yet the matter of German anti-Semitism since 1945, including such phenomena as the "inability to mourn,"[84] would seem to be complex since instances or absences of it were probably in many cases related to specific experiences within the social contexts created by Nazism. We simply need to know more about what happened in the realms of illness and health between 1933 and 1945 and the resultant effects on attitudes toward Jews. Anti-Semitism remained a significant force in Germany during the postwar period. In 1952 polling in West Germany found that 37 percent of the citizenry felt that it was better to have no

Jews in the country.[85] Although anti-Semitism has declined in the West with the passing of generations, new targets of prejudice and discrimination, such as the large Turkish community in West Germany, have emerged. And among professionals in West Germany, doctors and lawyers count the largest minorities still expressing anti-Semitic views.[86] This fact is especially troubling given the ever greater prestige, power, and technical capacity, even if compromised by institutional constraints and popular reaction, possessed by doctors in particular. The current Bundesärztekammer projections for the 1990s of 40–50,000 unemployed doctors are therefore particularly unsettling, because West German doctors have enjoyed prosperity since 1945 and because economic hard times were a major factor in their anti-democratic and racist radicalization before 1933.

Notes

1. *Leo Baeck Institute Yearbook* XXXVI (1991): 192–205. With permission of the Leo Baeck Institute.
2. *Manchester Daily Herald*, October 2, 1936, PC 4, reel 45, Wiener Library, London.
3. Rudolf Virchow, "Gegen den Antisemitismus," *Internationales Ärztliches Bulletin* 2 (1936): 16.
4. *Internationales Ärztliches Bulletin. Zentralorgan der Internationalen Vereinigung Sozialistischer Ärzte, Jahrgang I–VI (1934–1939) Reprint*, Beiträge zur Nationalsozialistischen Gesundheits- und Sozialpolitik, 7 (Berlin, 1989).
5. Michael Ignatieff, "The Rise and Fall of Vienna's Jews," *New York Review of Books*, June 29, 1989, p. 21.
6. Richard Evans, "From Hitler to Bismarck: 'Third Reich' and Kaiserreich in Recent Historiography," *Historical Journal* 26 (1983): 485–97, 999–1020.
7. Henry Friedlander, comment, "How to Remember: The Reichskristallnacht," German Studies Association, Milwaukee, October 7, 1989.
8. Fritz Stern, "The Burden of Success: Reflections on German Jewry," in idem, *Dreams and Delusions: The Drama of German History* (New York, 1987), p. 108. See also George L. Mosse, *Germans and Jews: The Right, the Left, and the Search for a "Third Force" in Pre-Nazi Germany* (New York, 1970), pp. 34–115. A subtext of my paper is the mutual support that older and newer modes of interpretation can provide in illuminating the history of Germany, just as, for example, Heinrich Mann's portrait of Diedrich Hessling in *Der Untertan* (1918) as a national type is given new dimension in Thomas Kohut, *Wilhelm II and the Germans: A Study in Leadership* (New York, 1991).
9. Werner Friedrich Kümmel, "Jüdische Ärzte in Deutschland zwischen Emanzipation und 'Ausschaltung'," in Gert Preisser, ed., *Richard Koch und die ärztliche Diagnose* (Hildesheim, 1988), p. 23. Kümmel incorrectly gives Hirschberg's name as Hirschfeld.
10. Uriel Tal, *Christians and Jews in Germany: Religion, Politics and Ideology in the Second Reich* (Ithaca, 1975); see also Donald Niewyk, "Solving the 'Jewish Problem': Continuity and Change in German Antisemitism 1871–1945," *Leo Baeck Institute Yearbook* XXXV (1990): 335–70.

11. Peter Gay, *Freud, Jews and Other Germans: Masters and Victims in Modernist Culture* (New York, 1978), p. 113.

12. Otto Dov Kulka and Paul R. Mendes-Flohr, eds., *Judaism and Christianity under the Impact of National Socialism* (Jerusalem, 1987).

13. Geoffrey Cocks, "The Professionalization of Psychotherapy in Germany, 1928–1949," in Geoffrey Cocks and Konrad H. Jaruasch, eds., *German Professions, 1800–1950* (New York, 1990), p. 314. Bias could mix with strategically expressed philsophical conviction, as in a preference for Jung over Freud: Paul Feldkeller, "Geist der Psychotherapie," *Deutsche Allgemeine Zeiting*, October 5, 1937; or be exploited directly: "Schuld an dem Konflikt ist der Jude Strauss.", Matthias Heinrich Göring to Herbert Linden, November 9, 1939, REM 2954, Zentrales Staatsarchiv, Potsdam.

14. Herbert Lüthy, *La banque protestante en France* (Paris, 1959), 1:90, quoted in Erwin Ackerknecht, "German Jews, English Dissenters, French Protestants: Nineteenth-Century Pioneers of Modern Medicine and Science," in Charles E. Rosenberg, ed., *Healing and History: Essays for George Rosen* (New York, 1979), p. 88.

15. Kümmel, "Jüdische Ärzte," p. 20.

16. Michael H. Kater, "Professionalization and Socialization of Physicians in Wilhelmine and Weimar Germany," *Journal of Contemporary History* 20 (1985): 689; David L. Preston, "The German Jews in Secular Education, University Teaching, and Science: A Preliminary Inquiry," *Jewish Social Studies* 38 (1976): 110–11, 114–16.

17. Michael H. Kater, "Hitler's Early Doctors: Nazi Physicians in Predepression Germany," *Journal of Modern History* 59 (1987): 35, n. 35; Karl A. Schleunes, *The Twisted Road to Auschwitz: Nazi Policy Toward German Jews, 1933–1939* (Urbana, 1970), p. 41. Nazi racial definitions raised the percentage of Jewish physicians in Berlin to around 60 percent: see "Die Juden in der Berliner Ärzteschaft," *Deutsches Aerzteblatt* 66 (1936): 1046.

18. Michael H. Kater, "The Nazi Physicians League of 1929: Causes and Consequences," in Thomas Childers, ed., *The Formation of the Nazi Constituency 1919–1933* (London, 1986), p. 147.

19. Donald W. Light et al., "Social Medicine vs. Professional Dominance: The German Experience," *American Journal of Public Health* 76 (1986): 79; Robert W. Proctor, *Racial Hygiene: Medicine Under the Nazis* (Cambridge, Massachusetts, 1988), pp. 251–81; Doron Niederland, "The Emigration of Jewish Academics and Professionals from Germany in the First Years of Nazi Rule," *Leo Baeck Institute Yearbook* XXXIII (1988): 294–5.

20. Kater, "Hitler's Early Doctors," p. 36, n. 35.

21. Proctor, *Racial Hygiene*, pp. 213, 286, 293, 297, 306; Stephen Jay Gould, *The Mismeasure of Man* (New York, 1981).

22. Robert M. Veatch, "Scientific Expertise and Value Judgments: The Generalization of Expertise," *Hastings Center Studies* 1:2 (1973): 29–40.

23. Rainer C. Baum, *The Holocaust and the German Elite* (Totowa, New Jersey, 1981), p. 266, quoted in Peter Hayes, *Industry and Ideology: IG Farben in the Nazi Era* (Cambridge, 1987), p. 382.

24. Sander L. Gilman, "Jews and Mental Illness: Medical Metaphors, Anti-Semitism, and the Jewish Response," *Journal of the History of the Behavioral Sciences* 20 (1984): 150.

25. Jan Goldstein, "The Wandering Jew and the Problem of Psychiatric Anti-Semitism in Fin-de-Siècle France," *Journal of Contemporary History* 20 (1985): 521–52.

26. Sherry Turkle, *Psychoanalytic Politics: Freud's French Revolution* (New York, 1978), p. 49.

27. Susan Gross Solomon, "David and Goliath in Soviet Public Health: The Rivalry of Social Hygienists and Psychiatrists for Authority over the *Bytovoi* Alcoholic," *Soviet Studies* 41 (1989): 269.
28. Susan Sontag, *Illness as Metaphor* (New York, 1978), p. 74.
29. Ibid., p. 76.
30. Peter Loewenberg, "The Unsuccessful Adolescence of Heinrich Himmler," in idem, *Decoding the Past: The Psychohistorical Approach* (New York, 1983), pp. 209–39.
31. Fritz Stern, "The Political Consequences of the Unpolitical German," in idem, *The Failure of Illiberalism: Essays on the Political Culture of Modern Germany* (New York, 1972), pp. 3–25.
32. Konrad H. Jarausch, "The Crisis of German Professions 1918–33," *Journal of Contemporary History* 20 (1985): 394.
33. Robert Gellately, "The Gestapo and German Society: Political Denunciation in the Gestapo Case Files," *Journal of Modern History* 60 (1988): 686.
34. Martin Broszat, "Politische Denunziationen in der NS-Zeit," *Archivalische Zeitschrift* 73 (1977): 25.
35. *Deutschland-Berichte der Sozialdemokratischen Partei Deutschlands (Sopade)* (Salzhausen, 1980) 6 (1939), pp. 926–7.
36. "Geschäftsgeist in Nazi-Deutschland," *Internationales Aertzliches Bulletin* 5 (1938): 20.
37. "Jewish Doctors Now Wanted," *Manchester Guardian*, September 15, 1939, PC 5, reel 106, Wiener Library.
38. Andrew Sharf, *The British Press and Jews under Nazi Rule* (London, 1964), pp. 161, 168–9.
39. Siegfried Ostrowski, "Vom Schicksal Jüdischer Ärzte im Dritten Reich. Ein Augenzeugenbericht aus den Jahren 1933–1939," *Bulletin des Leo Baeck Instituts* 24 (1963): 335–6.
40. "German Medical Services: Army's Difficulties," *Manchester Guardian*, January 12, 1942, PC 5, reel 106, Wiener Library; Proctor, *Racial Hygiene*, pp. 154, 156.
41. "Dr. Conti—Reichs-Totengräber," *Die Zeitung*, February 20, 1942, PC 5, reel 106, Wiener Library.
42. United States Office of Strategic Services, Research and Analysis Branch, *Notes on Air-Raid Damage and Health in Germany*, R & A No. 1801, March 10, 1944, p. 2, Hoover Library, Stanford University.
43. United States Strategic Bombing Survey, Morale Division, Medical Branch Report, *The Effect of Bombing on Health and Medical Care in Germany* (Washington, D. C., October 30, 1945), p. 163
44. Michael H. Kater, "Doctor Leonardo Conti and His Nemesis: The Failure of Centralized Medicine in the Third Reich," *Central European History* 18 (1985): 302–3.
45. Michael H. Kater, *Doctors Under Hitler* (Chapel Hill, 1989), p. 205.
46. *Reichsgesetzblatt*, August 2, 1938, pp. 969–70. According to Article 2, the Interior Minister was empowered to restore the right to practice upon recommendation of the Reich Physicians Chamber. It is not clear that this could have been used to allow practice by Jews on non-Jews. But there is at least some degree of potential ambiguity throughout the legislation regarding the possibility of the future practice of medicine by Jews, an ambiguity not in evidence, by contrast, in the legislation excluding Jews from the practice of law. Article I of that decree is a model of ruthless clarity: "Juden ist der Beruf des Rechtsanwaltes verschlossen." (*Reichsgesetzblatt*, October 14, 1938, p. 1403). The Nazis had

little use for lawyers generally, but of course had great need of doctors, in an emergency possibly even Jewish ones.

47. *Reichsärzteordnung* (Berlin, 1943), pp. 107, 139, 149.
48. Kater, *Doctors Under Hitler*, p. 205.
49. Raul Hilberg, *The Destruction of the European Jews*, rev. ed. (New York, 1985), 3:834, 850. There are also accounts of Jewish doctors being spared by *Einsatzgruppen* in the East, presumably for service in the ghettos and camps. Richard Breitman, personal communication, December 29, 1989.
50. Mrs. A., "Jewish Hospital Berlin," File 02/29. Yad Vashem Archives, Jerusalem.
51. Henry Friedlander, personal communication, May 10, 1989.
52. Gisella Perl, *I Was a Doctor in Auschwitz* (New York, 1948), pp. 152–3.
53. David Bankier, "Hitler and the Policy-Making Process on the Jewish Question," *Holocaust and Genocide Studies* 3 (1983): 1–20.
54. Christopher Browning, personal communication, May 31, 1989. Jewish doctors were also active on behalf of the resistance to the Nazis: see, for example, the account of a Jewish physician treating partisans in Russia in Nechama Tec, *In the Lion's Den: The Life of Oswald Rufeisen* (New York, 1990), pp. 190–1.
55. H. G. Adler, *Der verwaltete Mensch: Studien zur Deportation der Juden aus Deutschland* (Tübingen, 1974), p. 302; see also Jeremy Noakes, "The Development of Nazi Policy towards the German-Jewish 'Mischlinge' 1933–1945," *Leo Baeck Institute Yearbook* XXXIV (1989): 291–354.
56. Reichsminister des Innern to Regierungspräsident Frankfurt a.d. Oder, August 23, 1941, p. 3, Pr. Br. Rep 3 B Nr. 178. Staatsarchiv Potsdam. It was due to the shortage of doctors that in 1942 Conti opposed the plan of the Interior Ministry's Hans Stuckart to sterilize all first-degree *Mischlinge*. See Uwe Dietrich Adam, *Judenpolitik im Dritten Reich* (Düsseldorf, 1979), p. 323, n. 100. Conti's motive here was to prevent already overworked doctors from being burdened with sterilizations, but he also *might* have had in mind the deleterious effects on the future supply of doctors of the flight underground of half-Jewish physicians escaping sterilization.
57. Kölnische Gesellschaft für Christlich-Jüdische Zusammenarbeit, *Heilen und Vernichten im Nationalsozialismus* (Cologne, 1985), p. 126. This particular request would seem to exclude full Jewish doctors in mixed marriages.
58. UA 9/684. Universitätsarchiv der Universität zu Köln.
59. Marie Vassiltchikov, *Berlin Diaries 1940–1945* (New York, 1987), p. 224.
60. Horst-Eberhard Richter, *Die Chance des Gewissens: Erinnerungen und Assoziationen* (Hamburg, 1987), p. 37.
61. Konrad H. Jarausch, "The Perils of Professionalism: Lawyers, Teachers, and Engineers in Nazi Germany," *German Studies Review* 9 (1986): 107–37.
62. Auszug aus der Niederschrift über die 7. Sitzung der Rheinischen Arbeitsgemeinschaft für Wohlfahrtspflege am 4. Juli 1936 im Kreissparkassengebäude zu St. Goar, RW 53/455. Nordrhein-Westfälisches Hauptstaatsarchiv, Düsseldorf (hereafter cited as NWH).
63. F. Eichholtz, "Ermüdungsbekämpfung: Über Stimulantien," *Deutsche medizinische Wochenschrift* 67 (1941): 56.
64. Meldungen aus dem Reich, February 20, 1941, microcopy T175, reel 260, frame 3286. National Archives, Washington, D.C.; Heinz Boberach, ed., *Meldungen aus dem Reich* (Herrsching, 1984).
65. Jane Caplan, *Government without Administration: State and Civil Service in Weimar and Nazi Germany* (Oxford, 1988), p. 190.
66. Michel de Certeau, *The Practice of Everyday Life*, trans. Steven Rendall (Berkeley, 1984), p. 47.

67. Amt für Volksgesundheit to Ärztekammer Köln, August 22, 1944, Reg. Aachen 21308. NWH; "Doctors Warned," *Daily Herald*, March 29, 1940, PC 5, reel 106, Wiener Library.

68. Heinrich Böll, *What's To Become of the Boy? Or: Something to Do With Books*, trans. Leila Vennewitz (New York, 1984), pp. 39, 44–5, 68.

69. VO z. Sicherstellung der ärztlichen Versorgung der Zivilbevölkerung, 1942 [draft], R 18/5576. Bundesarchiv, Coblenz; Reich Interior Ministry to Reich War Ministry, July 22, 1942, Reg. Düsseldorf 54364III. NWH.

70. Such as the Nazi major of Stuttgart; Erich Kohler, personal communication, June 9, 1989.

71. Meldungen aus dem Reich, reel 261, frame 4481.

72. Edward Shorter, *Bedside Manners: The Troubled History of Doctors and Patients* (New York, 1985).

73. Jack Wertheimer, *Unwelcome Strangers: East European Jews in Imperial Germany* (New York, 1987). Jews from the East were widely viewed as a source of uncleanliness and disease: see idem, "The Unwanted Element"—East European Jews in Imperial Germany," *Leo Baeck Institute Yearbook* XXVI (1981): 26. Jewish organizations, however, established medical facilities for the immigrants: Trude Maurer, *Ostjuden in Deutschland 1918–1933* (Hamburg, 1986), pp. 542–3; see also Wertheimer, "The 'Ausländerfrage' at Institutions of Higher Learning—A Controversy over Russian-Jewish Students in Imperial Germany," *Leo Baeck Institute Yearbook* XXVII (1982): 187–218.

74. Löhner to Conti, March 4, 1943, microcopy T315, reel 17, frames 128–31. National Archives; Hauptarzt WBK, September 3, 1942, NSDAP Kreisleitung Eisenach, folder 00014a, Myers Collection, University of Michigan; Deutscher Gemeindetag Berlin to Deutscher Gemeindetag Düsseldorf, September 1, 1942, RW 53/466. NWH; Robert S. Cohen and Thomas Schnelle, eds., *Cognition and Fact: Materials on Ludwik Fleck* (Dordrecht, 1986), pp. 24–7.

75. Leonardo Conti, Stand der Volksgesundheit im 5. Kriegsjahr (1944), p. 6, Reg. Aachen 16486. NWH, Films like *Der ewige Jude* (1940) in fact utilized footage from the ghettos to emphasize to the German public the "unhygienic" habits of Jews.

76. R 18/5585. Bundesarchiv.

77. Christa Wolf, *Patterns of Childhood*, trans. Ursule Molinaro and Hedwig Rappolt (New York, 1980), pp. 149, 195–8.

78. Wehrwirtshcafts-Inspektion VII (Munich), 1937, microcopy T77, roll 248, frames 824–8. National Archives; Gesundheitsamt Düsseldorf, Jahresgesundheitsbericht, February 28, 1933, Reg. Düsseldorf 54708. NWH; Peter Loewenberg, "The Psychohistorical Origins of the Nazi Youth Cohort," in *Decoding the Past*, pp. 240–83.

79. Dr. Wolff, "Die Betreuung unserer Schwerverletzten," *Deutsches Aertzeblatt* 47/48 (1941), microcopy T78, roll 191, frames 677–82; Kommandeur, Sanitäts-Abteilung Chemnitz, Arbeitsbehandlung in den Res. Lazaretten, March 6, 1943, ibid., roll 189, frame 1409. National Archives.

80. Richter, *Chance des Gewissens*, p. 37.

81. Hilberg, *Destruction*, 2:627; David A. Foy, *For You the War Is Over: American Prisoners of War In Nazi Germany* (New York, 1984), pp. 128–31; Yoav Gelber, "Central European Jews from Palestine in the British Forces," *Leo Baeck Institute Yearbook* XXXV (1990): 327–8.

82. Omer Bartov, *The Eastern Front, 1941–45: German Troops and the Barbarization of Warfare* (new York, 1986), p. 109. Christian Streit, "The German Army and

the Policies of Genocide," in Gerhard Hirschfeld, ed., *The Policies of Genocide: Jews and Soviet Prisoners of War in Nazi Germany* (London, 1986), pp. 1–14.

83. Adam, *Judenpolitik*, pp. 342–3.
84. Alexander and Margarete Mitscherlich, *The Inability to Mourn: Principles of Collective Behavior*, trans. Beverley R. Placzek (New York, 1975).
85. Axel Schildt, "Popular Political Consciousness in Germany (after 1945)," paper presented at the University of Michigan, October 27, 1989.
86. Frederick Weil, "The Imperfectly Mastered Past: Anti-Semitism in West Germany Since the Holocaust," *New German Critique* 20 (1980): 143.

9

The Old as New: The Nuremberg Doctors' Trial and Medicine in Modern Germany[1]

On October 25, 1946, Brigadier General Telford Taylor, Chief of Counsel for War Crimes, filed an indictment before Nuremberg Military Tribunal I charging twenty-three German defendants with "murders, brutalities, cruelties, tortures, atrocities, and other inhumane acts."[2] Known officially as "The Medical Case," the subsequent proceedings also became known as "The Doctors' Trial" since twenty of the defendants were physicians. On August 20, 1947 fifteen of the defendants were declared guilty. The next day seven were sentenced to death and five to life imprisonment. The charges encompassed four crimes: the Jewish skeleton collection, the project to kill tubercular Polish nationals, the "euthanasia" program, and medical experiments on civilian and military prisoners. The experiments included the following: high altitude; freezing; malaria; mustard gas; sulfanilamide treatment of gas gangrene; bone, muscle, and nerve regeneration and bone transplantation; potability of sea water; epidemic jaundice, typhus and other vaccines; poison food and bullets; phosphorus incendiary bombs; biochemical treatment of sepsis with phlegmon; blood coagulation with polygal; toxicity of phenol; chemical, surgical, and x-ray sterilization. The victims included Germans, Russians, Czechs, Ukrainians, Poles, Yugoslavs, Jews, Sinti, Jehovah's Witnesses, communists, theologians, resistance fighters, mental patients, so-called "asocials," men, women, and children. The exact numbers are impossible to determine, but according to trial documents approximately 3,500 people were used as test subjects. At least 800 died, as many as 400 of the 1,100 test subjects in the Dachau malaria tests alone.[3] The human experiments constituted the bulk of the charges and this essay will attempt to show that their origins and aims stemmed from the social and professional trajectories of medicine in the history of modern Germany. These dynamics in turn demonstrate some problematic structural and attitudinal features of modern Western history in general and thus can alter our understanding of the place of German history in the history of the West. The Nuremberg Doctors' Trial, therefore, has significance even beyond the history of Nazi atrocities, the extent and limit of international justice, and the fragility of medical ethics.

It might seem at first that there is little to say about these acts from the perspective of law, ethics, or history. The cases at Nuremberg were simple and straightforward. They involved the murder of the involuntary subjects of medical experimentation.[4] Even the Nuremberg Code, which declared that "certain basic principles must be observed in order to satisfy moral, ethical, and legal concepts"[5] in medical experimentation on human beings, was originally ghettoized as "a good code for barbarians but an unnecessary code for ordinary physician-scientists."[6] In other words, the actions of the Nazi doctors were an aberration from well-established and well-observed principles of medical practice and research. They were clearly and unambiguously contrary to medical as well as general ethics. And when it comes to history, what do these atrocities tell us about the Third Reich—and Germany—that we do not already know? In the realm of law, the "Medical Case" at Nuremberg is significant in two fundamental ways. First of all, it was the first in a series of trials. In 1947 doctors charged with experimenting on human beings at Sachsenhausen and Auschwitz were tried in Berlin and Cracow, respectively. In East Germany trials were held in 1966 in Berlin and Magdeburg for like crimes committed at Neuengamme and Auschwitz. West Germany had held its own Sachsenhausen trial in Cologne in 1962.[7] But the reach of trials has been distinctly limited. Only a few of the many individuals involved in medical crimes have been brought to justice, not to mention the even more widespread unpunished complicity in the sterilization and murder of mental patients by the Nazis.[8] Moreover, legal actions cannot address the issue of those in medical authority who said or did nothing on the basis of suspicion or knowledge of what was going on in the camps and asylums. Much of the controversy over Alexander Mitscherlich's documentation of the Doctors' Trial arose from Mitscherlich's contention that knowledge and tolerance of medical atrocities were extensive and reached high into the ranks of the medical profession.[9] Many members of the medical leadership in West Germany in particular had continued or built careers in the Third Reich.

Second, the Nuremberg Code became the cornerstone for national and international legislation concerning human experimentation in research and treatment. The World Medical Association, founded in 1947, codified standards for human experimentation in the successive Declarations of Helsinki in 1964, 1975, 1983, and 1989. But while the original Nuremberg Code has as its first principle the "voluntary consent of the human subject,"[10] the Helsinki guidelines have made what many see as ethically dubious concessions at the expense of this first principle to the political and military requirements of states as well as to the medical and scientific interests of doctors and researchers.[11] Even these strictures are often not honored in the breach. The U.S. military employed four of the acquitted Doctors' Trial defendants both before and after their acquittal.[12] Debates have raged over the value and use of data from the Dachau experiments.[13] More recently, evidence has surfaced of experimentation on athletes and mental patients in the former DDR.[14] And in December 1990 the United States Food and Drug Administration "granted the Department of Defense a waiver from the informed consent requirements of the Nuremberg Code and existing federal law and regulations to use unapproved drugs and vaccines on the soldiers involved in Desert Shield."[15] Most recent are the revelations concerning American plutonium experiments conducted between 1946 and 1956 on less than fully informed human subjects.

When it comes to ethics, the Nazi doctors were guilty of violating two fundamental principles, "the prohibition against inflicting suffering on human beings and the Kantian categorical imperative prohibiting the use of persons as mere means to the ends of others."[16] Such moral imperatives provide the basis for arguments in favor of the universal application of a code of ethics for doctors and researchers. We are right to reserve special condemnation for doctors who cause and observe suffering and death. The invocation of an ethical imperative is also a necessary and effective response to the arguments from ethical and cultural relativism, from precedent, and from legal positivism, all of which were advanced by the defense at Nuremberg. Such principles are also especially vital in a modern age of professional functionalism and individual and corporate careerism. The Nuremberg defendants argued that as medical experts they could not be held responsible for judging matters of politics or law. This was more than an attempt to obscure the fact that it was mostly they as members of an influential scientific, medical, and military community who had initiated the experiments. It was also an obversion of an especially arrogant, destructive, and militarized Nazi medical "generalization of expertise" to which doctors among professionals everywhere have been particularly prone.[17]

The Doctors' Trial also tells us a great deal about history, about the history of professionalized medicine in Germany, about the history of Germany in general, and about one of the trajectories in the modern history of the West as a whole. In Germany doctors played an inordinate role in the development and application of racial biology both before and after the advent of the Nazis.[18] The defendants at Nuremberg were at some pains to avoid mentioning any professional or individual allegiance to Nazi racial aims. In this they were not alone. In Mario Puzo's 1955 novel about occupied Germany, *The Dark Arena*, a U.S. Army civilian personnel officer in Frankfurt laments, "'Never in the Party, never in the SA, never in the Hitler Youth. Christ, I'm dying to meet a Nazi.'"[19] At the Doctors' Trial this type of behavior reached one of its many low points when Karl Gebhardt denied knowledge of the purpose of the camps, blamed atrocities there on "the negative selection of...scum, conscripts, [and] foreigners," and defended the honor of "the decent Waffen SS."[20] Such disingenuous denial also, however, alerts us to motivating factors other than Nazi beliefs among these men (and one woman). The same is true of their rationalizations. Aside from attempting whenever possible to distance themselves from the experiments which had caused injury and death, the defendants vainly attempted to justify their actions. Several of these arguments had to do with the status of the human subjects: The prisoners in the experiments had been condemned to death; they were volunteers; they offered themselves in expiation for their crimes; those subjected to life-threatening experiments had been promised commutation if they survived. The defense also offered four arguments having to do with obedience to authority: It was wartime; the government had power and authority over the defendants; they had a right and a responsibility to help defend their country; there was no law in Germany or anywhere else against human experimentation. This last argument from authority was linked to an argument from precedent: Human experimentation had a long history. Finally, there was the argument from utility: The few must be sacrificed to save the many during a total war in which the lives of thousands of German soldiers and civilians were threatened by enemy action and by disease. This utilitarian argument was also in accord with the Nazi ideal of "*Gemeinnutz geht vor Eigennutz*" which was applied to military triage of German wounded during the Second World War.[21]

The prosecution at Nuremberg was forced to concede that there had been precedents for human experimentation. Cross-examination by the defense of prosecution expert witness Dr. Andrew Ivy also elicited the fact that the American Medical Association guidelines for human experimentation presented as evidence for the prosecution dated from 1946.[22] But the prosecution was hardly defenseless on this score. Aside from powerful arguments ranging from Western moral philosophy and the Hippocratic Oath to the ethical bankruptcy of the Nazi racism that informed the experiments, the prosecution was able to cite a preexisting ordinance regulating experiments on human beings. There was only the one, but it had been promulgated in 1931—in Germany.

On February 28, 1931 the Reich Interior Ministry published a circular concerning "Richtlinien für neuartige Heilbehandlung und für die Vornahme wissenschaftlicher Versuche am Menschen"[23] ("Guidelines for Novel Treatment and for the Undertaking of Experiments on Humans"). These guidelines, expanding on a similar Prussian directive from 1900, required, among other restrictions, consent of the patient for any nonemergency innovative therapy and of the subject of any nontherapeutic research.[24] There was debate at Nuremberg about whether these guidelines had the force of law. The Nazi regime apparently never specifically revoked these guidelines, but no such specific revocation would have been required. The Nazis abolished the Reichsgesundheitsrat, the five-man council which had issued the guidelines. More importantly, the Nazis destroyed the ethical autonomy of physicians upon which the guidelines were based. The Reichsärzteordnung (Reich Physicians Ordinance) of 1935, which declared that medicine was no longer a trade but rather a profession, subordinated the doctor to the dictates of the state, the will of the *Volk*, and what was termed the individual physician's own "*gesundes Volksempfinden*"[25] (healthy national instincts).

However, the 1931 guidelines have a history of their own which allows us to place the Doctors' Trial in a more extensive and fruitful context. Like the Prussian directive of 1900, the Reich circular of 1931 was largely the result of public outcry over well-publicized instances of medical malfeasance by doctors and hospitals. In the 1890s the *cause célèbre* was dermatologist Albert Neisser of Breslau, who inoculated four children and three adolescent female prostitutes with syphilis serum. In 1930 SPD Reichstag member Dr. Julius Moses decried the deaths of seventy-five children in Lübeck whose pediatricians were experimenting with tuberculosis vaccines.[26] By 1930 the medical establishment had already become extremely worried about the rising tide of public criticism. There was the danger that restrictions might be placed on their ability to try new treatments and to perform necessary medical research. In addition, German law as a whole was only gradually coming to reflect the need of doctors and medical researchers to experiment on patients and subjects.[27] The 1931 circular, therefore, was designed not to hinder experimental therapy and research but rather to allow it. This is clear from the first guideline:

> In order that medical science may continue to advance, the initiation in appropriate cases of therapy involving new and as yet insufficiently tested means and procedures cannot be avoided. Similarly, scientific experimentation involving human subjects cannot be completely excluded as such, as this would hinder or even prevent progress in the diagnosis, treatment, and prevention of diseases.[28]

The 1931 guidelines thus represented the success of doctors in establishing legally the principle of medical expertise and control within the bounds of law and traditional morality. The guidelines left enforcement to the individual doctor. The guidelines also expressed what must have been widespread agreement among doctors concerning the rights of patients and research subjects. Although the guidelines did contribute to the growing asymmetry of power and authority between doctor and patient, it seems fair to say that most doctors in Germany even in wartime would have been averse to the gross violations of human rights which were involved in the concentration camp experiments. There is even evidence in the published Doctors' Trial proceedings that there were degrees of culpability among the defendants which reflected not only function and fear but also reservation. Of course, very many doctors acquiesced in—or at least did not protest—these same illegal and unethical acts. In any case, the doctors on trial at Nuremberg could hardly have been unaware of this debate or unaffected by the conditions occasioning it. These physicians were representative of the mainstream of German medicine, not aberrant demons imposed by the Nazi regime upon the medical profession. They may not have been the cream of the German medical profession, but they came from the same bottle. Gerhard Rose, for one, was director for tropical medicine at the Robert Koch Institute. Karl Gebhardt, for another, had been an assistant at the University of Munich to Germany's leading surgeon, Ferdinand Sauerbruch, and since 1925 had specialized in reconstructive surgery and rehabilitation at Hohenaschau and Hohenlychen.[29] Their varying allegiances to Nazi racial ideals, along with their ambition and the prevailing political, social, and military conditions, simply led these doctors to reject humane standards.

But two broader historical conditions also worked significant influences on these doctors. The first was the rapid and pervasive medicalization of modern German society during the twentieth century. Doctors and medicine simply became more important and powerful during the period. This was common throughout the Western world; everywhere doctors and medicine began to play significant roles in the lives of individuals and in society. The second major historical influence on the Nazi doctors was the Nazis' own marked hypersensitivity to health and illness.

Whereas in earlier times illness and disease were closely linked in time with death and thus were matters of individual fate, modern medicine (and public sanitation and health policy) began to render illness and disease a matter of organized prophylaxis and treatment. As a result, for the first time the sick person became a social entity with an actual and perceived identity.[30] The ramifications of this development included significant social conflict. During the Weimar Republic many doctors believed that their status and well-being were threatened by certain political and economic forces and trends. Michael Kater has documented the large percentage of doctors led as a result into varying degrees of allegiance to National Socialism. Doctors on the political right warned of a "crisis in medicine" which was "variously construed as the bureaucratization, specialization, or scientization of medicine."[31] Often mixed in this were complaints about materialism, urbanism, and the pernicious influence of Jewish physicians. The political left criticized what they saw as capitalist inegalitarianism and the greedy hostility of the doctors' lobby toward the state health insurance system. This discontent was aggravated at the end of the decade by the ongoing increase in health premiums and decline in payments, even though businesses and government continued to pour increasing amounts of money into the system until at least 1930.[32] This situation—one not unfamiliar in the West today—was commented on regularly and angrily in a survey psychoanalyst Erich Fromm conducted among German blue and white collar workers in 1929.[33] Controversies among proponents and opponents of natural health, homeopathy, and "*Schulmedizin*" (academic medicine) also raged, though more across and within political, social, and occupational boundaries than along them. Relationships between patients and doctors were also problematic. By and large, doctors gained state-sanctioned expert authority—"practitioner control"—over their patients. The perverse extremity of this trend would be reached by Nazi human experimentation. People in general tended to like their own doctors, but to be suspicious of—or even hostile to—doctors as a group. (This is not unlike the present situation in the United States.) We have already referred to longstanding public unease over medical experiments on patients and the doctors' success in protecting themselves by issuing guidelines for therapeutic and nontherapeutic experimentation in 1931. Edward Shorter has argued that during the twentieth century doctors in the West gradually built a reputation for caring and competence in the minds of patients. For the first time doctors began to be able to diagnose, treat, and even cure illness. According to Shorter, it was after the Second World War that the impersonality of modern technical medicine began seriously to erode this generally happy relationship. Shorter's model holds generally for Germany, but, as we have seen, patients' and the public's attitudes toward doctors—and doctors' attitudes toward patients and the public—were deeply ambivalent. The mutual distrust Shorter demonstrates for the period after 1945 is clearly evident in Germany during the interwar period. The Third Reich only made things worse. Doctors were brought under the control of the state, educational standards in medicine deteriorated, and the many Jewish general practitioners and specialists in Germany and Austria were barred from practice in 1938. The introduction in the 1930s of medically effective mass-market drugs enhanced the popularity of doctors, but at the same time it could tend to make them the passive dispensers of comfort or cure instead of their active agents. During the war doctors were in even greater demand because the Nazis required *Atteste* (certifications) from physicians in order for people to miss work or get extra rations. But the growing vigilance of the authorities for slackers and malingerers (and doctors' cultivation of them) as well as chronic shortages of drugs diminished public appreciation of—and reliance upon—increasingly overworked and inexperienced doctors. Doctors, largely products of an authoritarian past now aggravated by an authoritarian present, often regarded patients as irresponsible in any number of ways.[34]

Nazi hypersensitivity to matters of health and illness was inherent in Nazi racism, with its obsession with a hierarchy of races based on specific physical and mental characteristics. The Nazis' Social Darwinism added the component of struggle against inferior races. Even war itself as the emotional and practical solution to the problem of inferior races was inherently problematic for the Nazis. In 1944 Reichsgesundheitsführer Leonardo Conti, echoing the concern of early race hygienist Alfred Ploetz and the antiwar stance of the Monist League before World War I, worried about the "dysgenic" effects of war whereby the fittest die at the front while the less fit burden already strained medical services at home.[35] The Nazis' obsession with strength expressed a preoccupation with weakness and threats to the physical integrity of the body. During the nineteenth century disease had become a pervasive metaphor for the "unnatural" while the rising anti-Semitism of the time drew on a long-standing association in the minds of many Europeans between Jews and illness.[36] The disease imagery of Hitler's *Mein Kampf* and the bloody misogynist fantasies of members of the Freikorps are two major cases in point.[37] On the basis of comparatively few responses to the questions "Are you afraid of illness?" and "Why (not)?" as well as a few other related questions in his survey of 1929, Erich Fromm concluded that Nazi voters (and the most active members of the KPD) betrayed a greater sense of hopelessness and internal conflict.[38] For example, Questionnaire 204 is that of a Nazi voter from Frankfurt am Main who saw Germany controlled by "the Jew" and who answered the questions about fear of illness with "*Ja*" and "*Da sie für uns nichts gutes Einbringen* (nothing good comes of it)."[39]

The Nazis' problems were aggravated from the start by the fact that the overall health of the German population had been adversely affected by the effects of malnutrition and the associated health and developmental problems stemming from the First World War, the inflation of 1923, the Depression, and the Nazis' own martial activities in the 1930s.[40] These problems had in their turn aggravated the already widespread significant health problems among Germans in the economically deprived classes. We must also remember that the Germans by and large constituted a society long concerned with matters of individual and collective *Sauberkeit* (cleanliness). Mobilization for war created a shortage of doctors, particularly among specialists, so much so that the misogynist Nazis were forced to admit unprecedented numbers of women into the medical schools and even to toy with the idea of allowing Jewish physicians to treat non-Jewish patients.[41] The war also led directly to the experiments on human beings in the concentration camps. The shortage of doctors, medical students, and military cadets as sources of traditional volunteers was advanced by the defense at Nuremberg as an additional compelling reason to use camp inmates.[42] In Russia German soldiers were exposed to bitter cold that, together with the Luftwaffe's concern for airmen down at sea, led to the hypothermia experiments.[43] Heavy casualties from gas gangrene on the Eastern front led to the sulfanilamide experiments.[44] The increasingly high operational ceilings attained by enemy aircraft led to the high-altitude experiments.[45] The exposure of German troops in Poland and Russia to typhus, malaria, jaundice, and cholera led to the vaccine experiments.[46]

There was also an important domestic aspect to the Nazi concern over the vulnerability of German soldiers to dangerous infectious diseases. The Nazis worried that not just slave laborers but returning soldiers from the East would be the sources for new epidemics in Germany. This concern was based on the epidemics that had broken out in Germany during the First World War, largely as a result of widespread malnutrition. It also rested on the assumption that Germans were more vulnerable because German public hygiene had rendered such diseases relatively rare. It was also thought that peoples in the East had built up tolerances against such scourges. This view reflected the Nazi emphasis on biology, their typical unconcern with the suffering of others, a studied ignorance of the role played by the disruptive effects of war, occupation, and exploitation, and a desire to use this suffering for propaganda about the "unhygienic" life-styles of "inferior" races. It was in fact Nazi concern over threats to the health of resident Germans as a result of the poor conditions under which Jews were forced to live which played an important role in the creation of the ghettos in Poland.[48] The German home front in fact never suffered from epidemics during the Second World War. This was due to the ruthless segregation of Eastern prisoners, an efficient mobilization of military and civilian health agencies, and the fact that the Germans were able to feed themselves at the expense of the many countries they occupied. Vaccinations, supported by the German drug industry, played only a small role. The German people suffered from the multiplication of common ailments, occasioned and aggravated by wartime conditions, especially in the large cities under attack from the air.[49] Illness also spread because it became one means of what Martin Broszat more broadly calls *Resistenz*[50]: in this case the largely unpolitical mitigation and avoidance of unpleasant and inconvenient obligations.

The principal ethical lesson contained in the history of the Doctors' Trial at Nuremberg concerns the dangers of social corporatism. Modern Germany consistently displayed such a corporatist ethic in its political and social organization. This solidarity can produce benefits for the whole and protect the members of the group against the depredations of individuals, as was the case with the German health care system.

But it can also lead to organized violation of the rights of individuals and of groups inside and outside the larger group in the name of solidarity. Corporatism cultivates a sense of duty, degrees of conformity, and even fanaticism. In Germany corporatism was part of a similarly generalized historical tradition of illiberalism which significantly affected the professions. These dynamics played a role in the Holocaust and among the doctors who performed experiments on human beings. This is not to say that the careerism and venality even more common as abuses within the liberal ethos were absent among these doctors.[51] And it is not to say that other large economic and political forces were not also responsible for these crimes.[52] But corporatism was the most pervasive phenomenon affecting the groups and individuals involved in these atrocities.

There is also an historical lesson in this story, one which allows us to see the old *Sonderweg* controversy in a new way. The lesson lies in the fact that the corporate tradition in Germany anticipated certain corporatist features of Western postliberal industrial statism. In the twentieth century corporatism became a major feature of, among other things, the professionalization of society. The organization of the interests of experts and their employers was accelerated by the growth of the state as a source of money to be granted and regulation to be influenced. These trends were magnified by the two world wars and the resultant "military-industrial complex." The world wars, which came about chiefly as a result of German difficulties, miscalculations, and ambitions, accelerated the "economic militarization" of modern societies throughout the West. The growth in scale and influence of what Michael Geyer has called the "organization of violence" by the modern state[53] helped further the trend toward corporate professional and technical service to the state. The growing influence of corporate bodies attempting to monopolize knowledge and technology marginalized the power of political parties and the public. Professionals became an important element of a postliberal state of large interlocking public and private institutions and organized interests.

Germany, therefore, did not follow a *Sonderweg* in the sense of a departure from a political standard achieved in the West. The false dichotomy between the "peculiar" and the "modern" that liberal historians have imposed upon German history was a function of the American and Western European struggle with their own political and social ambiguities as projected onto "the other" in the form, first, of Germany, particularly as a result of the two world wars, and then Russia, particularly during the cold war.[54] There was no "special path" in German history because there was no "path" which had led to an ideal liberal democracy in the West. Instead, in the West and in Germany there were elements of various political and social realities, including liberal democracy. But Germany, like any nation, has its own history and culture. And it was precisely some of that which was peculiar in kind and degree to Germany—here the military and professional corporatism preserved chiefly by Bismarck's *kleindeutsch* answer to the German question—that evolved under other conditions in Western nations in the twentieth century. Geyer has argued that the traditional portrayal of two Germanies, the one rational and industrial, the other militaristic and backward, was a function of "a corporate *pax Americana* and of 'America' as the imaginary fulfillment of the Western course of (liberal capitalist) development."[55] To the extent that a nation is a meaningful entity for a historian, there was of course only one Germany. The question is how to evaluate the specific conditions of German history without reducing that history to a function of Western ideological concerns. Germany was not the antipode of political developments in the West. Germany also was not simply a somewhat more illiberal version of the Western bourgeois state.[56] Part of the problem is that the primary subject matter of each of these approaches to German history—"premodern" elites and modern bourgeoisie, respectively—determines the nature and scope of the findings. If one studies the feudal one finds the feudal. If one studies the bourgeois one finds the bourgeois. Understanding Germany on its own unitary terms, however, permits us to avoid a static dichotomy posed around the standard of a liberal model and scale of modern historical development.

In Germany strong traditions of corporatism in society and state had been preserved and strengthened by the unique manner of German state-building through the unification of Germany by Prussia.[57] As in the West, powerful new commercial and industrial interests in the Reich too displayed inherent corporate instincts. Bismarck, like Napoleon III in France and Benjamin Disraeli in England only with more success, harnessed the new political forces of liberalism and democracy in service to old standards and structures of paternalistic governance. With little success, Bismarck attempted to woo the working class to the paternalistic state by means of a state health insurance system. Even Wilhelm II, that bumbling avatar of Prussianism, maintained some degree of royal authority through a striking and effective mix of old and new methods of rule.[58] This paternalism of thought and deed in

Germany contrasts with the liberalism of England during the same period, where greater economic and political individualism helped create the greater effectiveness of political parties and Parliament and also greater disparities between rich and poor.[59]

The process of professionalization itself was also problematic along these same lines. The growing power of professions in Germany was advanced by a traditional German respect for learning, the rapid industrialization of Germany, growing technical sophistication in disciplines like medicine, and, in the end, the Nazi demand for such organized technical expertise for purposes of racial selection, social control, and military expansion. Professions in the West, however, have traditionally been associated with liberal ideals such as individual liberty, a free market, meritocracy, and representative government. Had German professionals, therefore, represented a challenge to corporate traditions in Germany? This was most certainly not the case with the medical profession since 1869, when liberal Berlin physicians had completed a successful effort to establish medicine legally as a free trade rather than as a profession. From the founding of the Reich in 1871 onward, doctors (and, to one degree or another, most other professions) confronted and courted a powerful state bureaucracy. In the case of medicine, Bismarck's construction of a state health insurance system and the subsequent growth of socialist influence within it prompted aggressive collective action among doctors in defense of their interests. Such action included the threat of strikes to improve the position of doctors in the *Krankenkassen* (sickness funds) system, a campaign to gain recognition from the state as a profession (achieved with ambiguous political and professional effects in 1935), and ongoing attempts to regulate the market for physicians' services. Moreover, during the twentieth century—and especially with the national and economic disasters following the First World War—many doctors were radicalized toward the political right. More generally, the German experience of professionalization has alerted historians not only to what the "liberal" professions in Germany confronted, but also to what "liberal" professions are, or at least have become. Thus the recent study of the German experience of professionalization has contributed to an established critique of the Western ideal type of the liberal professional.

Charles McClelland has argued that "the German experience of professionalization, with its complicated tangle of private sphere and bureaucratically controlled dimensions, may prove more typical of professionalization throughout the twentieth-century world than the

Anglo-American 'model.'"[60] International legislation on human experimentation enhancing professional, state, and military claims at some expense of patients and subjects is a relevant example in the field of medicine. The trend toward "professional neocorporatism" began in late imperial Germany, according to Konrad Jarausch, when "professionals participated in the bourgeois shift from liberal to national attitudes," assuming a "postliberal" position based on a "rising tide of 'academic illiberalism.'"[61] This shift away from liberalism aggravated the tendency among professionals everywhere in the twentieth century toward using "the state to secure income and social position" and "rejecting its control over practice and organization."[62] In Germany this process drew upon an especially strong tradition of institutionalized corporatist thought, practice, and feeling at all levels of polity and society. Such a tradition encouraged both the obedience to state authority in pursuit of professional recognition and the defense of the profession's own corporate interests against the state and against competitors and clients. And particularly in medicine, even the enlightened liberal scientific ethic of individual and social improvement through technical and therapeutic intervention and prevention itself could help advance even inhumane state imperatives.[63]

Nazi Germany occasioned a fatal confluence of these trends and traditions. Genocide and *Krankenmord* were the direct result of Nazi racism. For genocide no other rationale or rationalization was advanced. The murder of the mentally and physically ill could be and was rationalized on the grounds of mercy or—especially during the war—utility. The experiments on human beings were racist in that they at least implicitly accepted the racist categorization of prisoners they used, in particular the Jews, Poles, and Russians upon whom the most dangerous experiments were usually conducted. But even though they were occasioned, informed, and exacerbated in effect by racism, these experiments, unlike those perpetrated by Josef Mengele and others at Auschwitz, were primarily military in origin and nature, thus providing ready rationalizations which have been defended and echoed at other times and places. The great majority of the doctors on trial at Nuremberg were in the military: seventeen of twenty-three were members of either the Luftwaffe, the army, or the Waffen SS. Most were not career military, but had worked on behalf of the military and had also subscribed to the militaristic ethos of the Nazi party and its affiliated organizations. During the war, as members of a military band of brothers, the Nuremberg doctors' professionalized corporatist instincts were intensified by a militaristic regime engaged in a campaign of racial expansion and extermination. They were thus relatively insulated from the atomization and individual competitiveness caused by Nazi dissolution of traditional social groupings.[64]

Moreover, the individuals who conducted the experiments were in great measure acting on principles and practices long embedded in their culture, their society, and their military identity. These principles and practices were then reinforced by much that was happening around them in the Third Reich. These doctors had been born, raised, educated, and in some cases had established themselves professionally before the Nazis came to power. Each one of them, had, as child, youth, and young adult, internalized values, habits, and attitudes of an Imperial Germany at the height of its powers and in the depths of its final crisis. World War I had an especially significant effect on doctors and psychiatrists, who were drafted in unprecedented numbers to deal with the staggering physical and mental casualties of industrial warfare. Military service itself only aggravated the authoritarianism common among doctors as increasingly effective and sought-after experts in matters of life and death. The same was even truer in the Second World War, especially on the embattled home front. By that time doctors had become even more therapeutically effective, largely through the medical and surgical advances of the First World War as well as the introduction of a wide range of drugs in the 1930s. The increasing initiative of patients only heightened doctors' defense of their prerogatives and authority, now backed up by ruthless Nazi wartime sanctions.

To be sure, the Nuremberg doctors tended to be the younger members of the medical profession who had been radicalized by the cultural and professional disruptions of World War I and its outcome, the inflation of 1923, and the *Weltwirtschaftskrise* of 1929. All of them were either in their twenties or their thirties in 1933: pediatrician Herta Oberheuser, who assisted Gebhardt with the sulfanilamide experiments at Ravensbrück, was twenty-two in that year; Sigmund Rascher, who conducted the high altitude experiments at Dachau, was twenty-four then. Such doctors were especially susceptible to Nazi propaganda promising national renewal and opportunities—professional and otherwise—for disillusioned yet ambitious youth. And the drastic political change of 1933 itself provided opportunities for many people on the way up within—or on the margins of—any establishment to establish themselves, often at the expense of departed Jewish colleagues, in positions of influence.[65]

The effects of all these experiences were intensified by the Nazi environment after 1933. In power were men violently acting out a "personal agony of armour-plated self-discipline."[66] In a very real sense, the Nazis were at war already from 1933 onward. While the Nazis may have atomized German society by dissolving traditional social groupings, the competitive "hierarchical continuum of achievement"[67] also allowed entities such as doctors to advance their corporate interests in both service and sacrifice to the state. It was a system that "foster[ed] the egotism of both individuals and groups."[68] The war cut both ways, creating both an environment of individual "survivalism" and of shared purpose and misery.[69] The professional, military, political, and national identities of the doctors experimenting on human beings fused under the press of war into a hard alloy of interest, duty, desire, allegiance, and rationalization. The very extremities of the camps and the condition of the people in them magnified the effects of Nazi racial propaganda.[70]

But the professional culture of the Nuremberg doctors had shaped them along the lines of a corporatist and statist professional ethos which antedated the First World War and anticipated general Western developments. These various corporate contexts reinforced each other during the Second World War. Their authority as medical experts over their test subjects reproduced in extreme measure their increasingly hard-won authority over their patients. At the same time, the doctors operated under the aegis of that most brutally powerful of state institutions, the military, while the war itself mobilized their loyalty to the nation. All of these corporate identities and loyalties tore at the capacity to make individual judgments about the individuals at their mercy. These doctors were not creatures simply of National Socialism and the Second World War, but of the history of modern Germany and the West. Germany, as a result of its own "peculiarities" and the forces of modernization, was an early postliberal state and society beset by a series of exceptional crises after 1914. In 1930 conservative politicians, military men, and bureaucrats assumed control of the Weimar Republic and three years later handed Hitler the keys to power.[71] The combination of these traditions and crises brought out the worst in German institutions and attitudes and permitted the worst to wield power. Among these worst were the doctors tried at Nuremberg. Their stations at the brutal intersection of the military, the medical profession, and the concentration camp system produced extreme actions nonetheless telling of multiple aspects of German and Western history in the modern era.

Notes

1. Manfred Berg and Geoffrey Cocks, eds., *Medicine and Public Health and Medical Care in 19th and 20th Century Germany* (Cambridge, 1996). Reprinted with permission of Cambridge University Press.
2. *Trials of War Criminals Before the Nuernberg Military Tribunals Under Control Council Law No. 10* (Washington, D.C., 1950), I:8; hereafter cited as *TWC* I, *TWC* II.
3. *TWC* I:289.
4. Michael A. Grodin, "Historical Origins of the Nuremberg Code," in George J. Annas and Michael A. Grodin, eds., *The Nazi Doctors and the Nuremberg Code: Human Rights in Human Experimentation* (New York, 1992), p. 139; Rainer Osnowski, ed., *Menschenversuche: Wahnsinn und Wirklichkeit* (Cologne, 1988).
5. *TWC* II:181.
6. Jay Katz, "The Consent Principle of the Nuremberg Code: Its Significance Then and Now," in *The Nazi Doctors and the Nuremberg Code*, p. 228.
7. Gerhard Baader, "Menschenexperimente," in Fridolf Kudlien, ed., *Ärzte im Nationalsozialismus*, (Cologne, 1985), p. 177; Brigitte Leyendecker and Burghard F. Klapp, "Deutsche Hepatitisforschung im Zweiten Weltkrieg," in Christian Pross and Götz Aly, eds., *Der Wert des Menschen: Medizin in Deutschland 1918–1945* (Berlin, 1989), p. 270; Günther Schwarberg, *The Murders at the Bullenhuser Damm*, trans. Erna Rosenfeld and Alvin Rosenfeld (Bloomington, 1984), pp. 112–19; Donald M. McKale, "Purging Nazis: The Postwar Trials of Female German Doctors and Nurses," *Proceedings of the South Carolina Historical Association* (1981), pp. 156–70.
8. Hans-Walter Schmuhl, *Rassenhygiene, Nationalsozialismus, Euthanasie. Von der Verhütung zur Vernichtung "lebensunwerten Lebens," 1890–1945* (Göttingen, 1987); Dirk Blasius, "Psychiatrischer Alltag im Nationalsozialismus," in Detlev Peukert and Jürgen Reulecke, eds., *Die Reihen fast geschlossen. Beiträge zur Geschichte des Alltags unterm Nationalsozialismus* (Wuppertal, 1981), pp. 367–80.
9. Alexander Mitscherlich and Fred Mielke, *Wissenschaft ohne Menschlichkeit. Medizinische und Eugenische Irrwege unter Diktatur, Burokratie und Krieg* (Heidelberg, 1949), v, 6, 279–98. This theme dominates the biomedical division of the recently opened Holocaust Museum in Washington, D.C.; see *Journal of the American Medical Association* 268 (1992): pp. 575–6.
10. *TWC* II:181.
11. Katz, "The Consent Principle," pp. 231–4; there are also legitimate challenges to Western individualism from Eastern and Southern cultures incorporating communal values: see Robert J. Levine, "Validity of Consent Procedures in Technologically Developing Countries," in Z. Bankowski and N. Howard Jones, eds., *Human Experimentation and Medical Ethics* (Geneva, 1982), pp. 16–30.
12. Linda Hunt, "U.S. Coverup of Nazi Scientists," *Bulletin of the Atomic Scientists* 41 (1985): 21–3; see also Stefan Kühl, *The Nazi Connection: Eugenics, American Racism, and German National Socialism* (New York, 1994); and Christian Pross, "Nazi Doctors: Criminals, Charlatans, or Pioneers? The Commentaries of the Allied Experts in the Nuremberg Doctors Trial," in Charles G. Roland et al., eds., *Medicine Without Compassion, Past and Present: Fall Meeting, Cologne, September 28–30, 1988* (Hamburg, 1992), pp. 253–84.
13. Robert L. Berger, "Nazi Science—The Dachau Hypothermia Experiments," *New England Journal of Medicine* 322 (1990): 1435–40; see also the exchange in

Lancet 151 (1946): 798, 830, 961, 152 (1947): 143; and the prophetic novel by Josephine Bell, *Murder in Hospital* (London, 1941). Not surprisingly, West German medical journals of the period (e.g., *Münchener medizinische Wochenschrift*, *Deutsche medizinische Wochenschrift*, *Medizinische Klinik*) do not discuss the Doctors' Trial; cf. Viktor von Weizsäcker, "'Euthanasie' und Menschenversuche," *Psyche* 1 (1947–48): 68–102. Only recently have the Japanese begun to confront similar human experiments carried out by the infamous Unit 731.

14. Steven Dickman, "East Germany: Science in the Disservice of the State," *Science* 245 (1991): 26–7; see also Annette Tuffs, "Germany: Horror Hospital," *Lancet* 338 (1991): 624.

15. George J. Annas, "The Nuremberg Code in U.S. Courts: Ethics versus Expediency," in *The Nazi Doctors and the Nuremberg Code*, p. 216.

16. Ruth Macklin, "Universality of the Nuremberg Code," in *The Nazi Doctors and the Nuremberg Code*, p. 255.

17. See Geoffrey Cocks, "Partners and Pariahs: Jews and Medicine in Modern German Society," *Leo Baeck Institute Yearbook* 36 (1991): 195–6.

18. Paul Weindling, *Health, Race and German Politics Between National Unification and Nazism, 1870–1945* (Cambridge, 1989).

19. Mario Puzo, *The Dark Arena* (New York, 1955), p. 45.

20. *TWC* II:146.

21. Johanna Bleker, "Zum Problem der Krankensichtung in der deutschen Wehrmachtsmedizin im Zweiten Weltkrieg," in Samuel Mitja Rapoport and Achim Thom, eds., *Das Schicksal der Medizin im Faschismus* (Berlin, 1989), pp. 184–7.

22. *TWC* II:85.

23. *Reichsgesundheitsblatt* 6 (1931): 174–5; *TWC* II:83.

24. Hans-Martin Sass, "Reichsrundschreiben 1931: Pre-Nuremberg German Regulations Concerning New Therapy and Human Experimentation," *Journal of Medicine and Philosophy* 8 (1983): 99–111; *Der Wert des Menschen*, p. 92; on the Prussian directive, see Grodin, "Historical Origins of the Nuremberg Code," pp. 127–8.

25. *Reichsärzteordnung* (Berlin, Vienna, 1943), pp. 7, 11.

26. Grodin, "Historical Origins of the Nuremberg Code," 127, 129.

27. Alfons Stauder, "Die Zulässigkeit ärztlicher Versuche an gesunden und kranken Menschen," *Münchener medizinische Wochenschrift* 78 (1931): 108. The same complaint was made by socialist physicians about the Nazi law banning vivisection: see "Die Vivisektion des Proletariats," *Internationales Ärztliches Bulletin. Zentralorgan der Internationalen Vereinigung Sozialistischer Ärzte, Jahrgang I–VI (1934–1939) Reprint*, Beiträge zur Nationalsozialistischen Gesundheits- und Sozialpolitik, 7, (Berlin, 1989), I (1934): 47–50. On Stauder's leading role in the *Gleichschaltung* of the medical profession, see Michael H. Kater, *Doctors Under Hitler* (Chapel Hill, 1989), pp. 182–4.

28. Grodin, "Historical Origins of the Nuremberg Code," p. 130; see also Friedrich Müller, "Die Zulässigkeit ärztlicher Versuche an gesunden und kranken Menschen," *Münchener medizinische Wochenschrift* 78 (1931): 104–7. The complete German text of the circular is in Sass, "Reichsrundschreiben 1931," pp. 107–9.

29. U.S. Nuernberg War Crimes Trial, Records Group 238, Microcopy M-887, Roll 29, frames 538–9; National Archives, Washington, D.C.; "Vermerk über die Besichtigung der klinischen Abteilung für Sport- und Arbeitsschäden der Heilanstalten Hohenlychen," R 89 13499, 129–33, Bundesarchiv, Coblenz; Karl Gebhardt, "Allgemeines zur Wiederherstellungschirurgie, " *Zentralblatt für Chirurgie* 63 (1936): 1570–6.

30. Claudine Herzlich and Janine Pierret, *Illness and Self in Society*, trans. Elborg Forster (Baltimore, 1987).
31. Robert N. Proctor, *Racial Hygiene: Medicine Under the Nazis* (Cambridge, Mass., 1988), p. 69.
32. David Abraham, *The Collapse of the Weimar Republic: Political Economy and Crisis*, 2nd ed. (New York, 1986), p. 241.
33. Erich Fromm, *The Working Class in Weimar Germany: A Psychological and Sociological Study*, ed. Wolfgang Bonss and trans. Barbara Weinberger (Cambridge, Mass., 1984). The analysis of responses to questions about health and illness was not published; see below, note 37.
34. Meldungen aus dem Reich, May 9, 1940, Microcopy T-175, Roll 259, frame 1485, and October 2, 1941, Roll 261, frames 4928–31, National Archives; Jahresgesundheitsbericht, Gesundheitsamt Grevenbroich-Neuss, January 31, 1940, Reg. Düsseldorf 54341, Nordrhein-Westfälisches Hauptstaatsarchiv, Düsseldorf; Edward Shorter, *Bedside Manners: The Troubled History of Doctors and Patients* (New York, 1985).
35. Leonardo Conti, "Stand der Volksgesundheit im 5. Kriegsjahr," p. 15, Reg. Aachen 16486, Nordrhein-Westfälisches Hauptstaatsarchiv, Düsseldorf.
36. Sander L. Gilman, "Jews and Mental Illness: Medical Metaphors, Anti-Semitism, and the Jewish Response," *Journal of the History of the Behavioral Sciences* 20 (1984): 150; Susan Sontag, *Illness as Metaphor* (New York, 1978), p. 74.
37. Klaus Theweleit, *Male Fantasies*, 2 vols., trans. Erica Carter, Stephen Conway, and Chris Turner (Minneapolis, 1987, 1989).
38. Erich Fromm Papers 1929–1949, Series 3: International Institute for Social Research, B. The German Worker Under the Weimar Republic, Box 12, F.5, Unsorted Fragments of Drafts in German, Contd., "Bearbeitung zu Frage 415/16 auf Seite 5a"; New York Public Library.
39. Ibid., Box 13, Tabulations of Questionnaires, F.5, #201-210.
40. Wehrwirtschafts-Inspektion VII (Munich), 1937, Microcopy T-77, roll 248, frames 824–28, National Archives; Friedrich Kortenhaus, "Verschlechterung der Volksgesundheit?" *Münchener medizinische Wochenschrift* 79 (1932): 1964–5.
41. Reichsminister des Innern to Regierungspräsident Frankfurt a.d. Oder, August 23, 1941, p. 3, Pr. Br. Rep. 3 B Nr. 178, Staatsarchiv Potsdam; Cocks, "Partners and Pariahs," pp. 197–200.
42. *TWC* I:323, 326, 330, 492–3.
43. *TWC* I:266.
44. *TWC* I:356.
45. *TWC* I:142.
46. *TWC* I:494, 508. Cholera experiments were carried out on prisoners of war in Russia: see Fridolf Kudlien, "Begingen Wehrmachtsärzte im Russlandkrieg Verbrechen gegen die Menschlichkeit?," in *Der Wert des Menschen*, p. 343.
47. Deutscher Gemeindetag Berlin to Deutscher Gemeindetag Düsseldorf, September 1, 1942, RW 53/466, Nordrhein-Westfälisches Hauptstaatsarchiv, Düsseldorf.
48. Christopher Browning, "Genocide and Public Health: German Doctors and Polish Jews, 1939–1941," *Holocaust and Genocide Studies* 3 (1988): 21–36.
49. Jahresgesundheitsbericht, Stadtkreis Krefeld, February 23, 1944, Reg. Düsseldorf 54291I, Nordrhein-Westfälisches Hauptstaatsarchiv, Düsseldorf; see also United States Strategic Bombing Survey, Morale Division, Medical Branch Report, *The Effect of Bombing on Health and Medical Care in Germany* (Washington, D.C., October 30, 1945).
50. Martin Broszat, "Resistenz und Widerstand: Eine Zwischenbilanz des Forschungsprojekts," in Martin Broszat et al., eds., *Bayern in der NS-Zeit*

(Munich, 1981), 4:691–709; for an instance of such "resistance"—and also reliance upon the popular amphetamine Pervitin—see Heinrich Böll's memoir, *What's To Become of the Boy? Or: Something to Do with Books*, trans. Leila Vennewitz (New York, 1984), pp. 73–74.

51. See the example of Sigmund Rascher discussed in Kater, *Doctors under Hitler*, pp. 125–6.

52. Achim Thom, "Verbrecherische Experimente in den Konzentrationslagern— Ausdruck des antihuman Charakters einer der faschistischen Machtpolitik untergeordneten medizinischen Forschung," in Achim Thom and Genadij Ivanovic Caregorodcev, eds., *Medizin unterm Hakenkreuz* (Berlin, 1989), pp. 397, 398–9.

53. Michael Geyer, "The Past as Future: The German Officer Corps as Profession," in Geoffrey Cocks and Konrad H. Jarausch, eds., *German Professions, 1800–1950* (New York, 1990), pp. 183–212. See also Michael S. Sherry, *In the Shadow of War: The United States since the 1930s* (New haven, conn., 1995); and Ian Buruma, *The Wages of Guilt: Memories of War in Germany and Japan* (New York, 1994).

54. The "domino effect" used by the United States to describe the spread of Communism was in part a carryover from Second World War descriptions of the inexorable spread of German and Japanese military expansionism.

55. Michael Geyer, "Looking Back at the International Style: Some Reflections on the Current State of German History," *German Studies Review* 13 (1990): 113.

56. David Blackbourn and Geoff Eley, *The Peculiarities of German History: Bourgeois Society and Politics in Nineteenth-Century Germany* (New York, 1984). On the distinctiveness of German liberalism, see Dieter Langewiesche, *Liberalismus im 19. Jahrhundert. Deutschland im europäischen Vergleich* (Göttingen, 1988).

57. John Breuilly, "State-Building, Modernization and Liberalism from the Late Eighteenth Century to Unification: German Peculiarities; Liberalism and Modernization in Wilhelmine Germany," *European History Quarterly* 22 (1992): 257–84, 431–8.

58. Thomas A. Kohut, *Wilhelm II and the Germans: A Study in Leadership* (New York, 1991).

59. Kenneth Barkin, "Germany and England: Economic Inequality," *Tel Aviver Jahrbuch für deutsche Geschichte* 16 (1987): 200–11.

60. Charles E. McClelland, *The German Experience of Professionalization: Modern Learned Professions and Their Organizations from the Early Nineteenth Century to the Hitler Era* (Cambridge, 1991), p. 10.

61. Konrad H. Jarausch, *The Unfree Professions: German Lawyers, Teachers, and Engineers* (New York, 1990), p. 24. "This characterization employs a historical Central European meaning of 'corporatism' as calling for a sociopolitical order based on *Berufsstände*. The prefix "neo" indicates the postliberal thrust of the attempt to reintroduce premodern elements into high industrial society." (p. 269n. 97). It can also be argued that no such turn from "liberal" to "national" was necessary to produce the type of corporate behavior Jarausch describes. Such an argument views liberalism as inherently corporate rather than as a more or less Western "ideal type" corrupted by special German conditions.

62. Ibid.

63. Michael Hubenstorf, "'Aber es kommt mir doch so vor, als ob Sie dabei nichts verloren hätten.' Zum Exodus von Wissenschaftlern aus den staatlichen Forschungsinstituten Berlins im Bereich des öffentlichen Gesundheitswesens," in Wolfram Fischer et al., eds., *Exodus von Wissenschaften aus Berlin: Frag-*

estellungen—Ergebnisse—Desiderate; Entwicklungen vor und nach 1933, Akademie der Wissenschaften zu Berlin Forschungsbericht 7 (Berlin, 1993), pp. 444–55; Alfons Labisch, *Homo Hygienicus: Gesundheit und Medizin in der Neuzeit* (Frankfurt, 1992), p. 133.

64. Detlev J. K. Peukert, *Inside Nazi Germany: Conformity, Opposition, and Racism in Everyday Life*, trans. Richard Deveson (New Haven, 1987), pp. 236–42.

65. See, for example, Geoffrey Cocks, *Psychotherapy in the Third Reich: The Göring Institute* (New York, 1985).

66. Peukert, *Inside Nazi Germany*, p. 169; Theweleit, *Male Fantasies*; Michael Burleigh and Wolfgang Wippermann, *The Racial State: Germany, 1933–1945* (Cambridge, 1991).

67. Peukert, *Inside Nazi Germany*, p. 95.

68. Michael Geyer, "The Nazi State Reconsidered," in Richard Bessel, ed., *Life in the Third Reich* (Oxford, 1987), p. 59.

69. Cf. Tilla Siegel, "Wage Policy in Nazi Germany," *Politics and Society* 14 (1985): 37; Christa Wolf, *Patterns of Childhood*, trans. Ursule Molinaro & Hedwig Rappolt (New York, 1984), p. 200.

70. For an argument for a similar phenomenon among German soldiers in Russia, see Omer Bartov, *Hitler's Army: Soldiers, Nazis, and War in the Third Reich* (New York, 1991).

71. For an analysis restricted to economic corporatism, see Werner Abelshauser, "The First Post-Liberal Nation: Stages in the Development of Modern Corporatism in Germany," *European History Quarterly* 14 (1985): 285–318. By concentrating on "corporatist interest mediation" (p. 287), Abelshauser posits a dichotomy between authoritarian "state" corporatism and "democratic welfare" corporatism that understates the historical confluence in modern German society and culture of "preliberal" and "postliberal" corporatist institutions and attitudes.

72. Detlev J.K. Peukert, *The Weimar Republic: The Crisis of Classical Modernity*, trans. Richard Deveson (New York, 1992), p. 280; see also Shelley Baranowski, "East Elbian Landed Elites and Germany's Turn to Fascism: The *Sonderweg* Revisited," *European History Quarterly* 26 (1996): 209–40.

Index

Abraham, Karl, 109
Adler, Alfred, 95; break with Freud, 15, 109. *See also* Adlerians
Adlerians, 10, 35, 66
Aichhorn, August, 20, 129, 132–33, 148n.46
Alexander, Franz, viii
Anschluss of Austria, 17, 125, 129, 131
Anti-Semitism, 7, 13, 23, 57, 58, 62–63, 79, 91, 125, 129, 161–62, 173–79, 184, 185–86, 187n.13, 200
Association for the History of Psychoanalysis, International, 15, 16
"Autocoordination" of German society, 34–35, 37, 113, 178

Basch, Michael, 141
Benedek, Therese, viii, x
Berlin Psychoanalytic Institute, viii, 32, 35
Bernfeld, Siegfried, viii, 79, 95, 98–99, 100
Bildungsbürgertum. See Middle classes
Bismarck, Otto von, 155, 159, 164, 174, 204, 205
Boehm, Felix, ix, x, 47, 116
Böll, Heinrich, 183, 212n.50
Brandt, Karl, 180

Character, 42, 115
Cimbal, Walter, 38
Community feeling, 35, 51, 115, 117
Confidentiality, suspension of, 36
Conti, Leonardo, 179–80, 181, 189n.56, 200
Corporatism, social, 24, 35, 165, 168, 195, 202–8, 212n.61, 213n.71

Deconstruction, 162–63
de Crinis, Max, 44, 45, 47
"Deprofessionalization," 35, 66, 178, 181

Depth psychology, 40, 65–66
Deutsch, Helene, viii, 92, 93
Doctors, 5, 108, 159, 168, 193–208; and patients, 50, 112, 159–61, 163–64, 179, 182, 183, 194, 197–98, 199–200, 207, 208; and National Socialism, 50, 62, 65, 66, 112, 114, 118–19, 159, 165–66, 169, 178–79, 185, 193–208; professionalization of, 50, 66, 108, 164–65, 165–6, 181–82, 195, 205. *See also* Medicine
Dörner, Klaus, 70, 109
Dührssen, Annemarie, 11–15

Ehrlich, Paul, 179
Eissler, Kurt, 133
Eissler, Ruth, 21, 126, 137, 138, 145
Eitingon, Max, viii
Erikson, Erik, xii, 141, 150n.88
Eugenics. *See* Nazis, eugenics
"Euthanasia" program, 32, 36, 65, 68–69, 70, 71, 107, 116, 167, 179, 184, 193, 194, 206

Fenichel, Otto, viii, 95, 97–98, 100
Final Solution, 6, 22, 66, 75, 130, 157–58, 174, 179, 180, 203, 206
Fleck, Ludwik, xi
Fliess, Wilhelm, 18, 19
Freud, Anna, 96, 136–37, 142
Freud, Sigmund, viii–ix, xii, 1–2, 7, 8, 12, 14, 15, 16, 17–19, 21, 57, 60, 75, 76, 87, 88, 91, 92, 94, 95–96, 109, 109–10, 119, 124–25, 136, 141; criticism, 91; escape, 110, 125, 129; rejection of, 187n.13. *See also* Freudian movement; Freudian theory; Freudians
Freudian movement, 11, 12, 32
Freudian theory, 9, 60, 133, 136, 142, 145–46
Freudians, 7, 12, 48, 57, 66, 95–99; as

DATE DUE